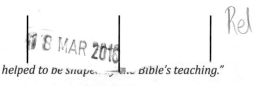
"Phil makes the deep truths of Scripture alive and accessible. If you want to grow in your understanding of each book of the Bible, then buy these books and let them change your life!"

– PJ Smyth – GodFirst Church, Johannesburg, South Africa

"Most commentaries are dull. These are alive. Most commentaries are for scholars. These are for you!"

– Canon Michael Green

"These notes are amazingly good. Lots of content and depth of research, yet packed in a Big Breakfast that leaves the reader well fed and full. Bible notes often say too little, yet larger commentaries can be dull - missing the wood for the trees. Phil's insights are striking, original, and fresh, going straight to the heart of the text and the reader! Substantial yet succinct, they bristle with amazing insights and life applications, compelling us to read more. Bible reading will become enriched and informed with such a scintillating guide. Teachers and preachers will find nuggets of pure gold here!"

– Greg Haslam – Westminster Chapel, London, UK

"The Bible is living and dangerous. The ones who teach it best are those who bear that in mind – and let the author do the talking. Phil has written these studies with a sharp mind and a combination of creative application and reverence."

– Joel Virgo – Leader of Newday Youth Festival

"Phil Moore's new commentaries are outstanding: biblical and passi_____ _____ _____ nd. God's Word _____ _____ od shines

– An_____ _____ dStories

"Want to understand the Bible better? Don't have the time or energy to read complicated commentaries? The book you have in your hand could be the answer. Allow Phil Moore to explain and then apply God's message to your life. Think of this book as the Bible's message distilled for everyone."

– Adrian Warnock – Christian blogger

"Phil Moore presents Scripture in a dynamic, accessible and relevant way. The bite-size chunks – set in context and grounded in contemporary life – really make the make the Word become flesh and dwell among us."

– Dr David Landrum – The Bible Society

"Through a relevant, very readable, up to date storying approach, Phil Moore sets the big picture, relates God's Word to today and gives us fresh insights to increase our vision, deepen our worship, know our identity and fire our imagination. Highly recommended!"

- Geoff Knott – former CEO of Wycliffe Bible Translators UK

"What an exciting project Phil has embarked upon! These accessible and insightful books will ignite the hearts of believers, inspire the minds of preachers and help shape a new generation of men and women who are seeking to learn from God's Word."

- David Stroud – Newfrontiers and ChristChurch London

For more information about the Straight to the Heart series, please go to **www.philmoorebooks.com**.

Acts

60 BITE-SIZED INSIGHTS

Phil Moore

MONARCH
BOOKS

Oxford, UK & Grand Rapids, Michigan, USA

First published in the UK in 2010 by Monarch Books
(a publishing imprint of Lion Hudson plc)
Wilkinson House, Jordan Hill Road, Oxford OX2 8DR, England
Tel: +44 (0)1865 302750 Fax: +44 (0)1865 302757
Email: monarch@lionhudson.com
www.lionhudson.com

ISBN 978 1 85424 989 0

Distributed by:
UK: Marston Book Services, PO Box 269, Abingdon, Oxon, OX14 4YN
USA: Kregel Publications, PO Box 2607, Grand Rapids, Michigan 49501

British Library Cataloguing Data
A catalogue record for this book is available from the British Library.

Printed and bound in the UK by JF Print Ltd.

This book is for my Dad.
When I wasn't interested in Jesus,
I saw his Holy Spirit at work in you.
Because you made the invisible God visible,
You convinced me that the message of Acts is true.

CONTENTS

THE GOSPEL TO THE GENTILES (37–47 AD)

THE GOSPEL TO ASIA MINOR (48–49 AD)

THE GOSPEL TO EUROPE (50–57 AD)

THE GOSPEL TO ROME (57–62 AD)

About the *Straight to the Heart* Series

On his eightieth birthday, Sir Winston Churchill dismissed the compliment that he was the "lion" who had defeated Nazi Germany in World War Two. He told the Houses of Parliament that *"It was a nation and race dwelling all around the globe that had the lion's heart. I had the luck to be called upon to give the roar."*

I hope that God speaks to you very powerfully through the "roar" of the books in the *Straight to the Heart* series. I hope they help you to understand the books of the Bible and the message that the Holy Spirit inspired their authors to write. I hope that they help you to hear God's voice challenging you, and that they provide you with a springboard for further journeys into each book of Scripture for yourself.

But when you hear my "roar", I want you to know that it comes from the heart of a much bigger "lion" than me. I have been shaped by a whole host of great Christian thinkers and preachers from around the world, and I want to give due credit to at least some of them here:

Terry Virgo, David Stroud, John Hosier, Adrian Holloway, Greg Haslam, Lex Loizides, and all those who lead the Newfrontiers family of churches; friends and encouragers, such as Stef Liston, Joel Virgo, Stuart Gibbs, Scott Taylor, Nick Sharp, Nick Derbridge, Phil Whittall, and Kevin and Sarah Aires; Tony Collins, Jenny Ward and Simon Cox at Monarch books; Malcolm Kayes and all the elders of The Coign Church, Woking; my fellow elders and church members here at Queens Road Church, Wimbledon;

my great friend Andrew Wilson – without your friendship, encouragement and example, this series would never have happened.

I would like to thank my parents, my brother Jonathan, and my in-laws, Clive and Sue Jackson. Dad – your example birthed in my heart the passion that brought this series into being. I didn't listen to all you said when I was a child, but I couldn't ignore the way you got up at five o'clock every morning to pray, read the Bible and worship, because of your radical love for God and for his Word. I'd like to thank my children – Isaac, Noah, and Esther – for keeping me sane when publishing deadlines were looming. But most of all, I'm grateful to my incredible wife, Ruth – my friend, encourager, corrector, and helper.

You all have the lion's heart, and you have all developed the lion's heart in me. I count it an enormous privilege to be the one who was chosen to sound the lion's roar.

So welcome to the *Straight to the Heart* series. My prayer is that you will let this roar grip your own heart too – for the glory of the great Lion of the Tribe of Judah, the Lord Jesus Christ!

Introduction: Ordinary People, Extraordinary God

When they saw the courage of Peter and John and realized that they were unschooled, ordinary men, they were astonished and took note that these men had been with Jesus.

(Acts 4:13)

In 30 AD, Jesus of Nazareth looked to have been an utter failure. If you don't understand that, then you will miss the message of the book of Acts. It is a record of survival through adversity, triumph against all odds, and victory snatched from the jaws of defeat. It is the story of a group of ordinary people who turned the tide of history through the power of their extraordinary God.

Jesus had failed to spread his message beyond the borders of Palestine. He had failed to convince the Jewish leaders that he was their long-awaited Messiah. He had even failed to keep the support of the rank-and-file people of Israel. He had been abandoned by the crowds, by his disciples, and even by God himself,[1] and had died a shameful criminal's death on a lonely hill outside Jerusalem. For all his early promise, by May 30 AD he had lost all but 120 of his followers,[2] and Luke goes out of his

---

[1] In my book *Straight to the Heart of Matthew*, I show that Matthew 27:46 was actually a cry of victory. Nevertheless, those who heard it at the time must have assumed it was a cry of utter defeat and despair.

[2] He appeared to a crowd of over 500 after his resurrection (1 Corinthians 15:6), but only 120 of them obeyed him enough to wait in Jerusalem as he commanded them (Acts 1:4).

way in the opening verses of Acts to tell us what an unimpressive bunch they were.

He stresses in verse 11 that they were *"men of Galilee"* – a group of uneducated barbarians from a far-flung corner of the Roman Empire. The gospel writers Matthew, Mark, and John were among the 120, and their gospels betray their provincial mindset. They refer to the hub of their little world as the *Sea of Galilee*, while Luke, the sophisticated Christian doctor from Antioch, knew enough about the wider world to call it simply a *lake*.[3] Jesus' vision for his Church to take the Gospel *"to the ends of the earth"* was not just stretching, but laughably over-sized.

As for their leader, Peter, and his fishing partner John, Luke tells us plainly that they were *"unschooled, ordinary men"*.[4] Their courage had failed them six weeks earlier on the night that Jesus was arrested, and verse 6 shows us that they still didn't fully understand his mission.[5] With generals like Peter and John presiding over the shattered remnants of his Kingdom army, Jesus' mission looked to have been a colossal failure.

Yet the Christian faith didn't die. Instead it grew, massively. The Gospel message ran from house to house across Jerusalem, then exploded through the cities of Samaria, Syria, Asia Minor, Greece, and Italy. It spread like wildfire across the Roman Empire, until its enemies complained that it had shaken the whole earth.[6] Incredibly and inexplicably, the Christian Church refused to roll over and die. Instead it conquered the world.

It was this success which brought the believers to the attention of Theophilus, the man to whom Luke dedicates his gospel and the book of Acts. We do not know his exact identity –

---

[3] Contrast Matthew 4:18; 15:29; Mark 1:16; 3:7; 7:31; John 6:1; 21:1, with Luke 5:1 and 8:26. The disciples' terminology is so embarrassingly inflated that some translators even replace the Greek word *sea* with *lake*.

[4] Acts 4:13.

[5] They ask Jesus when he will lead the Jews to throw off Roman rule. His real mission was far, far greater.

[6] Acts 17:6; 24:5.

his name means *Friend-of-God*, so it could even be a poetic name for Christians in general – but there is strong evidence that he was the judge for Paul's trial at Caesar's court in Rome.

For a start, Luke ignores the activity of nine of the twelve apostles, and in the second half of Acts he ignores the other three as well. Although his book has become known as "The Acts of the Apostles", its real focus is on the relative latecomer Paul, with detailed accounts of his missionary journeys, his arrest, his trials, and his journey to Rome. It isn't a biography, since it tells us neither the outcome of his trial nor how he eventually died, but it builds towards a cliff-hanger ending which leaves Paul awaiting judgment under house arrest in Rome. This only makes sense if Luke was writing to provide background for Paul's test-case trial of the Christian faith, and Luke confirms this by addressing his reader as *"most excellent Theophilus"*, which was the customary way for any Roman to address a judge in court.[7]

This is much more convincing than the view that Acts is a history of the spread of the Gospel from Jerusalem to *"the ends of the earth"*, in fulfilment of Jesus' command in Acts 1:8. Rome wasn't the ends of the earth, but the centre of it! She ruled the world from the centre of the Mediterranean Sea, which was Latin for the *Middle-of-the-Earth* Sea. The entire world revolved around her, even places at the true ends of the earth, such as Armenia and Britannia. Romans heard the Gospel on the Day of Pentecost itself,[8] and Paul wrote to a strong church in Rome in AD 57, five years before he arrived there in person. Therefore Luke didn't write Acts in AD 62 to describe the Gospel's arrival in Rome, but to guide a judge's verdict at the palace which

---

[7] The lawyer Tertullus and the defendant Paul both address the judge in Acts 24:3 and 26:25 in the same way that Luke addresses Theophilus in Luke 1:3. This is why Luke's recurrent theme in Acts is that Paul and the other Christians are innocent, and that their accusers are the real wrongdoers.

[8] Acts 2:10. The day of Pentecost was ten days after Jesus' ascension, in May AD 30.

dominated the earth. The prisoner Paul was about to stand before Caesar's court, and Judge Theophilus was about to pass his official imperial verdict over Paul and the Christian faith which had brought him there.

Luke gives Theophilus an outline of the Christian story so far. He tells him about the effect of the Gospel in Jerusalem (chapters 1–7), its spread to nearby Judea and Samaria (chapters 8–9), its acceptance by the Gentiles (chapters 10–12), its success in Asia Minor (chapters 13–15), its advance into Europe (chapters 16–20), and finally – with long speeches and careful attention to detail – the arrival of its leading exponent, Paul, in Rome (chapters 21–28). He does so using the best Greek in the New Testament, structuring his brief like the great Greek historians Herodotus, Xenophon, and Thucydides, on the basis of painstaking interviews with eyewitnesses.[9] As a result, the book of Acts was extremely successful: Theophilus ruled that Paul was innocent, and released him to continue his church-planting ministry.

Luke wrote this book for Theophilus, but he also filled it with essential, foundational teaching for any Christian who reads it today. We live in a world where the Church's mission can still feel as overwhelming and unattainable as ever. In the West, the Gospel has been sidelined, church attendance has haemorrhaged, and society at large views Christianity as the outdated and irrelevant creed of a foolish die-hard few. In parts of the world where church attendance is still strong, Christians have largely failed to transform the nations in which they live. Ours is still a world where Jesus' vision looks completely mismatched to his ragged bunch of followers. Yet Acts gives

---

[9] Luke 1:1–4. Luke was simply one of the best historians of the ancient world. When modern historians have criticized his work, archaeologists have repeatedly vindicated Luke at their expense. For example, scholars used to rubbish Luke's statement in 17:6 that the rulers of Thessalonica were called *politarchs* – until archaeologists dug up five separate inscriptions which proved that Luke was right and they were wrong.

ordinary Christians his blueprint for success – a much-needed manual from their extraordinary God.

If you feel like a very ordinary Christian, this should strike you as very good news indeed. Luke wrote Acts as far more than a legal brief for one of Caesar's judges in Rome. He wrote it as the story of ordinary Christians in the past, to encourage and equip ordinary Christians in the present. He wrote it to inform you, amaze you, excite you, and enthral you, but most of all he wrote it to *enlist* you. The Church's great mission is by no means over, and you have a role which is uniquely yours to play.

So hold on to your seat and get ready for the breathtaking message of the book of Acts. If you are an ordinary person, this book is for you: it is a call to ride to victory on the shoulders of your extraordinary God.

The Gospel to Jerusalem (30–33 AD)

The Promise (1:8)

But you will receive power when the Holy Spirit comes on you; and you will be my witnesses in Jerusalem, and in all Judea and Samaria, and to the ends of the earth.

(Acts 1:8)

When General Marshall became Chief-of-Staff to the US Army on the first day of World War Two, it consisted of only 174,000 poorly equipped soldiers. Five years later, he had turned it into the greatest army the world had ever seen, a mighty force of over 8 million men, which defeated the empires of Germany and Japan. Winston Churchill hailed Marshall as the *"organiser of victory"*, and declared that he had paved the way to triumph through his consummate brilliance as a strategist and trainer of men.

Luke wants to get one thing straight, right at the start of the book of Acts: the success of the Early Church was not down to any first-century equivalent of General Marshall. Their leader, Peter, took twelve years to realize he was even meant to take the Gospel to the Gentiles at all. When he did, he still needed to be rebuked to his face over his methods, *"because he was clearly in the wrong"*.[1] Paul, who rebuked him, was himself so lacking in the skills possessed by General Marshall that his critics in the church at Corinth complained that *"he is unimpressive and his speaking amounts to nothing"*.[2] We are so used to viewing the early apostles as superstars on a pedestal that we can easily

---

[1] Galatians 2:11–14.
[2] 2 Corinthians 10:10.

forget that they were pitifully inadequate for the task which they were given. Jesus told them not even to try to fulfil his Great Commission until they had first received *"the promise of the Father"*. Only that promise could turn this little band of zeroes into Christ's world-conquering heroes.

Not just *a* promise. *The* promise. The Old Testament contains 8,000 promises from God – one promise for every three verses – yet three times Luke tells us that one promise so encapsulates all the others that it can simply be called *"the promise of the Father"*.[3] It was the promise which Jesus said would result in believers being *"clothed with power from on high"*. It was the promise which was so indispensable that they must wait in Jerusalem and not try to start without it. It was the promise that God would baptize his People with his Holy Spirit – that he would come and live inside of them and carry them to victory through his own indwelling power.[4]

The 120 disciples knew what it meant to be filled with the Holy Spirit. They knew the story of Samson, who fought an entire Philistine army on his own when *"the Spirit of the Lord came upon him in power"*. He was an ordinary man, but when he was filled with the Holy Spirit he was more than a match for a thousand of his enemies.[5] They also knew the prophecies of Isaiah, that when God's New Covenant People were filled with the Holy Spirit then *"the least of you will become a thousand, the smallest a mighty nation"*.[6] They knew the book of Ezekiel, where the breath of the Holy Spirit turned a valley of old bones

---

[3] Jesus calls it *"the promise"* in Luke 24:49; Acts 1:4, and Peter calls it *"the promise"* in Acts 2:39. Not all English translations stick to Luke's literal phrase, but he uses it three times on purpose.

[4] Luke 24:49; Acts 1:4–5.

[5] Judges 15:11–15. We tend to view Samson as a muscle-man in his own right, but 16:17–21 tells us otherwise.

[6] Isaiah 60:22–61:1. Despite the chapter division, these two verses belong to one another.

into a mighty army.[7] They also knew the prophecy of John the Baptist that *"I baptize you with water for repentance. But after me... [Jesus] will baptize you with the Holy Spirit."*[8] The hundred and twenty had very little going for them in terms of natural gifting, but at least they had one thing in their favour: they knew the value of the baptism in the Holy Spirit, and they waited and prayed until it was given.

The Holy Spirit would enable them to be Christ's witnesses. Not just *do* his witnessing, but *be* his witnesses. He would transform their lifestyles from the inside out, so that they would bear the fruit of the Spirit. He would fill their hearts with love for one another, so that Paul could tell a church that he loved every single one of them because he was filled *"with the affection of Christ Jesus"*.[9] The Christians would be so transformed by their baptism in the Spirit that their Gospel message would become irresistibly attractive to the unsaved world.[10]

The Holy Spirit would turn them into Christ's fearless witnesses. This persecuted religious sect, led by a man who had denied Jesus three times in the face of hostile questioning, would bear bold and fiery witness to the resurrection of Jesus Christ the Saviour. They would not be head-down, hope-they-don't-notice Christians who practised their religion in private and kept it to themselves in public. They would be bold and unstoppable, as Michael Green comments in his excellent book, *Evangelism in the Early Church*: *"Neither the strategy nor the tactics of the first Christians were particularly remarkable. What was remarkable was their conviction, their passion, and*

---

[7] Ezekiel 37. The Hebrew word *ruach* in v. 6 is the word normally used for the Holy Spirit, and v. 14 shows us that this is intentional. What God promised he would do for ancient Judah, he will also do for his Church.

[8] Matthew 3:11.

[9] Galatians 5:22–23; Philippians 1:8. See also Romans 5:5.

[10] Titus 2:10. We will explore this more fully in the chapter "Just the Way You Are".

their determination to act as Christ's embassy to a rebel world whatever the consequences."[11]

They would not simply be witnesses, but witnesses *with power*. Like any good witness in court, they would come armed with a wealth of supporting evidence. "Exhibit A" would be their spiritual gifts, such as prophecy, tongues, and words of knowledge. "Exhibit B" would be their ability to heal the sick and drive out demons. "Exhibit C" would be their authority to issue blessings and curses through the power of Jesus' name.[12] By the time these powerful witnesses had finished their testimony, they would be so feared and respected that large crowds of non-Christian onlookers would repent, be saved, and join them in their mission.[13]

Suddenly, this begins to make sense of the phenomenal success of early Christianity in the absence of any first-century General Marshall. They didn't need one because they were baptized with God's Holy Spirit, and their success was simply the result of him coming to dwell inside them. When God filled Samson with his Holy Spirit, he conquered a mighty army; when God filled the Early Church with his Holy Spirit, they conquered the world.

And so the hundred and twenty gathered in the upper room in Jerusalem, and they prayed and waited. They waited because Jesus told them to. They waited because they knew there was no point in starting until the Holy Spirit came. They waited because they had grasped the secret of God's promise of indwelling power.

We, on the other hand, would rather not wait. We would rather look to a Christian celebrity or the latest Christian paperback as a catch-all solution for the problems that we face. Some churches have split over the baptism in the Holy Spirit. Others have accepted that they need it, but crowded it out

---

[11] Michael Green, *Evangelism in the Early Church* (1970).

[12] For example, in Acts 5:8–10; 8:20–24; 13:8–12.

[13] Acts 5:13–14.

under mountains of liturgy, activity, busyness, and distraction. The call to be baptized in the Holy Spirit is a call to die to our own strength and *wait*. It's very easy, but also very difficult.

Without the Holy Spirit, we can be busy for God but we cannot be successful. He has given us his plan, and he refuses to fulfil it any other way. The Church has only ever marched to victory through God filling her ordinary foot soldiers with his own extraordinary Holy Spirit. She has always floundered when she neglected this call. Jesus still makes this promise – *the* promise – to us today: *"You will receive power when the Holy Spirit comes on you; and you will be my witnesses... to the ends of the earth."*

Joseph Barsabbas (1:15–26)

> *So they proposed two men: Joseph called Barsabbas (also known as Justus) and Matthias…. Then they cast lots, and the lot fell to Matthias.*
>
> (Acts 1:23, 26)

You've got to feel sorry for Joseph Barsabbas. He was a follower of Jesus from the beginning, eager to play his role in Jesus' Kingdom Revolution. When Jesus healed the crowds in Galilee, he was there. When Jesus clashed with the Pharisees, he was there too. He was there to take notes on the Sermon on the Mount, there to see Jesus drive out a demon in the synagogue at Capernaum, and there when Jesus went up on a mountainside to pray over which twelve followers he was to choose as his disciples.

When Jesus came down from the mountain, Joseph Barsabbas was in for a nasty surprise. He was part of the shortlist, but he hadn't made it into the Twelve. His friends Peter, John and Matthew had. So had Andrew, James and Simon. Even Judas Iscariot was chosen. I mean, *Judas?!* What was Jesus thinking?! After months of following Jesus round and hanging on his every word, Barsabbas was put on the bench and told he hadn't made the first team. It must have been a bitter disappointment.

But he kept going. For two more years he followed Jesus, not as one of the Twelve but as a close follower nonetheless. He was there when Jesus fed the crowds with loaves and fishes, there when he sent out the Seventy-Two on their Gospel mission, and there when Jesus rode into Jerusalem on a borrowed donkey. He was there when the crowds turned against Jesus, there when he was crucified, and there when he appeared alive again after his resurrection. He was a witness to Jesus' life, ministry, death, resurrection and ascension. Jesus had chosen twelve disciples, one for every tribe of ancient Israel.[1] There couldn't be thirteen, so the only way to join the group was by filling "dead men's shoes". Judas was dead, which meant a vacancy had opened. Barsabbas' time had finally come.[2]

Once again he made the shortlist. Only he or Matthias could possibly be the right man for the job, so the Eleven would cast lots between them like the priests of ancient Israel.[3] It was a tried and tested way of letting God reveal his sovereign choice – and this time the lot fell to Matthias. *Matthias?! Why him?!* This was a man so unimpressive that Scripture tells us nothing about him, before or after he was chosen. Joseph Barsabbas had once again been poised to go down in history as one of the Twelve, and once again God had passed him by. He had not just been sidelined by the Eleven, but by God himself.[4] Of course I'm speculating about how Barsabbas must have felt in Acts chapter 1, but I'm pretty sure it hurt him. A lot.

So here's the reason why Joseph Barsabbas is one of my favourite Bible characters: he didn't let it spoil him. He stared

---

[1] Matthew 19:28; Luke 22:30.

[2] Luke had access to Matthew's earlier gospel, so his account of Judas' death in Acts 1:18–19 must complement rather than contradict Matthew 27:1–10. Evidently Judas' body fell from where it hung and split open on the ground. The priests then took the money he had returned to them and used it to buy the field as a burial ground for foreigners. This dealt positively with the way he had defiled the field with his blood.

[3] Exodus 28:30; Leviticus 16:8; Numbers 27:21; Ezra 2:62–63; Nehemiah 10:34. A few writers argue that, since Matthias is not mentioned again, the Eleven were mistaken to cast lots to replace Judas and should have waited three or four years for God to call the apostle Paul. This argument is weak because eight of the Eleven are not mentioned after this point either, and Peter did so out of inspired obedience to Psalm 109:8.

[4] The God-centred prayer – *"Lord, you know everyone's heart. Show us which one of these two you have chosen"* – must have made the sting of rejection particularly hard for Joseph Barsabbas.

God's sovereign choosing in the face and made a courageous choice of his own. He would let God be God and accept that the Church was Jesus' body, not his. It was a difficult choice, a mature choice, but it's a choice we all have to make if we want the extraordinary God to work through our ordinary lives. If we manipulate our way to leadership outside of God's choosing, we must lead out of our ordinary strength, but if we submit to God's choice of role, he empowers us to serve him with his own extraordinary strength.

Let me give an example from my own family life. My elderly relations are all British and all played a role in the war against Nazi Germany. One of them served in Montgomery's Eighth Army in North Africa. Another captured Pegasus Bridge in Normandy as part of a daring airborne raid in the early hours of D-Day. Still another flew RAF reconnaissance planes over enemy-occupied Europe. Meanwhile, several others played a more mundane role in the war as farmers, teachers, factory-workers and mothers back in England. My question is this: Which of these relatives were war heroes who defeated Nazi Germany? The answer, I hope, is obvious. They all were. All of them played their own particular role in the massive war effort which defeated Adolf Hitler. Wars are always truly won by a selfless team of willing nobodies, and in God's Kingdom it's the same.

The book of Acts is full of ordinary people who became great apostles, preachers and miracle-working church-planters, but it is also full of ordinary people who served in the background: Dorcas who sewed clothing for the poor; Mary who opened up her home for an all-night prayer meeting; Simon the tanner who offered lodgings to Peter; the businesswoman Lydia whose home became the base for Paul's church-plant in Philippi; the tent-makers Priscilla and Aquila, who discipled a zealous but ignorant young man named Apollos, little knowing that they were preparing an apostle of the future.[5] Which of these were the heroes of Acts?

---

[5] See the chapter on "Apostles and Elders".

They all were. Anyone who faithfully plays their God-given role can be a hero in God's drama.[6] The only losers are those who refuse their role, succumb to bitter disappointment and try to play in a position of their own choosing.

You may be like Joseph Barsabbas yourself. Perhaps you once had high hopes that God would choose you to lead, plant churches or perform great exploits in his name. He may yet do so, but first he calls you to serve faithfully in the little things, in the unglamorous and unnoticed sidelines of his Kingdom mission. He calls you to play your God-apportioned role with all the grace and humility of Joseph Barsabbas.

There's an epilogue to this story in 15:22, when the apostles choose a man called Barsabbas to deliver a letter to the churches of Antioch, Syria, and Cilicia. He is called *Judas* Barsabbas rather than *Joseph*, so it may have been a brother, but since Joseph was nicknamed *Justus* because he was *Just*, it is not unreasonable to assume that he was also nicknamed *Judas* because he was a man of *Praise*.[7] Luke tells us that Barsabbas was chosen alongside Silas, another Jewish follower of Jesus who had not quite made it into the original Top Twelve, and that together these *"leaders among the brothers"* prophesied, encouraged and strengthened the churches at a time of vital need. Barsabbas had refused to give in to bitterness and disappointment, and continued to serve God faithfully in whatever role he was given.

This should encourage you if ever you feel overlooked or devalued like Joseph Barsabbas. Don't despise the sovereign choice of God and don't let the knock-backs of yesterday spoil you for today. If you guard your heart and play your role, you too can be an ordinary person, empowered by your extraordinary God.

---

[6] Luke emphasizes this in the Greek text of 1:15 by telling us literally that there were *"about a hundred and twenty **names**"* in the upper room. Each of them was known to God by name, and he chose a role for them all.

[7] The names *Judah* (Hebrew) and *Judas* (Greek) both mean *Praise*. See Genesis 29:35.

Pentecost (2:1–13)

All of them were filled with the Holy Spirit and began to speak in other tongues as the Spirit enabled them.

(Acts 2:4)

Everybody loves a good birthday party, and Luke tells us that God does too. When the New Testament Church was born on the Day of Pentecost, God threw her a birthday party unlike any other. It started early; partygoers were accused of being drunk and disorderly; it spilled out onto the streets; and it was such a noisy, joyful affair that 3,000 onlookers rushed to join the party too. The 120 disciples had prayed and waited for ten long days since Jesus ascended to heaven, but when the Holy Spirit finally came he was definitely worth the wait.

It must have been frustrating to be part of God's People before the great birthday party of Pentecost. Moses had longed for a day when every believer would receive the Holy Spirit, and Old Testament prophets such as Ezekiel and Joel had promised that such a day would eventually come.[1] John the Baptist had promised it would come through Jesus, but Jesus told them to wait, because the time had not yet come.[2] Most of the books of the Bible date back to that long period when God's People waited for this *"promise of the Father"* to be granted, and although he gave a taster by filling a few individuals with his Spirit, it still seemed a very long time in coming. This helps us understand why the Church's birthday party was such a spectacular event.

---

[1] Numbers 11:29; Ezekiel 11:19–20; 36:26–27; Joel 2:28–29.

[2] Luke 3:16; John 1:33; 7:37–39.

The disciples were so intoxicated with joy that their neighbours assumed they must be early-morning binge drinkers.

They were intoxicated because they knew that their waiting was over. Jesus had told them not to begin their work of church-planting and world mission until they were *"clothed with power from on high"*,[3] but Peter knew on Pentecost morning that he should stand up and proclaim that the promised day had now arrived. Jesus of Nazareth had been raised to life and lifted up to heaven, he explained in verse 33, and had received the promised Holy Spirit to pour out on all his People. Because of Jesus' life, death, resurrection and ascension, a new era of life in the Spirit had begun.

Not every Christian gets as excited about this news as Peter and his fellow partygoers, so let me explain: The word *Pentecost* was simply the Greek word for the *fiftieth day* after the Passover, the date of the Feast of Weeks, the third most important festival in the Jewish calendar.[4] Originally, it had been a simple harvest-festival when the Israelites brought their early crops to the Lord's Temple to thank him that a greater harvest was on its way. Over time, it also became a celebration of the Law-giving at Mount Sinai, since this had taken place fifty days after the original Passover at the Exodus. Therefore God had not merely baptized his People with the Holy Spirit as promised. He had also done so on a day which promised that the Spirit would enable them to live the righteous life which the Law could not (as promised by Ezekiel and demonstrated in Acts 2:42–47), and that a mighty Gospel harvest was on its way (as promised by Joel and demonstrated in Acts 2:41). The disciples simply couldn't contain their excitement. Since *"the promise"* is also for us *"who are far off"*, we should be very excited too.[5]

---

[3] Luke 24:49.

[4] Exodus 23:16; 34:22, Leviticus 23:15–21, Numbers 28:26–31; Deuteronomy 16:9–12.

[5] Once again, Peter refers to the gift of the Holy Spirit as **"the promise"**. Although the phrase "baptism in the Holy Spirit" is not used in chapter 2, Acts

Sadly, not all Christians are. Some downplay the baptism in the Holy Spirit, convinced that they received it all invisibly at conversion and that visible signs like those at Pentecost were merely part of the heady, early years of Christianity. Of course they are right that not everything which happened on the Day of Pentecost is necessarily normative for today: wind and tongues of fire do not seem to accompany the baptism in the Holy Spirit anywhere else in the book of Acts; nor does the gift of speaking to foreigners in their own languages appear to be quite the same gift as speaking in prayer languages in private and public worship,[6] where a God-given interpretation is needed to make sense of what is said.[7] Yet, in spite of this, Peter refuses to let us downsize the Day of Pentecost to something smaller than it really is. He tells us in verse 39 that Christians in every generation can experience the same promise as him, and in 11:15–17 that we should expect our own baptism in the Holy Spirit to be *visible* like his.[8] The great preacher Martyn Lloyd-Jones asks a sobering question to anyone who expects anything less from the Holy Spirit today:

> [They say,] *"It happened when I was born again, at my conversion; there is nothing for me to seek, I have got it all". Got it all? Well, if you have "got it all", I simply ask in the Name of God, why are you as you are? If you have*

1:5 makes it very clear that this is what Luke is describing here.

[6] God thwarted the human race's self-worshipping goals at Babel in Genesis 11 by dividing them into different language groups. He released his Church's Christ-worshipping goals at Pentecost by enabling his followers to unite all language-groups in *"declaring the wonders of God"*.

[7] 1 Corinthians 10:12, 28; 14:1–28.

[8] Some people argue that Cornelius' experience cannot be normative either, but this raises a bigger question: Since all Scripture is *"profitable for doctrine"* (2 Timothy 3:16), and the experience-based questions of Galatians 3:2 and 5 assume that the baptism in the Holy Spirit is both visible and discernable, where are the additional Scriptures which warn us to expect it to be invisible today? There simply aren't any.

"got it all"... why are you so unlike the New Testament Christians?"[9]

Even those who ask for the baptism in the Holy Spirit and experience it for themselves can be tempted to treat it as a one-off experience rather than the beginning of a new way of life in the Spirit. Luke will not have us shrink the Father's promise down to an event instead of a lifestyle. He tells us that the same Peter who was baptized in the Spirit on the Day of Pentecost was also filled and refilled in 4:8 and 4:31.[10] Peter needed to go on being filled with the Holy Spirit day by day, and so do we. It is not enough to talk about our experience of the Spirit in the 1990s; what matters is whether we are full of him today!

Still others reduce the baptism in the Holy Spirit to a matter of personal experience alone. When Peter and friends received the Holy Spirit, they immediately preached the Gospel and called others to conversion. God wants us to enjoy being filled with his Spirit, but he does it because we are heirs to the mission he described with a quotation from Isaiah 61: *"The Spirit of the Lord is on me, because he has anointed me to preach good news to the poor. He has sent me to proclaim freedom for the prisoners and recovery of sight for the blind, to release the oppressed, to proclaim the year of the Lord's favour."*[11] Luke tells us in Acts 1:1 that Jesus only began his mission in the gospels and continues it now through his People; the reason he baptizes us with the Holy Spirit is so that we can carry out the next phase of his plan. One of the biggest reasons why we struggle to be filled or refilled with the Spirit is that we ask for the wrong reasons. The Spirit

---

[9] David Martyn Lloyd-Jones, *The Christian Warfare: An Exposition of Ephesians 6:10–13* (1976).

[10] In Acts 4:8 and 31, Luke deliberately uses aorist verbs to stress that Peter and friends were *filled* afresh and not merely *full* of the Holy Spirit. Similarly, Paul deliberately uses a present imperative in Ephesians 5:18 to stress that we must *"go on being filled with the Holy Spirit"*.

[11] Luke 4:14–21; Acts 1:1–2.

is still devoted to the mission of Isaiah 61, and he rushes to fill anyone else who is devoted to it too.[12]

God wants all Christians everywhere to navigate these pitfalls and be filled with his Spirit each day of their lives. All around the world, people are doing so today, and I want to end with a recent testimony from the United States, where a surprised pastor explains what happened to him when he asked God to do what he had promised:

> *Suddenly, without any warning, I experienced for the first time in my life a genuine baptism of the Holy Spirit. I was filled so fast with such an amazing and intimate joy and happiness, I began shouting and laughing... I laughed, I cried, I was overjoyed, and then without warning a flood of prophetic activity filled my mind, such as I've never experienced before. Then, as if all this was not strange and mysterious enough, I noticed my description of the things I was seeing was not in English! I was speaking in tongues! I got up the next morning, I worshipped with more intimacy than I ever have, I preached more passionately than I ever have, and people definitely noticed. Thank God for the baptism in the Holy Spirit. I can't wait to see what's next.*[13]

Whatever your background, God invites you to come and keep coming to be filled and refilled with his promised Holy Spirit. *"The promise is for you and your children and for all who are far off – for all whom the Lord our God will call."*

---

[12] Jesus tells us in John 15:26–27 that the mission of Isaiah 61 belongs to the Holy Spirit before it belongs to us.

[13] This story was told at the "Together on a Mission" conference at Brighton, UK, in July 2009.

WTNOTSO

The Message of Jesus (2:14–41)

Men of Israel, listen to this: Jesus of Nazareth was a man accredited by God to you by miracles, wonders and signs, which God did among you through him, as you yourselves know.

(Acts 2:22)

Witnesses speak. A judge like Theophilus knew that. So it must have come as no surprise to him that a book which began with the charge *"you will be my witnesses"* was also a book filled with speeches. There are twenty-four major speeches in Acts, almost one for every chapter, and together they account for over a third of its verses.[1] Peter has eight speeches, James has two, Stephen has one, and Paul has nine.[2] Theophilus must have expected this, not just because long speeches were part-and-parcel of any Greek history-book, but because he knew that a book about the lives of Jesus' witnesses must also explain what they bore witness *to*.

Theophilus understood something else about witnesses, something we can often forget. Witnesses do not simply speak. They speak specifically about what they have seen and heard. The Greek word *martus*, or *witness*, was not primarily a religious term but a legal one. It referred to anyone who bore testimony to what they had seen, heard, and experienced.

---

[1] 365 out of a total of 1,006 verses.

[2] The other four speeches are by non-Christians: Gamaliel, the Ephesian town-clerk, Tertullus and Festus. Not all of the Christian speeches are classic Gospel messages. Some are legal defences or talks for believers.

This is an important point for anyone who wants to communicate the Gospel effectively. Luke has given us a book of abridged Gospel messages in order to train us to be witnesses ourselves.[3] Not just *speakers*, who find engaging ways to talk about God's love, our sin, the cross, and salvation, but *witnesses* who tell people about Jesus' life, death, resurrection, and ascension. These are the events which Jesus lists in Luke 24:44–49 before he tells his disciples that *"you are witnesses to these things"*, and these are the things he has in mind when he tells them in Acts 1:8 that *"you will be my witnesses"*. Why else would the Eleven be so adamant that the replacement for Judas must be *"a witness with us of his resurrection"*, who had been there to see Jesus' life and ministry from his baptism in the Jordan right up to his ascension?[4]

Peter demonstrates what it means to be Christ's witness in Acts 2, when he delivers the first Gospel sermon of Church history. After eight verses which respond to the crowd's questions about the coming of the Holy Spirit, he launches straight into fifteen verses which give Jesus' biography: his life, his miracles, his crucifixion, his resurrection, his ascension, his identity as Lord and Christ, and his command to repent and be baptized. Since he is speaking to devout Jews, Peter backs this up with Old Testament quotations, but his message remains very simple: who Jesus is, what he has done, and what the hearer must do as a result.

This sets the tone for the other Gospel sermons in Acts as well. In chapters 3, 4, and 5, Peter preaches three more biographies of Jesus. In chapter 10 when he preaches to Cornelius and friends, he gives them a biography again – this

---

[3] Luke makes it clear that he abridges their words in v. 40. Although he was probably only present for seven of the twenty-four speeches, his account of each speech is still very reliable. Most of the speakers were his personal friends, and Luke 1:3 tells us that he painstakingly interviewed those who were there before he wrote.

[4] Acts 1:21–22.

time even talking about meals he shared with Jesus after his resurrection! Each time he stresses that he himself is a witness to these facts,[5] and each time he calls them to respond to Jesus the person. Philip echoes this approach in 8:35, when he tells Jesus' biography to the Ethiopian. The missionaries to Antioch and the young preacher Apollos do the same in 11:20 and 18:28. Paul does so repeatedly in the second half of Acts, although his final speeches are legal defences rather than classic Gospel sermons.[6]

This can't have come as a surprise to Theophilus, for he knew what was meant by the legal word *witness*. If we are surprised by the biographical nature of the sermons in Acts, Luke wants to make us sit up and take note.

Most Western Gospel messages treat the Gospel as a kind of spiritual equation – *sin plus the cross plus repentance equals salvation* – but this falls short of what we have truly been called to do. It treats the Gospel as a God-inspired formula, a set of well-crafted theological propositions, which the non-Christian hearer is asked to believe. It is nowhere near as powerful as introducing the hearer to the man Jesus Christ – to his life, teaching, miracles, death, resurrection and ascension. These are not opinions, but facts, and incontrovertible facts if the hearer will listen. What is more, Christians who find listening to Gospel sermons "boring" because they have heard the message so many times before, suddenly find them fascinating. The story of Jesus is simply too multifaceted ever to become boring. Instead, Christians find themselves falling more in love with him every time.

What's more, preaching the Gospel as a spiritual equation creates stillborn and self-centred "converts". Put simply, it

---

[5] Acts 2:32; 3:15; 4:20; 5:12; 10:39, 41.

[6] Examples are Acts 9:20, 22; 13:16–41; 17:3, 7, 18; 18:5; 28:23. Paul doesn't mention Jesus by name at all in Lystra or Athens in chapters 14 and 17, but this doesn't detract from this point. Both speeches are interrupted, and 17:31 shows that Paul was preparing the ground to speak about the life of Jesus.

presents Jesus as the solution to *my need* of forgiveness and reconciliation. If I accept it, I get up off my knees thinking that Jesus has made a transaction with *me*, and I wonder what other great things he can do for me too. Hearing the story of Jesus, however, is entirely different. I realize that the Gospel is not primarily about me at all; it's about *him*, and about his call to follow him. If I accept it, I get up off my knees understanding that I have made a transaction with *him*. I have received his forgiveness and been reconciled to God, but I have done so as part of being raised to a new life of following him as King. Although I know that he will bless me in a thousand different ways, my focus is on what I now need to do in obedience to *him*. I have actually understood that Jesus is Lord and Christ, and that my biggest need was not just forgiveness, but total repentance. This was Peter's message when it *cut people to the heart*, and it made them want to be baptized straight away.

Jesus has called you to be his witness too. I know you weren't there to watch his ministry in Galilee and Judea, but neither was Stephen, who is called a witness, or Paul who is called one too.[7] You are one of those that Jesus said are more blessed in John 20:29 because you believed what others told you and can now bear witness from your own experience that this first-century message is true. You are one of his modern-day witnesses, telling people the story they so desperately need to hear.

So tell people about Jesus: not just as the bridge, but as the destination; not just as the one who died to forgive, but as the one who lives that we might follow; not just as the one who helps, but as the one who humbles; not just as the one who balances the equation, but as the one who is its answer as well. That was Peter's message when 3,000 were converted, and it's still the message to which we are witnesses today.

---

[7] Stephen is called a *martus*, or *witness*, in 22:20, and so is Paul in 22:15 and 26:16.

True and False Conversion
(2:38)

> Peter replied, "Repent and be baptized, every one of
> you, in the name of Jesus Christ for the forgiveness
> of your sins. And you will receive the gift of the Holy
> Spirit."
>
> (Acts 2:38)

The Church's biggest danger has never been a lack of converts.
It has always been false ones. As Peter surveyed the anxious
crowds on the Day of Pentecost, he knew that the Church was at
a crossroads. This could be a moment of staggering growth for
the hundred and twenty, but it was also a moment of terrible
danger. Unless those who joined them were truly converted,
they would sink the tiny Church in its fragile first few days. Luke
outlines the response which Peter demanded from the crowds,
both here and in 3:19–20, because he wants us to do more than
simply preach the right Gospel message. He wants us to call for
the right response to it too.

Peter doesn't ask the crowd to say sorry for their sin. He
asks them to do something far more fundamental than that. He
tells them to *metanoeō*, or *repent*, which has at its root the idea
of *changing one's mind*. Repentance is about choosing to walk
on a completely new path, which is why Luke keeps referring to
the Christian faith as *"the way of God"*.[1] Peter insists in 3:19 that
the crowd must *"Repent, then, and turn to God"*, and Paul tells
King Agrippa in 26:20 that the Gospel message is that people
"should repent and turn to God and prove their repentance by their

---

[1] Acts 9:2; 18:25, 26; 19:9, 23; 24:14, 22.

deeds". True conversion is not about apologies or protestations of repentance. It's about a genuine, heartfelt change of mind, which results in a new way of life.

God has given us a helpful example of insincere repentance in the first chapter of 1 Kings. Adonijah, King David's oldest surviving son, tried to rebel against his younger brother Solomon when he was chosen by God as the heir to the throne. He failed and ran to lay hold of the brass altar in the Tabernacle, pleading for forgiveness on the basis of its blood sacrifices. This put Solomon in a dilemma: his brother was a sinful rebel who was worthy of death, but he was also appealing for forgiveness on the basis of God's blood sacrifice. Was he truly repentant, or did he just want forgiveness to live on as a rebel? Solomon couldn't tell, so he forgave him and let him prove his repentance through his deeds. Only a few verses later, however, Adonijah launched a second bid for the throne. His actions proved that his repentance was a sham, so even though his henchman Joab ran to lay hold of the bronze altar himself, Solomon quickly had them both executed for their sin. True repentance always bears fruit, and God wants us to grasp that conversion without heartfelt repentance is no conversion at all.

Peter tells the crowd that there is something specific they must do as a mark of their repentance. They must be baptized in water. He could hardly have asked the Jews to do anything more offensive, even though John the Baptist had prepared them for the news.[2] Water baptism was for Gentiles who converted to Judaism, so being baptized was to admit that no one could be saved by their Jewishness alone. It would mean burning their bridges and being ostracized by their fellow Jews.[3] It would mean throwing in their lot publicly and permanently with the hated and despised Galileans. Note that Luke tells us nothing about the Jews who paid lip-service to Peter's message, because

[2] It was in this sense that John the Baptist's baptism of repentance "prepared the way" for Jesus in Luke 3:4.

[3] John 9:22; 12:42; 16:2.

faith without obedience is of no use to anyone. He only tells us about the 3,000 who went through with Peter's difficult, unpalatable demand, because they were the true converts to Christ. Baptism is still the first demand which Jesus makes of all those who follow him, because only those who swallow their pride and obey their new Master at the first hurdle can become true disciples at all.

After two things which Peter called new converts to *do*, he moves on to two things which he calls them to *receive*. They must accept they are forgiven, which is not quite as easy as it sounds. Most churches are full of people who live with low-level guilt over their past and present sin, and who think it humility to refer to themselves as "sinners". Peter is not interested in recruiting an army of self-flagellating "sinners". He tells them to pass through the admission they are "sinners" towards faith that they have been made "saints" through the blood of Christ. Peter didn't need to tell the crowds to admit that they needed forgiveness – their agonized plea in verse 37 showed that they were well aware of that – but he did need to tell them to *believe* that they were forgiven. He needed to tell them to believe that their sins had been *erased* through the Gospel, and that the power of the cross was more than a match for their sin.[4] Conversion is not just an admission of failure. It is a confession of faith in Christ's great victory.

Finally, Peter tells the crowds that true converts will open themselves up to receive the gift of the Holy Spirit. He does not say this is automatic – we will look in the chapter on 19:1–6 at the barriers we can put in the way of receiving the gift – but he does say that the Gospel offers more than just the possibility of receiving. He assures them that if they repent, they *"will*

---

[4] The word Peter uses in 3:19 is *exaleiphthēnai*, which means literally *to erase* or *to blot out*. The much-quoted 1 Timothy 1:15–16 is not telling us to call ourselves sinners, but to call ourselves saved!

receive the gift of the Holy Spirit".[5] This is as certain as the gift of forgiveness, and essential if we are to live as true followers of Christ. Since Peter tells the crowds in 3:20 that to receive the Holy Spirit is to receive Christ himself,[6] it is ludicrous to think that anyone can repent and promise to walk his new path of forgiveness while refusing to let him come and dwell in their heart.[7] The message of 3:21 is that Jesus needs to stay bodily in heaven but longs to dwell through his Spirit in our bodies instead. Christian conversion is not just about receiving forgiveness, but about turning our lives over to Jesus so that he can continue his mission through us by the power of his Spirit.[8]

Luke encourages us through Peter's 3,000-strong response that God wants to use us to lead large numbers of people to salvation, yet at the same time he warns us to remember the Gospel's quality-control. Only those who repent, who are baptized, who receive forgiveness, and who open themselves up to the gift of the Holy Spirit can become true disciples in the army which Jesus is recruiting. He sets the bar high, and he forbids his witnesses to set it any lower.

Jesus Christ has stated his terms. Let's follow him wholeheartedly, and let's make other true converts who will follow him the same way too.

---

[5] Peter does not use a Greek imperative here, but a future indicative (*lēmpsesthe*) which means *you will receive* the Holy Spirit. This sense of certainty also pervades 3:19–20.

[6] Jesus also taught this himself in John 14:18.

[7] I am *not* saying that those who have not been baptized with the Spirit cannot be Christians. I am simply agreeing with Paul's consistent teaching that all true converts will want to be filled with the Holy Spirit. See Romans 8:9–17; 1 Corinthians 6:19; 12:12–13; Galatians 3:2–3; Ephesians 1:13–14.

[8] See Acts 1:1 where Luke tells us that Jesus *began* his mission in his own body. He now continues that same mission through his Spirit dwelling in our bodies too.

How to Grow As a Christian (2:41–47)

They devoted themselves to the apostles' teaching and to the fellowship, to the breaking of bread and to prayer.

(Acts 2:42)

A few months ago, my wife gave birth to our beautiful baby girl, Esther. We cuddled her, cleaned her, dressed her, and laid her in a cot in the maternity ward. We celebrated that the task of giving birth was over, but neither of us pretended that the job was now done. We both knew that the hard work was only just beginning. A new birth means new responsibilities, and 3,000 new converts on the Day of Pentecost must have seemed overwhelming to Peter and the hundred and twenty. Each of them had twenty-five baby Christians to look after.

The book of Acts tells the story of how churches grew fast without sinking. Luke told us in his first book that Jesus once gave Peter such a miraculous catch of fish that his nets *"began to tear"* and his boat *"began to sink"*, but that he didn't give him any more than he could handle.[1] On the Day of Pentecost, he gave Peter such great insight into how to disciple his converts quickly and effectively that he could cope with 3,000 at a time. Luke therefore follows up his teaching on true Gospel preaching

---

[1] Luke 5:6–7. The inference is that if Peter had had stronger nets and more business partners, Jesus would have given him more fish. How we disciple new converts can therefore be a real inhibitor to the number that God can entrust to us at any one time. We need to get this lesson right if we hope to grow.

and true conversion with several verses which teach about true discipleship as well.

Peter and the hundred and twenty did *not* disciple their new converts one-on-one. It's not just that they didn't have time to do so; they didn't want to. They were following Jesus' model, and Jesus had left them in no doubt as to what it meant to be his disciple. The word *mathētēs*, or *disciple*, was the Greek word for a *student*, a *learner*, a *follower*, or an *apprentice*. It was not for the teacher to pursue his passive pupils, but for the pupils to pursue their teacher and to follow him as their new master. Jesus had recruited the Twelve not with promises and incentives, but with a simple command to *"Follow me!"*, even though it meant leaving behind family, friends, fields, and fortune.[2] When Jesus commissioned them to *"Go and make disciples of all nations"*, he was not so much telling them to disciple the world as to call the world to become disciples.

Therefore Luke tells us that the apostles set up the structures and meetings which still form part of most local churches today. They organized large-scale meetings in the Temple courts, and an informal network of smaller meetings from house to house. Although it's fashionable today to despise such structured church life, it was actually the thing which saved the Church from sinking under the weight of its success. Luke doesn't bother mentioning the "converts" who agreed with the Christian message but refused to repent of their arrogant spiritual individualism. He focuses solely on those who were *added* to the Church (verses 41 and 47). They were the true converts to Christ, and the only ones he could use for the rest of his great story.

Meeting together provided a loving home in which the 3,000 converts could thrive. It is easy to assume that the *"they"* of verse 42 refers to the hundred and twenty, but in its context it has to refer to the three thousand as well. Because they were

---

[2] Matthew 4:19; 8:19–22; 9:9; 10:38; 16:24; 19:21, 27–30.

true disciples, they didn't need chasing and spoon-feeding and nappy-changing like my baby, Esther. Luke tells us that they *devoted themselves* to learning together, praying together, worshipping together, sharing together, fellowshipping together, laughing together, and breaking bread together, in exactly the same manner as had characterized the hundred and twenty.[3] They sold their possessions as gladly as the founder-members of the Church, and they had one heart and mind with their new brothers and sisters. The word which Luke uses is *koinōnia*, which means *oneness* or *fellowship* or *togetherness*. They were genuine converts, which meant they didn't need to be dragged to follow Jesus.

When Paul tells us that his Macedonian converts *"gave themselves first to the Lord and then to us"*, we begin to understand that Luke is not merely describing the practices of a one-off group of Christians in Jerusalem.[4] Every growing church has always been like this, from Antioch to Asia to Europe and (hopefully) to your own. Church leaders need to ensure that their preaching and programmes are relevant and full of content, but they mustn't wear their churches out in trying to disciple those who are not disciples at all. Treating new converts like passive little babies is a sure-fire way to wear out church members, stifle church growth, and put an end to a church's advance with the Gospel. Calling new converts to *"follow"* by devoting themselves to their local church, however, is an equally sure-fire way to discover which ones are truly converted, and to help them grow into mature believers that God can build with.

The three thousand gave up their lives to become part of the alternative community which lived for Jesus in Jerusalem. Master rubbed shoulder with slave, and both treated one

---

[3] The Greek word *proskartereō* in vv. 42 and 46 means *to stick to something determinedly*, and is the word Luke uses in 10:7 to describe a servant *sticking determinedly* to his master. He told us in 1:14 that the 120 *stuck determinedly* to corporate prayer, and now he tells us that the 3,000 did so too.
[4] 2 Corinthians 8:5.

another as brothers. Jews from Africa, Europe, Asia and Judea shared their homes and their lives with one another.[5] They were consumed with Christ, and they poured out their lives to be part of his new community. Far from swamping the Church, the three thousand made it stronger, so that not a day would go by without more unbelievers being saved and added to their number.

Luke doesn't tell us that the apostles needed to exhort the three thousand to go out and bring their unsaved friends to Christ. He simply tells us in 5:42 that every time they met in the Temple courts or from house to house, there were always newcomers present to discover the Good News that Jesus is the Christ.[6] It's hardly surprising, when such a beacon of hope had been lit in their midst.

Two of the commonest questions I am asked as I travel round churches are *"How can I grow as a Christian?"* and *"How can I make my church grow?"* Luke has given us his answer to both questions in these verses. If we preach the true Gospel and ask for true conversion, we will build churches of true disciples who devote themselves to their Lord, to one another, and to the unbelievers who are drawn irresistibly to their flame.

---

[5] Acts 6:1 stops us from being unrealistic about the Jerusalem church. It was united but not problem free.

[6] Luke uses the verb *euangelizō* in 5:42, meaning *to evangelize*. Non-Christians constantly came to the church meetings to find out more, and if we live this way, they will certainly come to our meetings as well.

Just the Way You Are
(3:4, 12)

Then Peter said, "Look at us!"… When Peter saw this, he said to them: "Men of Israel, why does this surprise you? Why do you stare at us…?"

(Acts 3:4, 12)

One Sunday morning at the turn of the twentieth century, Mahatma Gandhi decided to go to church. The young lawyer, who would go on to become the father of the modern state of India, had been impressed by what he read of Jesus in the gospels, and decided that he wanted to know more. Biographers are not agreed on what exactly happened as he tried to enter the church near his offices in Natal, South Africa, but it certainly put him off the Gospel for the rest of his life. One of the white ushers apparently barred the "coloured" newcomer from taking a seat at the back of the whites-only church building, and Gandhi was suddenly confronted with the great gulf between the Jesus of the gospels and the Jesus who is often found in church. He looked back on this experience in later life and complained that, *"I like your Christ – I do not like your Christians. Your Christians are so unlike your Christ."* Mahatma Gandhi went to church to look for Jesus, but he didn't find him there. The billion-strong modern nation of India was founded by a Hindu instead.

The early Christians knew that outsiders would judge Jesus based on how his Church behaved. For a time, Jesus had been able to say that *"Anyone who has seen me has seen the Father"*,[1] but that was before his ascension. The world needed a new place

---

[1] John 14:9.

in the post-ascension world where they could look to discover what the Living God is like. That new place was his Kingdom community, the Church. Jesus had told them moments before his ascension that from now on, *"You will be my witnesses."* Not just witnesses who bore testimony through their words, but also witnesses who bore testimony through their lifestyle. As John put it in one of his letters, *"No one has ever seen God, but if we love one another, God dwells in us."*[2]

So when Peter told the lame man at the Beautiful Gate to *"Look at us!"*, he was doing something far more than turning the beggar's attention from his wallet to his face. He was commanding him to gaze at him and John because they were part of the new face of Jesus on the earth. They were part of Jesus' body, the Church, and to meet them was to meet Jesus himself. Stephen displayed this to the Sanhedrin in 6:15, when they *"saw that his face was like the face of an angel"*, and it was this more than anything else that convinced the world that the Christian Gospel was true.

Aristides of Athens gives this explanation for why he and so many others were converted to Christ through the Church's message:

> *They walk in all humility and kindness, falsehood is not found among them, and they love one another. They do not despise the widow or grieve the orphan. He that has, distributes liberally to him that has not. If they see a stranger they bring him under their roof, and rejoice over him as if he were their own brother; for they call themselves brothers, not after the flesh, but after the Spirit and in God. When one of their poor passes away from the world and one of them sees him, he provides for his burial according to his ability; and if they hear that any of their number is imprisoned or oppressed for the*

---

[2] 1 John 4:12.

name of their Messiah, all of them provide for his needs,
and if it is possible that he may be delivered, they deliver
him. And if there is among them any man who is poor and
needy, and they have not an abundance of necessaries,
they fast two or three days so that they may supply
the needy with the food they need. And they observe
scrupulously the commandments of their Messiah.[3]

Aristides had been deeply impressed by the lifestyle of the early believers, and such radical, authentic Christianity is still deeply impressive today. The Gospel did not spread like wildfire through the Roman Empire simply because the apostles motivated rank-and-file Christians to "become more evangelistic". It did so because the Early Church was filled with the Holy Spirit and therefore became a new kind of community: pure, loving, caring, and sincere. The world has always been sick and tired of *talk-talk*, but it has never failed to respond to genuine *walk-walk*. The citizens of Jerusalem, Antioch, and the rest of the Roman Empire were simply so baffled and intrigued by the alternative lifestyle modelled by the Church that – against their natural preferences – they began to suspect that Jesus really might be Messiah Christians claimed that he was, and that his Kingdom might truly have come as they said.

Paul told Titus that the way Christians live can *"make the teaching about God our Saviour attractive"*. He uses the Greek word *kosmeō*, which is the word Peter uses for women making themselves look beautiful for their husbands, and the word John uses for the Bride of Christ making herself gorgeous for her Wedding Day.[4] He chose that word for a reason. The Church is Jesus' Bride, and she can make him look gorgeous or make him look ugly. The Church which Aristides saw was the same Church as Acts, which made Jesus look gorgeous and attracted

---

[3] Aristides of Athens, *Apology* (chapter 15), dedicated to the Emperor Hadrian, c. 125 AD.

[4] Titus 2:10; 1 Peter 3:5; Revelation 21:2.

the world. The Church which Gandhi saw was very different: it made Jesus look ugly and repulsed him away from the Gospel.

Jesus is in heaven where the world cannot see him, but through his Spirit he also dwells in *us* where they can. That's why the real test of a church being filled with the Holy Spirit is not the liveliness of their meetings or their enjoyment of charismatic gifts. The real test is whether a church becomes Jesus' witnesses, a beautiful Bride dressed up for her glorified Husband. It is whether she lives like him, loves like him, and walks like him. It is whether she can tell people *"Look at us!"* (verse 4) as a prelude to telling them to look beyond her to see *Jesus* in her (verse 12).

Mahatma Gandhi rebuked Christian missionaries by claiming that *"If Christians would really live according to the teachings of Christ, as found in the Bible, all of India would be Christian today."* We shouldn't need a Hindu to remind us of the message of Acts. We will not convince the towns, cities and nations of the world that the Gospel of Jesus is true through new methods or programmes or initiatives. The answer is much more fundamental than that. The answer is just the way we are.

What I Have (3:6)

*Then Peter said, "Silver or gold I do not have, but
what I have I give you. In the name of Jesus Christ of
Nazareth, walk."*

(Acts 3:6)

Peter and John didn't have very much going for them. They didn't
have any silver. They didn't have any gold. They didn't have any
schooling or professional religious qualifications. They didn't
have great strategic minds which might turn the Church's global
vision into reality. They were just ordinary people who relied on
their extraordinary God.

They did, however, have one thing in their favour, which
Peter refers to mysteriously as *"what I have"*. When he and
John were accosted by a beggar en route to one of their prayer
meetings at the Temple, he was convinced that this one thing
was enough to offset all his personal inadequacies. Part One of
the book of Acts is the section where Luke tries to teach us the
secrets of effective Christian ministry, so there's a reason why
he gives us Peter's cryptic statement here. He wants us to stop
and do some detective work – and discover that we have what
Peter is describing as well.

Luke has already given us a first clue in his former book to
Theophilus. In Luke 12:32, Jesus promised the disciples: *"Do not
be afraid, little flock, for your Father has been pleased to give you
the kingdom."*[1] Jesus is King, and his Kingdom is not a matter of
talk but of power. He promised nobodies like Peter and John –

---

[1] Note that Luke uses the past tense here. The Father has already made up his
mind that the Kingdom is ours for the asking.

and us – that he would rule through them as his spokespeople on the earth. A few chapters later, Luke gives a second clue to show us how.

It is Luke 19 and Jesus is passing through Jericho on the way to die in Jerusalem. The streets are filled with cheering crowds, but Jesus picks out a corrupt little tax collector who has climbed a tree for a better view of the Messiah. He invites himself to Zacchaeus' house, and as the tax collector responds to his love and forgiveness by repenting and returning his ill-gotten fortune to those he had cheated, Jesus excitedly exclaims that this is why he came down to earth in the first place. *"The Son of Man came to seek and save what was lost,"* he explains. Not *those who were lost*, but *what was lost*. That's a very interesting way of putting it. It sounds awfully similar to what Peter says in Acts 3 when he tells the lame beggar he will give him *"what I have"*.[2]

The English poet John Milton grasped what Luke was saying here, and it inspired his two epic poems, *Paradise Lost* and *Paradise Regained*. The first, more famous poem tells the story of how Adam lost the Garden of Eden when he fell for Satan's temptation and sinned. The second poem tells the story of how Jesus reversed this loss when he resisted Satan's temptation and lived a completely sinless life. Milton's two poems form a stark contrast between Adam-the-Loser and Jesus-the-Victor because he understood what Luke is trying to tell us here.[3]

God made Adam to rule over a perfect world. He was a "king" of sorts, but he blew it. He and his wife ate forbidden fruit and brought a terrible curse upon the universe. They chose to believe Satan's lies over God's loving commands, and they made

51

---

[2] The word *to apolōlos* in Luke 19:10 is a neuter noun which cannot refer to lost *people*. It must refer to **"what was lost"**, just as Peter promises to give the lame beggar *"what I have"*.

[3] Paul teaches this explicitly in Romans 5:12–17 and 1 Corinthians 15:21–22, 45. John Milton published *Paradise Lost* and *Paradise Regained* in 1667 and 1671 respectively.

room for Satan build his foul kingdom on their planet. Death and sickness and trouble and pain began to infest their world, and did so with legitimate authority. When Satan tempted Jesus with a view of all the kingdoms of the world and a promise that *"I will give you all their authority and splendour, for it has been given to me, and I can give it to anyone I want to"*, his temptation was powerful because it contained an element of truth.[4] Sin doesn't merely separate us from God, it also strips us of his authority, but Jesus came to reclaim "what was lost". Paul wrote to the Galatians that *"Christ redeemed us from the curse of the law by becoming a curse for us, for it is written: 'Cursed is everyone who is hung on a tree.'"* He follows this up by telling the Colossians that he *"disarmed the powers and authorities... triumphing over them by the cross".*[5]

Now back to Peter and the lame beggar at the Beautiful Gate. The man wants money, but Peter doesn't have any. He only has the Gospel: the message that what Adam lost, Jesus has won. He looks at the beggar, lame from birth sitting in the dust, and remembers that when Jesus died on the cross he *removed* the curse of sin, *broke* Satan's authority, and *disarmed* him of his powerful weapons such as sickness. Peter grasps that the Gospel is not just a message of forgiveness for the beggar (which the man will discover later when he joins them for their Temple prayer meeting),[6] but also a message of healing and restoration. He turns to the beggar and gives him what he has – the ability to rule over Satan through the Gospel through the power of Jesus' name. He commands him, *"In the name of Jesus*

---

[4] Luke 4:5–6.

[5] Galatians 3:13; Colossians 2:15.

[6] Lame people were banned from the Temple (Leviticus 21:18 and probably 2 Samuel 5:8), so the beggar was about to enter the Temple for the first time in his life. When Peter says in v. 16 that the man now possesses *holoklēria*, or *complete healing*, he hints that he found forgiveness as well as healing through the Gospel.

Christ of Nazareth, walk!", and the lame man springs to his feet.[7] The crowds who witness the miracle are amazed, but confused. Is Peter a saint with special powers from God? Peter explains that it is all a question of *authority*, if only God's People will have *faith* in the Gospel they profess.

Recently, I discovered a cat in my shed. It had made a lot of mess and was cowering in the corner as I entered. *"Come on, cat, out you go,"* I said gently, but the cat refused to move. I looked at the damage it had done to my shed and suddenly felt very cross. I turned to the cat and shouted with a very different tone: *"You! Cat! Get out now!"* In an instant the cat fled, its tail between its legs because it knew I meant business, and even as it left I felt God speak to me: *"I have given you real authority over sin and sickness and Satan, yet all too often you act gently towards him. Rebuke him like that, and he will flee from you."*

I've been learning "what I have" through the Gospel, and God wants you to learn that it's "what you have" too. This week, for example, I rebuked the pain in a man's knee in the same way as the cat in my shed, and his knee was instantly healed by the power of Jesus' name. Not exactly a lame man, I know, but at least it's a start. When we grasp that the Gospel is "what we have", we find a faith which is more than big enough to override all our personal inadequacies.

---

[7] This was a double miracle, because the forty-year-old man had been lame from birth yet did not need to learn to walk (3:2; 4:22).

To Boldly Go (4:1–22)

When they saw the courage of Peter and John and realized they were unschooled, ordinary men, they were astonished and they took note that these men had been with Jesus.

(Acts 4:13)

The Kite Runner is the critically acclaimed story of a coward-turned-hero.[1] A young Afghan boy named Amir sees a local bully about to rape his best friend, Hassan, but he is too scared to help and abandons him to his fate. Twenty years later, he is still haunted by the guilty memory of his cowardice when he hears of a sudden chance for redemption. That same bully is now a leader of the Taliban, deep inside Afghanistan, and he has taken Hassan's son to become his sex-slave. This time, Amir does not hesitate. He smuggles himself back over the border, confronts the bully, and rescues Hassan's son in a breathtaking reversal of the past. Amir's transformation from coward to hero makes for a very inspiring story.

Unlike *The Kite Runner*, Luke's description of a coward-turned-hero is a true story. At Passover in 30 AD, Simon Peter denied Jesus three times, then ran and hid while his Master was crucified.[2] Theophilus knew from Luke's first book that Peter loved his life more than Christ, so in his second book, Acts, Luke gives him a very surprising ending to the story. Like an ugly caterpillar emerging from its chrysalis as a beautiful butterfly, the Peter who stands before the Sanhedrin a few

---

[1] *The Kite Runner* is a novel by Khaled Hosseini (2003), which was also turned into a film in 2007.

[2] Luke 22:54–62.

weeks after his denials is virtually unrecognizable.[3] He tells the Jewish leaders they are unsaved rebels, exposes their sin and hypocrisy, and then accuses them of murdering God's Messiah. The Sanhedrin are so startled by his new-found courage that they offer to release him if he will promise to stop preaching in the name of Jesus, but Peter is not about to cut a deal. *"Judge for yourselves,"* he barks in reply, *"whether it is right in God's sight to obey you rather than God."*[4] His would-be judges have no idea how to resist such raw courage and determination, so release him unharmed. Peter and John take on the seventy-one leaders of the Jewish nation and they win. It's a sudden transformation which demands an explanation.

Luke tells us that the Sanhedrin assumed that Peter and John were courageous because they *"had been with Jesus"*. That was true, but Peter had been with Jesus for three years before he denied him as well. It was *how* Peter had been with Jesus in the weeks since his denials which gave him the courage of Acts 4.

First, Peter had not merely been with Jesus, he had been with the *resurrected* Jesus. Peter boasted at the Last Supper that he would rather die than deny Jesus, but death was more frightening than he thought and he couldn't follow through. Jesus appeared to Peter at least six times after his resurrection,[5] and showed him that death was now a defeated foe. Peter wrote about this later when he said:

> *Praise be to the God and Father of our Lord Jesus Christ! In his great mercy he has given us new birth into a living*

---

[3] Acts 4 is technically undated, but 2:41, 2:47, and 4:4 mean that it must have happened weeks after Pentecost.

[4] In Plato's *Apology*, the great hero Socrates tells the judges at his trial that *"I honour and love you, but I shall obey God rather than you."* Luke may be hoping to paint Christianity in the same light for Theophilus – as the great heroic truth which cannot be silenced. See also 5:29.

[5] Luke 24:33–34, 36–49; John 20:26–31, 1–25; Matthew 28:16–20; Acts 1:4–12.

hope through the resurrection of Jesus Christ from the dead... If you should suffer for what is right, you are blessed. "Do not fear what they fear; do not be frightened." But in your hearts set apart Christ as Lord.[6]

Peter had seen that Jesus was Lord even over death itself, so he no longer feared dying. The man who is not afraid to die can never be silenced.[7]

Second, Peter had resigned himself to dying a martyr's death. When Jesus met him on the beach at Galilee, he told him plainly in John 21:18-19 that he would die for the Gospel. In the TV series *Band of Brothers*, the leader of a group of paratroopers tells his men that *"You hid in that ditch because you think there's still hope. But... the only hope you have is to accept the fact that you're already dead."*[8] Jesus knew that Peter would only find courage to spearhead the Church's mission when he lost all hope of dying peacefully in his bed. He defied the Sanhedrin, and even slept soundly on death row in Acts 12, because he already considered himself to be Christ's dead-man-walking.

Third, Peter had been baptized with the Holy Spirit. Luke tells us that the key mark of this was not his ability to speak in tongues, lead charismatic meetings, or heal the sick. The Holy Spirit is the Spirit of Courage who emboldened the shepherd-boy David to confront Goliath, and who still emboldens people like us to confront the world.[9] That's why Luke tells us in verse 8 that Peter refused to back down because he was *"filled with the Holy Spirit"*, and in verse 31 that the whole Church were *"filled with the Holy Spirit and spoke the word of God boldly"*.

It is difficult to overestimate the role which this raw

---

[6] 1 Peter 1:3; 3:14–15.

[7] The French playwright Pierre Corneille puts it succinctly: *"He who does not fear death cares naught for threats."*

[8] *Band of Brothers*, Episode 3: "Carentan".

[9] 2 Timothy 1:7; 1 Samuel 16:13, 18.

courage played in the astonishing growth of the Early Church. Michael Green puts it this way:

> *Here were men and women of every rank and station in life, of every country in the known world, so convinced that they had discovered the riddle of the universe, so sure of the one true God whom they had come to know, that nothing must stand in the way of their passing on this good news to others... They might be slighted, laughed at, disenfranchised, robbed of their possessions, their homes, even their families, but this would not stop them. They might be reported to the authorities as dangerous atheists, and required to sacrifice to the imperial gods: but they refused to comply. In Christianity they had found something utterly new, authentic and satisfying. They were not prepared to deny Christ even in order to preserve their own lives; and in the manner of their dying they made converts to their faith.*[10]

It is tempting to believe that the Early Church grew through better programmes or preachers or practices than our own, but Luke gives us a far simpler, far costlier explanation. He tells us that Spirit-filled men like Peter and John knew the risen Jesus and believed his Gospel, and that this made them unafraid to die for the sake of his mission. We may or may not be called to die for our faith, but we will all face threats and opposition if we refuse to stay silent.

The French philosopher Blaise Pascal converted to Christ with the statement that, *"I only believe the stories of witnesses who get their throats cut."*[11] The world is still looking for similar witnesses today, who demonstrate by their courage that they truly believe what they say. Our own stories still have room for a

---

[10] Michael Green, *Evangelism in the Early Church*, 1970).

[11] Blaise Pascal's 593rd *Pensée* (1670): *"Je ne crois que les histoires dont les témoins se feraient égorger."*

surprise ending like Peter's. God calls us to be cowards-turned-heroes through the transforming power of the Holy Spirit.

Given Name (4:12)

Salvation is found in no one else, for there is no other name under heaven given to men by which we must be saved.

(Acts 4:12)

First-century Palestine was home to two great religions which detested each other. Roman paganism was brash and self-assertive, and its desire to dominate is still felt in the names of our planets and the months of our calendar.[1] The Roman masters of Palestine offered worship and sacrifices at the temples of their gods in a fearful attempt to avert divine wrath and curry divine favour. Rome despised its monotheistic Jewish subjects, but tolerated their religion as the unpleasant price of peace in the provinces.

Judaism was ancient and sophisticated. Its Scriptures were without equal, and the Pharisees had turned the Law of Moses into an elaborate mechanism for pleasing God. Synagogues throughout the land taught how to win God's approval through strict adherence to the Mosaic Law, and the crowds at the Temple in Jerusalem brought sacrifices which they were told would secure his forgiveness. One day, they hoped, the Messiah would come and rid their land of the Romans and their paganism. In the meantime, they distanced themselves so strongly from the "Gentile dogs" that they refused to cross the threshold into any of their polluted homes.[2]

Peter and John had grown up in Palestine as believers in

---

[1] For example, the god *Janus* and January, the god *Mars* and March, and the goddess *Juno* and June.

[2] Acts 10:28; John 18:28; Galatians 2:12.

Yahweh through the lens of first-century Judaism. They were so steeped in its thinking that even in Acts 1:6 they still hoped for a Messiah who would drive the Romans back into the sea. Yet something significant had happened to them which had changed their perspective and set them at odds with the rest of their culture. As the Sanhedrin noted in Acts 4:13, they had been with Jesus and let his teaching undo all their preconceived ideas. They stood before the Sanhedrin, which had crucified their Master only a few weeks earlier, and they dared to announce their unspeakable conclusion: Roman paganism and Jewish Judaism were not as different as they had been taught, but were simply two faces of the same basic idea. They were two different ways to offer worship and sacrifices to earn God's forgiveness and favour. For all their superficial differences, they were both human attempts to work our own way to salvation.

Jesus of Nazareth had taught something radically different from either paganism or Judaism. He told a leading Pharisee that his pious devotion had done nothing to gain him God's forgiveness or favour. He was trying to buy his salvation through human endeavour, but God is too big to need any gifts from his creatures. He doesn't save because people give, but because *"God so loved the world that he gave"*.[3] He gave his only Son, Jesus, as the perfect sacrifice for sin so his justice would be satisfied and his favour extended. Jesus did not come to be served, as if God needed our service, but to serve humankind with an offering of his own.[4] Jesus' death and resurrection had proved once and for all that both paganism and Judaism were misguidedly flawed. Both tried to buy God's salvation through human sacrificial giving, but we can only be saved if we let God be the Giver.

We live in a world like first-century Palestine, only more so. Our nations play host to a myriad of religions, all with their

---

[3] John 3:1–8, 16.
[4] Mark 10:45.

own devoted group of disciples. Islam, Judaism, Hinduism, and Churchgoing are superficially different but fundamentally the same. They are all attempts to earn God's favour through our worship, devotion, and morality; they simply disguise themselves in different sets of clothes. Peter and John tell us they are all doomed to failure because God has already blazed his own trail of salvation. He sees our gifts as little more than a shabby attempt to bribe our Judge to ignore our guilt, when he has already given his Son's blood to be both just and the one who makes the foulest sinner clean. God the Giver is a blood donor who is not looking for fellow donors, but for humble recipients.

The message that salvation is found in Jesus Christ alone is a major taboo in our multifaith society, but it was just as taboo in first-century Palestine. It was this Gospel message which drew the ire of the Sanhedrin and, later, the persecution of the emperor as well. So long as people assumed that they were preaching a way of giving to God, the apostles were received by the Jews as brothers and by the pagans as gods. At soon as they discovered that they were preaching God the Giver, however, both Jew and Gentile turned on them and tried to stone them to death.[5] Only the humble can receive the message of Jesus as the good news of salvation. The proud find it bad news because it denies them a share in the glory for their salvation. Salvation is a gift freely given, so the glory goes to God alone.[6]

Luke wants the Church in every generation to see the same fruit as the Early Church in verse 4 of this chapter, so he urges us to find it by preaching the message of verse 12. Not through multifaith dialogue, but unflinching evangelism. Not through confused insecurity, but bold exclusivity. Through preaching this message which both enrages and engages in equal measure. This, he says, is the God-given Gospel to which we are witnesses.

---

[5] Acts 13:15, 45; 14:11–19. This turnaround was provoked by the clear message of 13:38–39.

[6] See Matthew 5:3; Romans 1:16–17; 4:5.

Prayer Which Moves God (4:23–31)

After they prayed, the place where they were meeting was shaken. And they were all filled with the Holy Spirit and spoke the word of God boldly.

(Acts 4:31)

A few months ago, my wife found a Buzz Lightyear costume in a charity-shop. It was exactly the right size for our five-year-old son, Isaac, and she knew it would make an ideal present for the start of the summer holidays. He would happily spend most of the summer dressed up as Buzz and fighting aliens in our back garden, but there was one minor hurdle in the way: Isaac had never even heard of Buzz Lightyear.

Not to be put off by such a trivial detail, we began to prepare him for his surprise. We started talking about stars, planets and space-travel, and we watched *Toy Story* together as a family. We did Buzz impressions over breakfast, and built space rockets out of cardboard boxes, until one day Isaac asked if we would buy him a Buzz Lightyear costume. It was neatly folded away at the back of the cupboard, but still we didn't reveal our hand. We watched *Toy Story 2* and talked about satellites and aliens and moon-landings, until one day, at the start of the school holidays, Isaac could think of no better present than a Buzz Lightyear costume and was ready for his surprise. He played, ate and slept in that costume throughout the summer, because his parents had created in him a desire for the very thing we wanted to give him. He still doesn't know that it was in the cupboard long before he ever knew that Buzz existed.

Luke tells us that it's often the same when we pray. We may feel as though we are bending God towards our own desires, but he is the one who gives us those desires in the first place. He isn't playing games with us – he really wants to give us all we ask for – but he is committed to working out his rule on the earth through his Church. Therefore in Acts 4:24–30 Luke gives us the longest recorded Christian prayer in the New Testament because he wants us to grasp what happens when we pray. We do not pray to *change* God's will, but we must pray if we want to see God's will come to pass. Let's stop and examine what Luke teaches us in his school of effective prayer.

The believers address the Lord as *despotēs*, meaning *Sovereign Lord*, which is the very same word which the Greek Old Testament uses to translate *Adonai Yahweh*.[1] Effective prayer always begins by reminding God of his names in Scripture. He has revealed himself through a wealth of names in the pages of the Bible because he wants to build our faith that his character holds the answer to our every need. Do you need provision? He is *Yahweh Jireh*, the Lord Who Provides. Do you need healing? He is *Yahweh Rophek*, the Lord Who Heals You. Do you need protection and deliverance? He is *Adonai Yahweh*, the *despotēs*, the *Sovereign Lord*. The believers in Acts 4 address the Lord by one of his own names in Scripture and remind him to be who he has promised he will be. They have chosen to obey him instead of their government, so God the *Sovereign Lord* must deliver them.

Next, the believers remind the Lord of his promises towards them. They quote from Psalm 2, again from the Greek translation of the Old Testament,[2] reminding him of his promises through David and asking him to do as he has promised. Their

---

[1] Two of the earliest examples are in Genesis 15:2, 8.

[2] Luke shows us that the church in Jerusalem used the Greek rather than Hebrew Old Testament. Peter's first quotation in Acts 1:20 *only* works in the Greek Septuagint, because the Hebrew speaks of a *fortress* being empty rather than a *dwelling*, and so does James' quotation in Acts 15:16–18. Luke always

quote reads *"Why do the nations [ethnos] rage and the peoples [laos] plot in vain? The kings [basileus] of the earth take their stand and the rulers [archōn] gather together [sunagō] against the Lord [kurios] and against his Anointed One [christos]."* Watch what they then do in their prayer: *"Indeed Herod* [who thought of himself as a basileus] *and Pontius Pilate* [who was our archōn] *met together [sunagō] with the Gentiles [ethnos] and the people of Israel [laos] in this city to conspire against your holy servant Jesus, whom you anointed [chriō]."*[3] Can you see what they are doing here in prayer? They quote God's promises back to him, using his own words in Scripture to ask to do the very thing he has promised. He has pledged that whenever the nations and peoples gather together to conspire against the Lord and his Christ, he will bring their plans to nothing. Of course God will answer their prayers, protect them, and enable them to defy the threats of their enemies – they are praying for the very things he has trained them to desire from him!

Finally, the believers remember that God's Old Testament promises must be read in a New Covenant context. They could have continued their prayer by asking him to stop the persecution or crush their enemies like pottery, but they understand the Gospel far too well to do that.[4] Instead, they understand that God wants to save the nations, not destroy them, so they ask for boldness and for miracles which will lead them to believe. As they close their prayer, God shakes the room as he answers their prayer by filling them with his Holy Spirit. He answered swiftly and completely because they were praying in exact accordance with his will. They were simply praying back to him

---

follows the Greek rather than Hebrew in Acts, and this quotation from Psalm 2 is word-for-word from the Septuagint.

[3] In fact, even though the *people* of Israel should be singular, the believers refer to Israel as the *laoi*, or *peoples*, to strengthen the link back to God's promises in Psalm 2.

[4] This would have repeated the mistake for which Jesus rebuked them in Luke 9:54–56.

the names and promises which he had given them to pray. They were simply asking him to give them what was folded away in his cupboard.

This is how the great men and women of Church history have always prayed. A friend of Martin Luther, the sixteenth-century reformer, wrote this about his prayers:

> *Not a day passes in which he does not spend in prayer at least three hours, such as are most precious for study. On one occasion I chanced to hear him pray. Good Lord, what a spirit, what faith spoke out of his words! He prayed with such reverence that one could see he was speaking with God, and with such faith and such confidence as is shown by one who is speaking with his father and friend. I know, said he, that Thou art our Father and our God. Therefore I am certain that Thou wilt confound those who persecute Thy children... Standing at a distance, I heard him praying in this manner with a loud voice. Then my heart, too, burned mightily within me, when he spoke so familiarly, so earnestly, and reverently with God, and in his prayer insisted on the promises in the Psalms, as one who was certain that everything he prayed for would be done.*[5]

When you do not know what to pray, this is your answer. Go to the names and promises of God in Scripture and pray them back to him. God has many gifts for you, folded away like a Buzz Lightyear costume in his cupboard, just waiting for you to ask for them as you are stirred by his name and his promises. This is what Jesus meant when he promised that *"If you remain in me and my words remain in you, ask whatever you wish, and it will be given you."*[6] Come and ask, expecting your prayers to move God, and when he answers just remember: You only moved him because first he moved you.

---

[5] Veit Dietrich wrote this in a letter to Philip Melanchthon on 30th June 1530.
[6] John 15:7.

Insider-Dealings (4:32–37)

There were no needy persons among them. For from time to time those who owned lands or houses sold them, brought the money from the sales and put it at the apostles' feet, and it was distributed to anyone as he had need.

(Acts 4:34–35)

The newspaper I read has pages of speculation about the future prices of stocks and shares. Business analysts from around the world give their hottest tips and deadliest warnings about the companies listed on the London Stock Exchange. I find their opinions interesting, but there's one report which I always find most compelling of all. It's the section entitled "Directors' Dealings". Senior executives have a legal duty to disclose any sale or purchase they make of their own company's shares, and it sends an important signal to investors. Last week, when a large retailer announced its ambitious plans for the future, one of its directors bought 50,000 extra shares and convinced the analysts that the bullish rhetoric might be true. The week before, however, a utility company issued an upbeat statement on the back of disappointing sales figures, and analysts quickly smelt trouble when a director sold 200,000 shares. Investing in stocks and shares can be a very risky venture, so it's always important to check that the directors' walk matches up to their talk.

The Gospel of Jesus Christ is an even riskier venture still. It demands a person's everything – their hopes, their plans, their time, their money and their energy – and can even cost them their lives. It should come as no surprise then, really, that unbelievers analyse the lives of the Christians around them to decide if their Gospel is true. This was one of the reasons that the Early Church grew so rapidly, and it may be a reason why the Western Church is declining just as rapidly too. That's what it means to be a Christian witness: someone whose walk, not just talk, convinces the jury of the world that Jesus Christ has truly risen and is Lord.

In Jerusalem, their verdict was clear. The Church of Acts 4 was dramatically different from the city in which it dwelt. Israel was a nation obsessed with the Promised Land, and righteous Naboth had been willing to die rather than sin against the Lord by selling some of his family estate.[1] But there were strange insider-dealings going on in the Church at Jerusalem. There were rumours that the believers had a hope which was greater than a piece of real estate in Palestine, and had begun to sell off their family properties. They were not investing the money (as any wise landowner would), but simply "squandering" it on the poor that they now called "brothers" and "sisters".[2] When the Jews of Jerusalem confirmed these financial rumours, they began to take the Christian Gospel very seriously indeed. Non-Christians know how to analyse the Church's insider-dealings, and to read whether its members really believe that the message they preach is true.

There was another rumour on the lips of the analysts in Jerusalem. Their Scriptures prophesied that the Messiah would *"defend the afflicted among the people and save the children of the needy"*, and that he would *"deliver the needy who cry out...*

---

[1] 1 Kings 21:1–16. Naboth refused to sell his vineyard because the Lord had commanded him not to in Leviticus 25:23 and Numbers 36:7. The detached way in which the early Christians treated their property in Palestine shows us that the New Covenant has changed the modern-day importance of the Promised Land.

[2] 1 Timothy 5:3–16 suggests that the money was actually not "squandered", but given based on wise criteria.

and save the needy from death".[3] The rumour that "there were no needy persons" within the new church family made them wonder if the Messiah had actually come. The Jews had long paid lip-service to the Law of Moses and its Jubilee principles of care for the poor, but they had never truly practised what they preached.[4] When they saw a community in which rich shared with poor, landowner shared with labourer, and master shared with slave, it gave credence to the message that the Old Covenant had truly been fulfilled in Jesus. Judge Theophilus was well accustomed to gauging the character of witnesses, so he cannot have been surprised that such insider-dealings had impressed the Jews of Jerusalem.

Rumour also had it that these Christians were not merely giving to each other as *they* saw need. They were doing something far more radical than that. They were bringing their money and laying it at the apostles' feet, trusting their God-anointed leadership to allocate it to those in greatest need. They weren't just philanthropists who gave their fortunes in their own name to their own favourite causes. They brought their money to God's leaders, with no strings attached, because their giving to the needy was primarily a gift to the Lord himself, administered by the leaders he had chosen.[5]

This kind of insider-dealing won the respect of Jerusalem, and ultimately of the world,[6] but it is always costly and never

---

[3] Psalm 72:4, 12, 13. This psalm of Solomon was a Messianic psalm and is linked closely to Acts 4:34.

[4] Theophilus also knew that his own Greco-Roman culture had never done so either, for all they admired Aristotle's fine-sounding suggestion that friends should live in community and with everything in common.

[5] Proverbs 19:17. This should challenge us not merely to give to the causes of our choice but, where possible, to do so through our local church. We give as part of a wider body, not as independent benefactors.

[6] There is no evidence that the other New Testament churches followed the exact same *practice* as Jerusalem, but they all followed the same *principle*. Each local church can work out the right practical detail for its own particular context. Hebrews 10:34 tells us that the Jewish leaders eventually confiscated

pain-free. It was not many years after Luke wrote the book of Acts that one church leader was forced to warn his readers that

> When non-Christians hear from our mouths the words of God, they are amazed at their beauty and majesty; but when they discover that our actions do not match up with the words we say, they turn from wonder to blasphemy, saying that it must all be a myth and delusion.[7]

We need to make constant checks that our walk always matches up to our talk.

When I worked at the American company Procter & Gamble, I rubbed shoulders with some very smart investors. One director was particularly cold towards my talk about Jesus, until the day I tendered my resignation to work for a church. He took me to one side and told me he would offer me more money to stay if he didn't already know I was leaving for half of what he was paying me. Then he said something which has stayed with me ever since. He looked me in the eye and told me: *"I have never taken you seriously when you talked about religion – until today."*

Every week, those around us compile a subconscious report on the basis of our lives, which marks the Christian message "up" or "down" as a credible investment. Like it or not, that's what being a witness means. People don't always believe what we tell them, but they always take note of our insider-dealings.

Christian property as part of their persecution in the 60s AD, so anyone who hung on to their property lost it anyway.

[7] 2 Clement 13:3. Some historians believe that Clement wrote these words in the 90s AD, but most believe that 2 Clement was written by a later church leader in about 150 AD.

The Fifth Column (5:1–11)

> *Then Peter said, "Ananias, how is it that Satan has so filled your heart that you have lied to the Holy Spirit and have kept for yourself some of the money you received for the land?"*

(Acts 5:3)

In the early months of the Spanish Civil War, as the Nationalist forces marched on Madrid, General Emilio Mola made a radio broadcast to the nation. He had been asked which of his four columns of troops would be the most instrumental in capturing the capital, and he gave a famous reply. Victory would not belong to any of his four columns, he boasted to his listeners. He had a *"fifth column"* of Nationalist sympathizers dwelling unnoticed within the city itself. They were the troops which would be instrumental to the victory. They would sabotage Madrid's defences from the inside out, and would lay her wide open for capture.[1]

In Acts 3 to 7, Satan attacks the young Church with four dangerous columns. The first column is *Persecution*, as threats, beatings, and imprisonment seek to weaken the believers' resolve. The second and third columns are *Division* and *Distraction*, as the apostles struggle to unite the Grecian and Hebraic believers without losing their focus amid the ever-increasing demands of church leadership. The fourth column, which spills over into chapter 8, is *Scattering*, as Stephen's martyrdom provokes panic and all the believers except the apostles flee the city of

[1] Emilio Mola's boast was in fact misplaced. The city of Madrid resisted his attack in the autumn of 1936. Franco captured it in 1939, however, due to a genuine *"fifth column"*.

Jerusalem. These form four formidable columns with which Satan attacks the walls of the Church, but the greatest danger in these chapters is the "fifth column" within. Satan couldn't break the walls of the Church from the outside in, so he worked under cover to destroy her from the inside out.

The Devil has quite a track record of working this way. Centuries earlier, when the Israelites arrived at the border of the Promised Land, he used his man Balaam to seduce them into idolatry and sexual sin in a last-ditch attempt to stem their advance.[2] Later, when they crossed the River Jordan and entered the Promised Land, he used Achan to commit sin within the Israelite camp, so that God opposed their army in battle.[3] Like any general who knows that his enemy is too strong for him, Satan has long been forced to pin his hopes on the success of his "fifth column".

Ananias and Sapphira were oblivious to this fact, and actually thought that they were doing God a favour. They had sold a piece of property and came to lay a bag of coins at the apostles' feet. They looked like virtuous people, generous givers, and exactly the kind of people who were needed in the growing church at Jerusalem, but Peter was too full of the Spirit not to spot Satan's "fifth column". He confronted Ananias and challenged him over his hypocrisy, accusing him of pretending to give generously while all the while holding back a proportion of the proceeds for himself. When Ananias denied it, Peter told him that Satan must have filled his heart because he was lying to the Holy Spirit, and then suddenly, without Peter explicitly cursing him, he fell to the ground and died! Three hours later, his wife appeared and repeated his lie, so Peter rebuked her and she fell down dead too! Peter was too spiritually aware to fall for

---

[2] Revelation 2:14. See also Numbers 25:1–9; 31:16.

[3] Luke uses the Greek word *nosphizomai*, or *to embezzle*, in 5:2–3 because it is the very word used in the Greek Old Testament to describe Achan's sin in Joshua 7:1. He is therefore making a deliberate link here.

Satan's agents on the inside, and the "fifth column" was swiftly repulsed.

Many modern readers find this episode terribly offensive. What kind of God gets this angry with his People, and why couldn't he be a bit more lenient? Hasn't anybody told him that patience is a virtue? It is one thing for him to judge Balaam and Achan in the Old Testament, but this side of the cross it just seems so out of place. Why did it really matter if a couple in the church chose to give slightly less than the entire proceeds of their sale?

Luke tells us that in some ways it didn't matter at all. Peter does not criticize them for bringing less than the sale price for their land, but goes out of his way to emphasize that the property and its sale-price was entirely theirs to dispose of as they wished. The issue was not about *stealing* at all. It was about *lying* and *hypocrisy*, which are altogether more serious.

Luke shares none of our misgivings towards God's judgment of Ananias and Sapphira. In fact, he seems to stress the importance of God's action by using the word *ekklēsia*, or *church*, for the first time in verse 11.[4] This was one of the words which the Greek Old Testament used for the *assembly* of Israel in the desert, when Israel succumbed to Satan's "fifth column" under Balaam and Achan. Luke seems to use it here for the first time in order to remind us that it is incredibly serious when the Church starts play-acting at devotion like the Pharisees and pagans. The advance of the Church is firmly linked to her pure and attractive witness to the person of Jesus Christ. If Satan soils and corrupts her under a veneer of discipleship, it is *game over* for the Church. Like a surgeon dealing with a cancerous melanoma, God gets out his scalpel and operates fast. Soon Ananias and Sapphira are lying dead on the floor of his surgery, but the body of Christ has been spared.

---

[4] Luke uses the word *ekklēsia* three times in a secular sense simply to mean the Ephesian *assembly*, but he also stresses the continuity between Israel and the Church by using it in 7:38 to refer to Israel in the desert.

We would sound more convincing in our complaints against God's judgment in Acts 5 if our churches were growing as fast as the one in Jerusalem. In the aftermath of these two deaths, the whole city was gripped with reverent awe towards God. Satan's "fifth column" dramatically backfired, as it always does when church leaders get serious over sin in their midst, so that the half-hearted fringe of the Jerusalem church either got gloriously saved or too scared to keep coming. Perhaps it's time we treated sin a bit more seriously ourselves.

If you are a church leader, you need to recognize the Christian tendency to judge sin too harshly in unbelievers and too leniently in believers. Paul wrote to the Corinthians to tell them

> *not to associate with sexually immoral people – not at all meaning the people of this world who are immoral... You must not associate with anyone who call himself a brother but is sexual immoral... What business is it of mine to judge those outside the church? Are you not to judge those inside? God will judge those outside. "Expel the wicked man from among you."*[5]

Luke warns church leaders to be vigilant for Satan's "fifth column", and to confront it as Peter does, both here and in 8:18–23. He calls them to be jealous for the Church with a godly jealousy, as those who must present her one day to Christ her Husband.[6] Luke warns every Christian in the Church to be vigilant in their own life too, to ensure that how they live matches up to what they sing and pray. Sin scuppers churches, but passion for Jesus keeps them strong. The loyal citizens of Madrid rose up and defeated Emilio Mola's "fifth column", and by God's grace you can defeat Satan's "fifth column" as well.

---

[5] 1 Corinthians 5:9–13.

[6] Paul uses this terminology in 2 Corinthians 11:2–3.

Primary Witness (5:12–16)

Crowds gathered also from the towns around Jerusalem, bringing their sick and those tormented by evil spirits, and all of them were healed.

(Acts 5:16)

Don't watch the beginning of *Saving Private Ryan* unless you want to see twenty-four minutes of brutal, stomach-churning slaughter. Director Steven Spielberg reproduces one of the bloodiest moments in World War Two, and it is horrific.[1] Unlike the soldiers who landed on the other four beaches on the morning of D-Day, the infantrymen on Omaha Beach were forced to do so alone. Their naval support was insufficient, their bomber support failed altogether, and over half of their tanks were sunk before they ever reached the shore. The American GIs who attacked the German defences at Omaha were forced to do so without the artillery support which proved so decisive elsewhere. As a result, fifteen times as many men fell taking Omaha as any other beach on D-Day.

Jesus told the Early Church not to attempt their dangerous mission until they were baptized in the Holy Spirit. He didn't want Jerusalem to become their Omaha, so he warned them to wait for the artillery to arrive. The Holy Spirit would fill them and turn them into Jesus' witnesses, but he would also go one vital step further. The Holy Spirit would also be the Primary Witness himself.

Most of our problems in evangelism stem from the

---

[1] *Saving Private Ryan* (Paramount, 1998). *Empire* magazine voted this *"the best battle scene of all time"*.

mistaken assumption that we need to persuade God to join us in *our* mission. Joshua made this mistake when he entered the Promised Land, and was reminded by an angel he was fighting in God's mission and not the other way round.[2] Jesus issued the same warning to the disciples in John 15:26–27 when he promised, *"When the Counsellor comes, whom I will send to you from the Father... he will bear witness about me. And you also must bear witness."*[3] Unless you understand that the Holy Spirit is the Primary Witness and that we merely play the role of secondary witnesses, you will find the Great Commission rather like the opening scene of *Saving Private Ryan*. The Holy Spirit destroys Satan's defences with his miraculous covering fire, so that we can march forward to lead people to repentance through the Gospel.

Whichever way you read the book of Acts, one constant fact should be clear: The Church grew rapidly in its early years because the Holy Spirit empowered God's People to perform amazing miracles of healing and deliverance. In Jerusalem, the non-Christian crowds lined the streets to be healed by Peter and the other apostles. In Samaria, there was *"joy in the city"* over miracles so amazing that even a magician got his wallet out and tried to buy himself a franchise. In Judea, whole regions came to faith when they saw a lame man healed and a dead woman raised to life. Even the opponents of the early Christians were forced to confess that *"Everybody living in Jerusalem knows they have done an outstanding miracle, and we cannot deny it."*[4] We cannot hope to see such mighty advance for the Gospel by merely proclaiming to people that Jesus is King. We need to make room for the Holy Spirit to open up his bombardment and prove that the message we are preaching is true.

Luke's promise that the Holy Spirit wants to play the role

---

[2] Joshua 5:13–15.

[3] The Greek word *martureō* is the verb of the noun *martus*, and means *to be a witness*.

[4] Acts 2:43; 3:6–10, 5:12–16; 6:8, 8:6–7, 13, 18; 9:32–42.

of Primary Witness is enormously encouraging, yet it is all too tempting to continue to assault the beaches by ourselves. Few of us deny the Holy Spirit's role altogether, but we can often relegate him to a supervisory role. We argue that *that was then and this is now*, and assume that such miracles of healing belong to a bygone generation. We forget that Jesus himself was accredited to the world by his miracles through the Spirit,[5] and that he promised to accredit anyone who followed him by doing *"greater things than these"* when he filled them with his Spirit.[6] We forget that such miracles were a vital factor in all four of Paul's missionary journeys,[7] and that we mustn't embark on any ventures of our own without working with the Spirit in exactly the same way.

Perhaps we find it easier to leave miracles to the history books because we are profoundly aware of our own inadequacies. We reel from past disappointments and persuade ourselves that such healings belong to a superior class of Christian, like the apostles. Peter, Paul and Luke disagree. Peter asks us incredulously, *"Why do you stare at us as if by our own power or godliness we had made this man walk?... By faith in the name of Jesus, this man... was made strong."*[8] Paul asks similarly, *"Does God give you his Spirit and work miracles among you because you*

---

[5] Acts 2:22; 10:38. Luke places a surprising amount of emphasis in 10:38 on Jesus' humanity and his dependence upon the Holy Spirit. He promises us that God will do the same miracles through us as well.

[6] Jesus told the disciples in John 14:12 that such miracles would be possible *"because I am going to the Father"* – in other words, because he was about to receive and pour out the promise of the Holy Spirit (Acts 2:33). Since this promise is for every generation (Acts 2:39), we dare not ignore this offer of covering fire.

[7] Acts 14:3, 8–10; 16:16–18; 19:11–20; 28:8–9. If you are tempted to point out that Luke does not report any miracles in Thessalonica, Berea, Athens, or Corinth, this chapter is particularly for you. We know from Paul's letters that he performed miracles in those places too (2 Corinthians 12:12; 1 Thessalonians 1:5; Romans 15:18–19). Luke doesn't mention it because he feels you should already be convinced.

[8] Acts 3:12, 16.

observe the law, or because you believe what you have heard?"[9]
Luke tells us literally in 14:3 that the Lord bore witness alongside
Paul and Barnabas, by performing great miracles which proved
that their message was true.[10] God agrees with you that you are
inadequate, but insists this means you need the Holy Spirit's
artillery more, not less, than they did.

I was once very sceptical about all this. I had read the
book of Acts but assumed it was a hero story for my admiration,
not imitation. Then, through the goading of a mature Christian
mentor, I began to take risks and to ask God to heal people
whenever I preached the Gospel. When the Holy Spirit – to my
complete surprise and amazement – started healing a few of
those I prayed for, I saw a sudden increase in the number of
people who responded for salvation. Just last Sunday, for example,
I was able to tell people that they *knew* what I was preaching
was true, because they had just seen Jesus heal someone before
their very eyes.[11] I'm still a very ordinary infantryman, but I'm
not sceptical any more. I've started making room for the Holy
Spirit to be the Primary Witness, and discovering that he makes
us very fruitful when we do.

I still feel dry-mouthed with fear every time I pray for
healing, like Tom Hanks at the start of *Saving Private Ryan*. I still
make mistakes and get embarrassed, and I still get confused
and disappointed. But I'm through with Omaha Beach and asking
the Holy Spirit to play a backseat role. I'm following Luke's
instruction to let the Holy Spirit be the Primary Witness as I work
with him to heal and to deliver. Whatever your own background
and whatever your current experience, I encourage you to leave
Omaha Beach behind today. The Holy Spirit has his artillery
ready and is looking for modern-day secondary witnesses.

---

[9] Galatians 3:5.

[10] Again Luke uses the word *martureō*, or *to witness*, in Acts 14:3.

[11] Importantly, the most significant healing was of a *Christian*. I am not suggesting
that healing is simply an evangelistic tool for unbelievers. Jesus called it *"the
children's bread"* in Matthew 15:26.

Betty Zane (6:1–7)

It would not be right for us to neglect the word of God in order to wait on tables.... We will give our attention to prayer and the ministry of the word.

(Acts 6:2, 4)

The year was 1782 and the American War of Independence was in its final year. The well-trained armies of Great Britain had been humiliated and outmanoeuvred by George Washington and his Continental Army. Yet the war was not quite over, and the British still hoped that an alliance with the Native Americans might give them control of the Ohio River. They needed to capture the lonely Fort Henry, so in September 1782 the British and their native helpers attacked.

The Americans in the fort were horribly outnumbered, but they had powerful artillery to defend their position. A first attack was driven back under a hail of musket and cannon shot. Second and third attacks were also repulsed, but as the fourth and most ferocious attack fell upon Fort Henry, the defenders experienced two terrible setbacks. First, Ebenezer Zane, one of the fort's most senior officers, was hit by an English bullet and died where he stood. Second, Colonel Shepherd shouted to the men under his command that they had no more gunpowder left below – in the next few minutes their cannon and muskets would be forced to fall silent. The fort would surrender to the British.

It was at this point that a young teenaged girl named Betty Zane entered the history books. Betty arose from the body of her dead father and announced her plan to Colonel Shepherd:

"My father's house is not a hundred yards from this fort; he has a store of gunpowder hidden beneath the floor – let me run and get it, so the fort will not be taken." With his reluctant consent, Betty Zane slipped over the wall of the fort and ran the gauntlet of enemy fire all the way to her father's house. She quickly filled a tablecloth with gunpowder, hoisted it over her shoulder, and ran back through the gunfire to rescale the wall. Shaking with fear and grateful to still be alive, she ran to the guns with her precious supply of gunpowder. Immediately, Fort Henry's artillery rang out with fresh cannon fire and the British began to take flight, never to return. Fort Henry had survived.

In the previous chapter we talked about the artillery fire of the Holy Spirit. It is one thing to learn the role of his artillery, but quite another to stay at all times stocked with gunpowder. The Devil wants to distract you, as he tried to distract the apostles, from the disciplines which can help you partner with the Holy Spirit. If we want to become ordinary people who advance through the artillery of our extraordinary God, we must resist the Devil with the single-minded focus of Betty Zane. She knew where the gunpowder lay, and she let nothing distract her from her life-or-death pursuit.

The apostles appointed seven assistants because they were determined not to be distracted from *prayer*. They began the book of Acts in prayer (1:14), they taught their converts to devote themselves to prayer (2:42), and they continued in their steadfast prayer throughout the book of Acts.[1] I've never met a Christian who doesn't want to see the Church grow and multiply like in the pages of the book of Acts, but it is one thing to want it and quite another to run daily for the gunpowder which makes it possible. The uneducated fishermen who shook the world with the Gospel in the pages of Acts were only able to do so because

---

[1] Acts 1:24; 3:1; 4:24; 6:6; 7:59; 8:15; 9:40; 10:9; 12:5; 13:2–3; 14:23; 16:16, 25; 20:36; 21:5; 22:17; 28:8.

"these men had been with Jesus".[2] We will be empowered to do the same as them if we copy their lives of prayer.

Luke emphasizes this in Acts 14:15 when he reports that Paul told the crowds that he was *a man just like them*. He uses the word *homoiopathēs* in Greek, which is only used in one other place in the whole of the New Testament. James, the leader of the church in Jerusalem, wrote a letter to the scattered Jewish believers in which he used the same word to encourage them that *"Elijah was a man just like us. He prayed earnestly that it would not rain, and it did not rain on the land for three and a half years. Again he prayed, and the heavens gave rain."* Luke, who must have had access to James' earlier letter, wants to echo his words to us that *"The prayer of a righteous man is powerful and effective."*[3] Prayer is the gunpowder through which we lay hold of the Holy Spirit's artillery so that he bombards the Devil's battle lines and empowers us to stride to victory.

The apostles also appointed seven assistants because they were determined not to be distracted from the *Word of God*. We saw in the previous chapter that faith is a vital factor in unleashing heaven's cannonade, yet *"faith comes from hearing the message, and the message is heard through the word of Christ"*.[4] There was a reason why the apostles were undaunted in the face of complaints, backsliding, persecution, and scattering. They were attentive to the gunpowder of the Word of God, and they had built themselves up with a faith which was equal to their fight. This was also why their preaching both disturbed and converted an empire. They were those who rose early to read Scripture and who did as Jesus commanded: *"What I tell you in the dark, speak in the daylight; what is whispered in your ear, proclaim from the roofs."*[5]

Note also that Luke specifically tells us that they refused to

---

[2] Acts 4:13.

[3] James 5:16–18.

[4] Romans 10:17.

[5] Matthew 10:27.

be distracted from *ministering* the Word of God to others. It is not enough to devote ourselves to prayer and Bible reading – we must also create room for him to flow through us to others. He is the Primary Witness and he has an agenda of his own. He is not interested in empowering our self-absorption, but in enabling the advance of those who share his passion for the needs of the world.

The book of Acts shows us that God does not use the strongest, the most gifted, or even the most passionate members of his army. He uses any ordinary person who runs single-mindedly to his gunpowder like Betty Zane. Someone once said that *"the secret of Christianity is Christianity in secret"*, and Luke tells us that this is most definitely true. If you run to prayer, if you run to study Scripture and if you run to minister to others, you will never be caught short when you need the Holy Spirit to open fire.

Can you hear the Enemy beating at the gates of the Church? It is time for you to rise up and run for gunpowder like a girl called Betty Zane.

Jerusalem Rejects the Gospel (6:8–7:60)

You stiff-necked people, with uncircumcised hearts and ears! You are just like your fathers: You always resist the Holy Spirit!

(Acts 7:51)

The martyrdom of Stephen forms the grand finale to Part One of the book of Acts. Unless you understand that, you will find his speech to the Sanhedrin a long-winded and aggressive misjudgment in preaching. It wasn't at all. It was a God-inspired masterpiece which backed the leaders of Jerusalem into a corner and propelled the Gospel on its journey to the rest of the world.

Stephen serves as a one-man summary of everything Part One of Acts has told us we must be. He is Joseph Barsabbas and Simon Peter rolled into one – equally at ease serving humbly in obscurity or preaching boldly in adversity. He preaches the Gospel so wisely that no one can resist him, and he lives the Gospel so faithfully that he looks just like an angel. This is a man who studied Scripture, prayed bold prayers, performed great miracles, and made bitter enemies. In fact, he is such a model Christian that Luke deliberately portrays him as the perfect witness to Christ.[1]

---

[1] Like Jesus, Stephen is tried by the high priest and Sanhedrin, is accused by false witnesses of threatening to destroy the Temple, is condemned for speaking about the Son of Man at the right hand of the Father, prays forgiveness for his murderers, and commits his spirit to the Lord as he dies. Stephen is the perfect witness for Christ, which is why his trial decides whether the city of Jerusalem will accept or reject Christ himself.

Stephen and his friends were fast winning over the whole city of Jerusalem. In chapter 5 the high priest and his Sadducee friends grew jealous and angry that the dead formalism of their Temple was being eclipsed by the uneducated yet Spirit-filled disciples. They confronted them at the end of chapter 5, hoping to silence them with threats, but Peter stood his ground and accused them of murdering their Messiah, leading an unsaved nation to destruction, and missing out on the gift of the Spirit because they refused to obey God.[2] Three years of uneasy co-existence between first-century Judaism and Spirit-filled Christianity were coming to an end. Jerusalem was so full of the Gospel in 5:28 that the city either needed to convert en masse to Christ like many of the priests in 6:7 or reject his message outright like the Diaspora Jews in 6:9. It was time for the Sanhedrin to pass an official verdict upon the Gospel of Jesus Christ, and the fate of the *"Holy City"* was hanging in the balance.[3]

That's why Stephen's speech – the longest in the book of Acts – is neither rambling nor insulting, but the perfectly pitched challenge of a skilled barrister. Stephen is on trial before the Sanhedrin, but he very quickly turns the tables to put the Sanhedrin themselves on trial.[4] They put him on trial for blasphemy against *"this holy place"* (the Temple), and against God and his Law, but his defence reveals that they themselves are the real blasphemers.[5]

They are the true blasphemers against God and his *"holy*

---

[2] Acts 5:27–32. Note Luke's use of Gamaliel's speech in 5:33–39 as a subliminal warning to Judge Theophilus!

[3] Nehemiah 11:1; Isaiah 52:1; Matthew 4:5; 27:53. From this point on, Scripture only ever uses the phrase *"holy city"* to refer to the *New* Jerusalem.

[4] The Sanhedrin was the highest Jewish court in the land, consisting of the high priest, chief priests and elders of Israel. See 5:21, where the 71-member Sanhedrin overlaps with Israel's *gerousia*, or *body of elders*.

[5] Acts 6:11, 13. Stephen's speech is a New Testament version of Ezekiel 20, where God attacks his People's rose-tinted view of their history and gives them his own perfect view of their history instead.

place". Yahweh had appeared to Abraham in Mesopotamia, Joseph in Egypt, and Moses at Mount Sinai – all of them outside of the borders of Israel. Even when Joshua led God's People into the Promised Land, God dwelt in Moses' Tabernacle and not in Jerusalem. The Sanhedrin were the ones who truly dishonoured God, because their obsession with the Temple sought to box God into one building. Even the great Temple-builder Solomon had confessed that his structure was far too small to ever truly house God's greatness.[6]

They are the true blasphemers against Moses and the Law of Sinai. Moses had warned the people in Deuteronomy 18:15–19 that one day *"God will send you a prophet like me from your own people"*,[7] and had threatened God would punish those who refused the Prophet when he came. Stephen reminds the Jewish leaders that their predecessors rejected Joseph, Moses, God's prophets, and even God himself, preferring to worship a golden calf than submit to his true image.[8] He is about to carry on with more examples when the stony faces of the Sanhedrin provoke him in verse 51 to pass his withering verdict there and then. They are *"stiff-necked"* and have *"uncircumcised hearts"*, just like their rebellious Old Testament forebears, but they have actually gone even further than ancient Israel at her worst.[9] They have rejected the Prophet Jesus, and in a staggering act of Lawbreaking have betrayed and murdered him even though he is their Messiah and God. The Sanhedrin and the city they lead are guilty of blasphemy as charged. They must repent and receive the Gospel, or suffer the terrible consequences.

---

[6] Acts 7:49 is a quotation from Isaiah 66:1–2, but it also corresponds to Solomon's own words in 1 Kings 8:27.

[7] Stephen quotes this in 7:37 because this "Prophet" was the Messiah. See John 1:21; 7:40; Acts 3:22–23.

[8] Stephen quotes in 7:42–43 from Amos 5:25–27 where God addresses the northern kingdom of Israel, but he deliberately changes *Damascus* to *Babylon* in order to redirect its message to the city of Jerusalem.

[9] Exodus 32:9; 33:3, 5; 34:9; Deuteronomy 9:6, 13; 31:27; Jeremiah 4:4; 6:10; 9:26.

The Jewish leaders do not realize that it is they who are on trial, not Stephen. They are furious with his message and drag him outside the city to stone him to death. He remains Christ's perfect witness even as he dies, full of the Holy Spirit and describing a vision of Jesus getting up from his heavenly throne to receive him as the first Christian martyr. His judges reveal their wicked anger and hatred, but Stephen reveals nothing but peace and love. He commits his spirit to Jesus, asks forgiveness for his lynch mob, and then goes to join his glorified Saviour in heaven.[10]

The leaders of Jerusalem think they have passed their verdict upon Stephen and fail to grasp that he had actually just passed Christ's verdict over them. Three years earlier the city of Jerusalem had called for Jesus' blood and had him crucified outside their walls, but in God's grace he rose again and sent his followers back into Jerusalem. Now, in 33 AD, as they drag Stephen outside the city walls to kill him, the mob reject Christ a second time through his Church. Stephen's murder would scatter the believers from Jerusalem, and they would settle in Judea, Samaria and more distant lands instead.

Luke ends Part One of the book of Acts with something far greater than a long speech from a brave Christian preacher. He ends it with a showdown between the Jewish leaders in Jerusalem and the church within their city walls. Part Two of Acts will begin with the believers mourning over Stephen's death, but it was the city of Jerusalem which was in direst need of mourning. The Early Church was scattered, but her story had only just begun.

---

[10] It is not out of place in v. 60 for Luke to describe Stephen's bloody death as him "falling asleep". This was a phrase used by the early Christians for anyone dying and going to be with Jesus in heaven. Note that elsewhere Scripture always refers to Jesus *sitting* at the right hand of the Father in heaven, never *standing* (Matthew 26:64; Mark 14:62; 16:19; Luke 22:69, Colossians 3:1; Hebrews 1:3; 8:1; 10:12; 12:2).

The Gospel to Judea and Samaria (33–37 AD)

Reproducing Lilies (8:1–8)

Those who had been scattered preached the word wherever they went.

(Acts 8:4)

Part Two of the book of Acts is very much the sequel to Part One. That may sound obvious, but it's actually a crucial point to make. In the first seven chapters of Acts, Luke lays down several foundational principles which turn ordinary Christians into extraordinary world-changers. In chapters 8 and 9, he shows us those principles in action. Although the action in Part Two moves from Jerusalem to Judea and Samaria, Luke wants us to notice that the principles remain the same. The ordinary deacon Philip brings revival to Samaria and spreads the Gospel to black Africa, simply because he knows his authority, works with the Holy Spirit, and is ready to share the message of Jesus. The ordinary Christian Ananias is able to lead the Church's arch-enemy to Christ, simply because he walks closely with Jesus and has the courage to do whatever he says. The ordinary Christian Dorcas is so effective in her unglamorous work with the poor in Joppa that Peter has to raise her from the dead so that her work can continue.[1] Part Two introduces an impressive array of very ordinary Christians, and it deliberately leaves many of them anonymous.

Take for example the anonymous Christians who fled Jerusalem at the start of chapter 8 at the height of the persecution which began with Stephen's death. They had

---

[1] Since 1 Timothy 5:9–12 talks about an order of widows in the Early Church who devoted themselves to helping the poor, it appears from Acts 9:36, 39 that Dorcas led an order of widows in the church at Joppa.

escaped with their lives, but had left behind jobs, homes, and livelihoods for the sake of the Gospel. If a group of Christians has ever been entitled to hit the dirt and lie low for a while, it was this band of scattered refugees who made their new homes in Judea, Samaria, Damascus, and Antioch.[2] But they didn't. Luke tells us in 8:4 that they evangelized and shared the Gospel wherever they went.[3] In fact, the historian Kenneth Latourette demonstrates that

> *The chief agents in the expansion of Christianity appear not to have been those who made it a profession or made it a major part of their occupation, but men and women who carried on their livelihood in some purely secular manner and spoke of their faith to those they met in this natural fashion.*[4]

The leaders of the Early Church did not abdicate this responsibility to church members, like a World War One general issuing orders to his frontline troops from the comfort of his cosy command-centre. Luke is very clear in verses 25 and 40 that the Christian leaders were just as active in sharing their faith wherever they went too. Yet they understood something so startlingly obvious that we mustn't forget it either.

I felt God remind me of this principle recently when I visited the Natural History Museum in London. Like most of London's museums, it is full of interactive puzzles for children, and like most of London's parents, I like to do the children's puzzles for

---

[2] Luke tells us in 11:19 that these refugees made it even further than Judea and Samaria. They settled as far north as Phoenicia, Antioch and even the island of Cyprus.

[3] Although Luke tells us in 8:5 that Philip *publicly preached* (*kērussō*) the Gospel, he tells us in 8:4 that every believer *evangelized* (*euangelizō*) their friends and neighbours.

[4] Kenneth Scott Latourette, *History of the Expansion of Christianity*, Volume 1 (1945).

myself. Here's the one that really spoke to me – let's see if you can answer it:

> *There are two lilies in five square miles of water. Each lily reproduces every day, so that on day two there are four lilies, on day three there are eight lilies, and so on. The lilies take four months to cover two and a half square miles of water – how many more days will it take them to cover the rest of the lake?*

The answer, of course, is *only one day*. Even though it took the lilies four whole months to cover half of the water, since every lily is actively reproducing they will finish the job in only one more day. So long as every lily keeps on playing its part, their exponential growth potential is limitless.

And so it was in the Early Church. The Christians deliberately scattered into every area of their local communities, so that the Christian writer Tertullian was able to boast that

> *We are but of yesterday, but we have filled every place among you – cities, islands, fortresses, towns, marketplaces, even the camps, tribes, companies, palace, senate, forum – we have left nothing to you but the temples of your gods... We are not Indian Brahmins or fakirs living in woods and exiling themselves from ordinary life... We go to your forum, your market, your baths, your shops, your workshops, your inns, your fairs, and the other places of trade.*[5]

Once they had infiltrated themselves as reproducing lilies throughout the whole expanse of their communities, the Christians then gave themselves to personal evangelism, day in and day out, until they won their own little network of contacts

---

[5] Tertullian wrote this in his *Apology* (chapter 37) in about 197 AD.

to Christ. They were so successful that Celsus, one of the most vocal early opponents of Christianity, complained bitterly that

> *We see in private houses workers in wool and leather, laundry-workers and the most illiterate and bucolic yokels, who would not dare to say anything at all in front of their elders and more intelligent masters. But they get hold of the children privately, and any women who are as ignorant as themselves... "Come along with your playmates to the leather shop or the laundry and you will get the full story."*[6]

Luke reminds us in verses 5 to 8 that there is still an important role for anointed public preachers and miracle-workers, but he will not have us attribute the success of the Early Church to a small group of platform-speaking apostles and deacons. General Patton's battle maxim was that *"Generals and staff-officers don't win wars. Soldiers win wars,"* and Part Two of the book of Acts tells us the same. The success of the Church can never depend on a few extraordinary leaders. It's God's army of ordinary, Gospel-sharing, reproducing lilies which together will conquer the world.

If you long to see the Kingdom of God come in your town or city as it did in the book of Acts, be a reproducing lily yourself. If you are a church member, don't leave it to your leaders, and if you are a leader, don't leave it to your church members. God may even want to scatter you to a new city or nation to be one of the first reproducing lilies in a new pond. Wherever God places us, Luke reminds us in Part Two of Acts that the principles of Part One remain the same. Regardless of geography, wherever ordinary Christians live as active witnesses for Christ, they will quickly reproduce themselves until God's glory fills the whole earth.

---

[6] Celsus wrote this in about 175 AD, but his own writings have not survived. We only know what he wrote because Origen quotes liberally from him in his *Contra Celsum* in about 248 AD.

Grief and Hope (8:2)

Godly men buried Stephen and mourned deeply for him.

(Acts 8:2)

I have an elderly friend whose husband died several years ago. They had been married since the late 1940s, and she was naturally devastated. Fortunately, she had a large group of friends who rallied round to support her, but one of them grew very impatient with her in her grief. *Why was she so upset?*, her friend demanded. *Didn't she realize that her husband was now with Jesus in a far better place? Why wasn't she rejoicing in the knowledge that he was now free from his worn-out body and enjoying the delights of heaven?* Whether she meant to or not, the friend was serving a side-plate of guilt to a woman who was already choking on her main dish of grief and loneliness. It was a well-intentioned act of cruelty.

The truth is, there is nothing wrong with Christians grieving at all. Luke tells us that Stephen's friends were being *godly* when they beat their chests in deep grief over his death.[1] What is more, John tells us in his gospel that Jesus himself mourned deeply at the death of his close friend Lazarus. He wept so much outside Lazarus' tomb that even the cynical crowds of Bethany exclaimed, *"See how he loved him!"* He was so moved as he drew near the dead man's house that John tells us literally that his spirit was *"stirred up"* within him and he *"snorted with anger on*

---

[1] The Greek word *kopetos* in Acts 8:2 does not merely mean *grief* or *mourning*. It comes from the word *koptō*, which means *to cut* or *to hit*, and means literally *to beat one's chest as a sign of intense grief*.

the inside".[2] If Jesus treated death as a repugnant intruder, even when he knew that he was about to raise his friend back to life again anyway, there can be nothing wrong with Christians today grieving deeply and in agony over those they love. We, above all people, know that humans were never created to die in this way, so perhaps we should even grieve more than unbelievers who don't know any better. Since the Psalmist tells us that the death of believers is *"precious in the sight of the Lord"*, we should not be browbeaten into thinking we honour him by treating their deaths as less precious than he does.[3]

The reason we fall for this muddled way of thinking is that the insensitive comforter was not completely wrong. As Christians, we have more reason to grieve over death than unbelievers, but we also have more God-given insight to combine our deep grief with an even deeper hope. One of my friends is a very gifted professional artist, who has felt unable to put brush to canvas for several years since the death of his young son to cancer. It is a privilege to watch him learn to live in the good of what Paul teaches in 1 Thessalonians 4:13: *"Brothers, we do not want you to be ignorant about those who fall asleep, or to grieve like the rest of men, who have no hope."* By God's grace, he is learning to hope in the midst of grief and return to his painter's easel. By God's grace we can all learn to grieve with hope like him.

We can grieve with hope because we know that death is not the end, but the beginning. Just as Jesus rose from his heavenly throne to greet his battered martyr, Stephen, so too he rises to greet any of our loved ones who die in faith as his followers.

---

[2] John 11:33, 36, 38. John uses the same Greek word *tarassō* to describe water being *churned up* in John 5:4. His word *embrimaomai* could be used to describe warhorses snorting in readiness for battle, which explains why Jesus snorts as he asks how to get to Lazarus' tomb so he can go at once and raise him from the dead. Jesus did not treat death with equanimity, but as Satan's attack upon the once-deathless human race.

[3] Psalm 116:15.

My elderly friend's husband was freed from his crippled legs the moment he died and his disembodied spirit rose to be with Christ in heaven. One day, when Jesus comes back, he will run with legs that will never grow old when he receives his resurrection body.[4]

We can also grieve with hope because the Gospel gives life meaning, even when it is cut off in its prime. Stephen's exit from life was tragic, as his spiteful enemies dashed his skull, but they could never rob his days of their meaning or significance. His untimely death was victory, not defeat, even as his name meant *Victory-Crown* in Greek. Few people have ever fulfilled as much as Stephen did the passage I quoted earlier from Michael Green, that *"in the manner of their dying [the early Christians] made converts to their faith"*. Stephen's life had meaning even as he lay dying because he sowed seeds of future salvation in the heart of Saul of Tarsus who was watching from the sidelines.[5] He had thrown away his life as a willing pawn in the great chess game of Church history, and God ensured that his sacrifice checkmated the Devil across the Roman Empire.

We can also grieve with hope because *"we know that in all things God works for the good of those who love him, who have been called according to his purpose"*.[6] When the godly King Josiah died, the whole of Judah mourned so deeply for him that the prophet Jeremiah composed laments for them to sing for many years to come. Nevertheless, God sent the prophetess Huldah to announce that his untimely death was in fact an act of mercy.[7] The Lord had blessed him with an early grave to spare him from the judgment which was coming on his land.

---

[4] I address these issues of "life after death" in heaven and "life after life after death" in the new heavens and new earth in much more detail in my book *Straight to the Heart of Revelation*.

[5] See Acts 26:14 and my explanation of its meaning in the chapter on "Saul of Tarsus".

[6] Romans 8:28.

[7] 2 Chronicles 35:24–25; 2 Kings 22:19–20; Isaiah 57:1–2.

Luke doesn't tell us why God saved the lives of the apostles in chapter 5 but not the life of Stephen in chapter 7, but simply hints that it was a blessing and not a curse for the young deacon. Like the Old Testament hero Samson, who did more in the purposes of God through his death than he ever did through his life, Stephen's death drove the Christians out of Jerusalem and planted churches throughout Judea, Samaria, Phoenicia, Antioch, and Cyprus.[8] Even when loved ones die young and in the most baffling of circumstances, we can grieve with hope because our God can bless his People, even in death.

So let's grieve for those who die, and let's do so with clear conscience, knowing that we are following in the footsteps of Jesus and the godly friends of Stephen. Let's grieve deeply and for as long as we need to, but let's always grieve with hope. Death is not the end and neither is it always tragic. Because we follow the extraordinary God, even days of grief can be days filled with everlasting hope.

---

[8] Acts 8:1–4 and 11:19 are to Stephen what Judges 16:30 is to Samson.

Starting Points (8:35)

Then Philip began with that very passage of Scripture and told him the good news about Jesus.

(Acts 8:35)

Because Philip shared the Gospel as the message of Jesus, he saved an Ethiopian eunuch and sent him back to save his nation.[1] Think about it. If Philip had been a man who preached the Gospel as a spiritual equation, he would never have connected with the man in a chariot on the Gaza road. If he had simply tried to make him listen to his message that *sin plus the cross plus repentance equals salvation*, he would not have been ready to listen. His questions were about the identity of the Suffering Servant in Isaiah 53, and he wasn't interested in Philip's message until he saw how it was relevant to his starting point. Philip captured his attention because he told him the story of Jesus as the answer to the very questions he was asking. He did all that Luke taught us to do in Part One of the book of Acts. *"Philip **began with that very passage of Scripture** and told him the good news about Jesus."*

He was like the engineers who built the Channel Tunnel between England and France when I was a child. I still remember watching the celebrations on TV when the French and English tunnellers finally met each other at the bottom of the sea. They

---

[1] The inhabitants of the ancient kingdom of Ethiopia in modern-day Sudan were black (Jeremiah 13:23), but some of them were also Jewish. This explains why the eunuch was reading the book of Isaiah on the way back home from worshipping at the Temple in Jerusalem. This was therefore *not* a case of the Gospel going to the Gentiles, but to a far-flung Jewish community. The Gospel would only go to the Gentiles in chapter 10.

had halved their construction-time by digging one tunnel from England and another from France, and by using the very latest technology to ensure that they met in the middle. Each team kept a constant focus on the other team's position so that nothing would make them miss each other and their final moment of breakthrough.

Philip and the other early believers were experts at digging Gospel tunnels towards non-Christians. They had no interest in trying to force them to listen to a one-size-fits-all presentation of the Gospel. They were interesting in finding starting points from which to captivate their listeners with story of Jesus Christ. They never changed the Gospel itself – that option was never open to them[2] – but they constantly changed their manner of sharing it, so that anyone who met them was in no doubt as to the significance of the life, death, and resurrection of Jesus to the questions they were asking.

The Ethiopian was not asking questions about sin or judgment or forgiveness, even though Isaiah 53 is one of the greatest Old Testament passages about the atonement. He was simply looking for an explanation of the Scriptures he had heard people reading on his trip to the Temple in Jerusalem. Philip *"began with that very passage"* and used it as a launch pad to tell him that Jesus was the person he was looking for. He did the same thing as Peter and the other apostles when they discovered people's starting points were confusion over tongues-speaking, surprise over supernatural healing, indignation over claims to spiritual authority, and accusations of blasphemy.[3] It really didn't matter which tunnels they found their Jewish hearers digging; they could always find ways to dig to meet them and to show them that Jesus of Nazareth was the person they were looking for.

---

[2] Paul makes it very clear in Galatians 1:6–12 and 2 Corinthians 11:2–4 that God has entrusted his Gospel to us as his messengers. We have no more right to alter its content than a postman has to open and alter our mail.

[3] Acts 2:14–21; 3:12–16; 4:7–12; 6:11 – 7:53.

This skill became even more important once the Christians moved to the cities of Asia Minor, Greece, and Europe. Very few of the pagans they met had any real interest in the God of Israel or the Jewish Messiah. Instead, the Christians needed to take time to discover their starting points, and to tunnel towards them with Jesus as the answer to their questions. In backwater Lystra, the barbarian peasants had very few spiritual questions other than how to ensure a good harvest and avoid offending the gods like the villains of Greek mythology.[4] Therefore Paul preached a message about the true Lord of the Harvest, and would have used this starting point to talk about his Son Jesus had he not been interrupted. The educated Athenians asked different questions about how to appease unknown gods. Therefore Paul preached a different message in Athens which used the writings of their own philosophers and poets to convince them that the Unknown God had sent him to answer their questions by telling them about a man who was raised from the dead. In every place, the early Christians found the local starting points and built Gospel tunnels to those very places to explain how Jesus was the answer to the questions they were asking.

We, however, tend not to be as good at listening as the early Christians. Because we know that Jesus is the Answer to the ultimate human question, we rarely take the time to present him as the answer to people's smaller questions too. Francis Schaeffer used to say, *"Give me an hour with an unbeliever and I will listen for the first fifty-five minutes, and then in the last five minutes I will have something to say."* We tend to try it the other way around, yet wonder why unbelievers are not interested in what we have to say. Unless we are prepared to discover where

THE GOSPEL TO JUDEA AND SAMARIA (33–37 AD)

98

[4] The Roman writer Ovid published a folk tale from Asia Minor in his *Metamorphoses* in c. 8 AD, in which the gods Zeus and Hermes came to earth but were refused hospitality by the people they visited. This explains why the superstitious Lystrans responded to Paul and Barnabas in the way they did in 14:11–18.

people are truly digging, we will
them and lead them to Jesus as the An.

I'm trying to become more like Phili,
Christians, and I'm finding that it works w.
starting points like they did. I want to talk to my you
about Jesus, but they just want Dad to make some popco
up with them on the sofa, and watch *Finding Nemo* and *Sh.*
I don't need much persuading, and when we turn off *Finding
Nemo*, I find a chance to tell them about God the perfect Father
who comes to seek and save the lost. When we turn off *Shrek*, I
tell them about the God who sees ugly sin in the hearts of self-
proclaimed Prince Charmings, yet who loves to save each ogre
who admits their faults and asks him to love them anyway. I
want to talk to my Muslim friends about Jesus, but I find they
just want to tell me about Ramadan and their story of Eid al-
Adha. I've learned to stop and listen, before telling them that
Jesus fasted forty days and nights to beat sin for them, and then
died as Abraham's sheep sacrifice to reconcile them back to
God. I want to talk to other friends about Jesus, but they just
want to talk about DVDs or pop music or sports. I'm learning to
spot questions in their favourite films and lyrics and to explain
how Jesus is the answer.

It's still the same Gospel message, but told from the place
where people *are*, not from the place where I'd like them to be.
Sharing the Gospel this way is what Philip did, what Paul did and
what Luke tells us to do as well. It's very, very effective when we
tell people the message of Jesus from the place where they are
digging. People will listen, so long as we listen first, when we tell
them the Good News of Jesus from their own particular starting
point.[5]

---

[5] We will explore this idea further in the later chapters "Knitting", "Bridges and
Walls", and "Tour Guides".

Baptism (8:36–40)

As they travelled along the road, they came to some water and the eunuch said, "Look, here is water. Why shouldn't I be baptized?"

(Acts 8:36)

If you've ever played the board game *Risk*, you know the importance of watching your enemy's moves. *Risk* is a game in which each player has a secret mission to complete, and each must second-guess their opponents' missions from the moves they see them make. Wherever they attack hardest is where the game will be won or lost, so those who win *Risk* read the other players' intentions and prepare their own defences.

Satan wants to play *Risk* for the nations of the earth, but we mustn't let him. We must watch his attacks and get ready to defend those areas that he considers to be of greatest importance. Luke wants to warn us of this and prepare us to resist him, and he does so by flagging the importance of a much-neglected territory. He warns us not to neglect the importance of *baptism in water*.

Baptism is more important than many of us realize, but its vital importance has not escaped Satan's attention. He took it seriously when Jesus told his disciples in the Great Commission to *"go and make disciples of all nations, **baptizing them** in the name of the Father and of the Son and of the Holy Spirit"*. He took it seriously when Peter told the crowds on the Day of Pentecost that the way to be saved is to *"Repent and **be baptized"*.[1] He has taken it seriously throughout Church history. When the third-

---

[1] Matthew 28:19; Acts 2:38.

century bishops decided to introduce a three-year probation-period before new converts could be baptized, he was there.[2] In Reformation Europe, when the Anabaptists were executed for their "rebaptism" as adults, he was there too.[3] In fact, even today, we still find him working when people are saved out of Islam or nominal Christianity. Their friends and family seem to cope with the news that they are now attending church. It's when they tell them they are getting baptized that the sparks begin to fly.

Philip was too smart to neglect the importance of baptism as part of conversion. When he pioneered the Gospel among the mixed-race Samaritans, he made sure to baptize everyone who believed.[4] Even more tellingly, the Ethiopian eunuch understood so little about the Christian Gospel that he thought Isaiah 53 might be about Isaiah himself, yet after Philip briefly outlined the Gospel message for him, his natural response in verse 36 was *"Look, here is water. Why shouldn't I be baptized?"* Luke wants us to see that the Early Church preached and practised water baptism as an essential part of Christian conversion. The Devil attacks it because it is pivotal to his mission, but we must not let its importance escape us.

Paul wrote a letter to the Romans which outlined why he baptized his converts all over the Empire: *"Don't you know that all of us who were baptized into Christ Jesus were baptized into his death? We were therefore buried with him through baptism into death in order that, just as Christ was raised from the dead through the glory of the Father, we too may live a new life."*[5] He explains it still further in 1 Corinthians 10:2, where he likens it to the Israelites crossing the Red Sea. The Israelites were not

---

[2] Hippolytus of Rome lists many such hurdles for baptismal candidates in his *Apostolic Tradition* (c. 215 AD).

[3] See Thieleman van Braght's book *The Martyrs' Mirror* (1660).

[4] Acts 8:12, 13, 16.

[5] Romans 6:3–4. See Paul's commitment to water baptism in Acts 9:18; 16:15, 33; 18:8; 19:5.

saved through their "baptism", but through the Passover, yet something definitive happened at the Red Sea as they "died" to Egypt and stepped into new life on the far shore. Their "baptism" was where Pharaoh lost any last hope of bringing the Israelites' past back to haunt them. Whatever our Christian denomination or tradition, this serves as a strong warning that baptism is far more than mere symbolism, and we had better beware not to fall for the Devil's attack.

It should make us question the practice of *infant baptism*. Although Luke tells us that whole households were baptized, he also tells us that whole households *believed* as well.[6] Similarly, although Paul likens baptism to Israel crossing the Red Sea (babies and all) and circumcising their children, he also tells us that we can only become part of *New Covenant* Israel through faith, not through our parentage.[7] In fact, when Peter told us to *"Repent and be baptized"* (in that order), he was expressing his belief that water-baptism is *"the pledge of a good conscience towards God"*.[8]

It should make us question the practice of *sprinkling people* at their baptism. The Ethiopian cannot have set out on his long desert journey without drinking water, but when he understood the true meaning of baptism in terms of death, burial and resurrection with Christ, he pointed to an oasis into which he and Philip could "go down" and "come up". Similarly, when Scripture tells us that John the Baptist *"was baptizing at*

---

[6] Compare Acts 16:15; 18:8. Historians cannot agree on the origin of infant baptism in the Church, but it appears to have been linked to high rates of infant mortality and the wish to ensure that babies were "Christianized" before they died.

[7] See Romans 2:28–29; 3:22–30. Colossians 2:11–12 likens water baptism to circumcision, but it does so with specific reference to the baptized person's faith.

[8] Acts 2:38; 1 Peter 3:21. A "pledge of good conscience" means a first sign of obedient faith. That's why I love to call people to respond to the Gospel, but feel I haven't fully preached the Gospel until I have talked about water baptism, and they haven't fully responded to the Gospel until they have been baptized.

Aenon near Salim because there was a lot of water there", it is urging us not to rob baptism of its identification with Christ.

It should also make us question the practice of *delaying* water baptism due to the reticence of either the new convert or their church leaders. Philip had just had a terrible time in Samaria when the new convert Simon Magus subsequently floundered.[9] Yet when the Ethiopian asked him *"Why shouldn't I be baptized?"*, he did not reply *"Because I just had a bad experience and am once-bitten-twice-shy"*! Paul also baptized his converts quickly and without a prolonged probation period, because Lydia asks him after her baptism whether or not he considers her a true believer.[10]

There are many reasons to neglect Luke's instructions about believers' baptism through full immersion, but not one of them convinces me. Instead, when I look at the way that the Devil has attacked it through 2,000 years of Church history, I begin to suspect that it is integral for our mission and devastating for his own. Let's not allow him to win his game of *Risk* for the nations of the earth. Luke tells us what is written on Satan's mission card and tells us to *"go and make disciples of all nations, baptizing them in the name of the Father and of the Son and of the Holy Spirit"*.

---

[9] Acts 8:9–24. Luke tells us in v. 13 that Simon truly *believed*, even if he did not genuinely convert to Christ.

[10] Acts 16:15.

Saul of Tarsus (9:1–19)

*Go! This man is my chosen instrument to carry my
name before the Gentiles and their kings and before
the people of Israel. I will show him how much he
must suffer for my name.*

(Acts 9:15–16)

Saul of Tarsus was not like Neo in *The Matrix*,[1] but it's amazing
how many people act as though he was. They assume that his
conversion was sudden, like the movie-hero Neo's when he
swallows a little red pill. They assume he was given the mission
of his dreams, like Neo when he meets his mentor Morpheus.
They assume that his success was due to a series of instant
knowledge-downloads like the ones which Neo receives within
the Matrix. Luke, however, is determined to debunk any myths
like these about the life of Saul of Tarsus – or the apostle Paul as
he is better known[2] – because he wants us to use him as a model
for our lives. Paul was not a Christian superhero any more than
Peter, John or the other apostles. He was an ordinary person
whose life is an example of how we ourselves can follow our
extraordinary God.[3]

It is common, even in secular English, to refer to any sudden

---

[1] Played by Keanu Reeves, *The Matrix*, Warner Brothers Pictures (1999).

[2] Luke, a stickler for chronology, starts calling him *Paul* after he meets Sergius
Paulus in Acts 13:9. It appears that he renamed himself after the procurator
at the start of his First Missionary Journey because the Greek name *Paul*
made him more acceptable to the Gentiles than his Hebrew name *Saul* (see 1
Corinthians 9:22).

[3] Paul was an amazing person, but he reminds us in Acts 14:15 that he was
only a person. He himself urged people in 1 Corinthians 11:1 to *"Follow my
example, as I follow the example of Christ."*

change of belief as a "Damascus road conversion". Saul of Tarsus was the arch-enemy of the Christian faith, but after meeting Jesus on the road to Damascus he became its leading exponent and apostle. Since this was one of the most remarkable turnarounds in history, it is tempting to view this as a case of God saving someone instantly, and to ask him to do so in our own towns and cities today. It sounds like a God-glorifying conclusion, but it actually leads to unreality and disappointment, because it is not what Luke describes here at all.

Paul tells the story of the Damascus road in his own words in chapters 22 and 26, and he warns us to expect people to take time before coming to genuine conversion. He tells us that even his own Damascus road experience was not a "Damascus road conversion"! First, he tells us in 26:14 that Jesus didn't just ask him, *"Why do you persecute me?"* He also followed it up with a warning that *"It is hard for you to kick against the goads."*[4] My father-in-law used to be a cattle-farmer, so I have seen a goad in action. It's basically a big stick which a farmer uses to force a stubborn animal to move forward. Jesus told Paul to stop resisting his painfully persistent call to believe the Gospel, and that it was time to surrender after a long process of conviction. God had beaten stubborn Paul with the beautiful lifestyle and miracles of the Jerusalem church which he had hated from afar. He had beaten him again as he watched Stephen die gracefully with words of faith and forgiveness on his lips. He had beaten him again as he read the Old Testament Scriptures and was confronted by prophecies about the Messiah.[5]

Even then, the vision of Jesus was still not enough to

---

[4] These words also appear in 9:5–6 in the "Textus Receptus" Greek manuscript, which is why they appear in the King James Version and in other older English translations. The most reliable Greek manuscripts have these words in 26:14 but not in 9:5–6, so most modern translators leave them out.

[5] Since Paul speaks about "casting his vote" in 26:10, he was probably a member of the Sanhedrin which tried Peter too. Since Tarsus was the capital of Cilicia, he was probably also one of Stephen's opponents in 6:9–10.

convert him straight away. He tells us in 22:16 that he only surrendered to Christ after three days of soul-searching when Ananias prodded him with the final goading question, *"What are you waiting for?!"* We need to be careful not to view Paul's conversion as a sudden turnaround, or unreality will lead to disappointment in our own personal evangelism. People take time to process the Gospel and surrender to Christ. Jesus warned it would be so when he told the disciples that *"A man scatters seed on the ground. Night and day, whether he sleeps or gets up, the seed sprouts and grows... As soon as the grain is ripe, he puts the sickle to it, because the harvest has come."*[6]

It is also easy to assume that Paul gratefully accepted his God-given calling, but he tells us that this was not the case either. He went to Jerusalem and debated with his Grecian Jewish friends there, convinced that he was the perfect man to reach them because of his history as a Pharisee and former persecutor of the Church.[7] He even tried to argue with Jesus when he appeared to him in a vision at the Temple, adamant that no one was better suited to reach the Jewish nation than him. He had to learn the lesson of Joseph Barsabbas, that we can only play the role which Jesus has assigned to us, and that since the Jews would not receive him he would be sent *"far away to the Gentiles"*.[8]

It is also very easy to assume that Paul received a sudden impartation of power through the Holy Spirit which meant that he was able to preach with insight, power and authority which can never be matched in our own lives. Again, however, Scripture refuses to let us place him on such an unhelpful pedestal. First, Galatians 1:17–18 tells us that Paul spent his first three years as a Christian in obscurity in Arabia. Second, Acts 9:30 and 11:25 tell us that he spent a further six years in obscurity back in

---

[6] Jesus told this Parable of the Growing Seed in Mark 4:26–29.

[7] Acts 9:28–31; 22:17–21.

[8] Acts 22:21; Galatians 2:8; Romans 11:13. Acts 9:15 tells us he had a calling to preach to Jews overseas too.

Tarsus. In fact, Paul did not launch his ministry onto the world stage until more than a decade after his conversion. Instead, he did all the things Luke has laid as a foundation in Part One of the book of Acts. He spent years in serious Bible study and prayer, hearing God's will for his life and gathering the insights and understanding which would make him so effective as a missionary to the Gentiles.[9] We must not assume that Paul's understanding came as a divine download like Neo's martial-arts or Trinity's helicopter skills in *The Matrix*. He spent years in diligent obscurity, studying Scripture and praying in private, and as a result he was one day ready to go public.

It is very easy to treat Saul of Tarsus as a Christian superhero, but Luke is determined not to let us. That's why he tells us Paul's complaint in Acts 14:15: *"Men, why are you doing this? We are only men, human like you."* If we treat Paul's conversion as a sudden turnaround, for the mission of his dreams, empowered by a supernatural download of information from the Holy Spirit, we will write him off as in a league of his own and fail to follow his example.

Christian activist Dorothy Day once famously rebuked a journalist with the words: *"Don't call me a saint – I don't want to be dismissed that easily."* Paul would rebuke us in the same way today. He was an ordinary person, called to an extraordinary work and equipped by God as he gave himself faithfully to the foundational principles of the Christian life. He got baptized in water, he was filled with the Holy Spirit, he joined a group of Christians, he turned away from his former life of sin, and he gave himself to Bible study, prayer, evangelism, and praying for the sick. God wants to make you more like Paul today, as you pull him off his pedestal and copy him as he copied Christ.

---

[9] Paul tells us in Romans 15:20–22 that the Lord gave him his clear calling to preach the Gospel in unreached nations while he was studying Isaiah 52:15. He also tells us in Romans 16:25–26 that he only understood the riches of the Gospel when the Holy Spirit spoke to him as he read the books of the Old Testament prophets.

Ordinary Ananias (9:10–19)

In Damascus there was a disciple named Ananias....
The Lord said to Ananias, "Go!"

(Acts 9:10, 15)

If we tend to think too much of Saul of Tarsus, we definitely tend to think too little of Ananias of Damascus. He was the ultimate Joe Nobody, a rank-and-file believer like you and me. Even those who refuse to tear Paul down from his saintly pedestal cannot fail to see their own reflection in ordinary Ananias. That's why Luke uses him as a challenge to us about the scope of all God wants to do through us today.

We don't know much about Ananias at all. He is even less famous than the wicked Ananias who died with his wife Sapphira in chapter 5. What we do know is that he was a faithful Christian who lived out the righteous lifestyle which Luke showcased for us in Part One of Acts. He was *"a devout observer of the law and highly respected by all the Jews"* (22:12), and his generous heart comes out in 9:17 when he greets the murderous persecutor Saul as a dear Jewish *brother.*[1] His commitment to prayer is evident from the way he describes believers in 9:14 simply as *those who call on God's name*, and he was evidently a man filled with the

---

[1] Some people argue that Ananias calls Saul his *brother* because he knew he had become a Christian on the road to Damascus. They use this to prove that baptism in the Holy Spirit is a "second blessing" quite separate to repentance. Whether or not this is true in practice, we cannot argue it from that verse. Acts 22:16 suggests that Saul did not become a Christian until Ananias challenged him to respond to his vision, and Luke tells us that Jews referred to each other as *brothers* in 2:29, 37; 3:17; 7:2; 13:15, 26, 38; 22:1; 23:1, 5–6; 28:17, 21.

Holy Spirit. He was one of the typical, ordinary Christians that Jesus used in the first century to change the world.

Part of this was due to his courage. However difficult Philip found it to obey the Lord in 8:26–27 and exchange Samaria in the midst of revival for a lonely desert road, Ananias must have found it many times harder here. Saul of Tarsus had gone from house to house in Jerusalem to find and imprison both male and female believers, with a bloodthirsty hatred for the Church of Jesus Christ. He was known to be travelling to Damascus with letters of authority from the high priest to do the same thing there. In fact, even the apostles thought his talk of a heavenly vision must be a treacherous ruse to infiltrate the Church and to destroy it root and branch.[2] It was absolute lunacy for Ananias to go and reveal himself to his would-be assassin, which is why he protests that *"Lord, I have heard many reports about this man"* – probably one of the greatest understatements in the New Testament! Yet ordinary Ananias made an extraordinary difference for Christ by simply doing as he was told in obedient faith. His faithful visit to Paul at Judas' house on Straight Street was a vital first step in the Church's global expansion.

Ananias was also used because of his devotion to Christ. It is clear from the way he ministers to Paul that he knew that the Gospel was "what I have" and that he had learned to live in the good of it. When Jesus appeared to him in a vision, he was able to go on his perilous mission because he trusted his Lord enough to do what he said. He knew Jesus well enough to grasp that he is not looking for advisers to assist him in his strategic war-room, but simply foot soldiers on the battlefield who will carry out his commands. Jesus was able to use Ananias because he was a true Betty Zane. He had devoted himself to knowing the Lord through Bible study and prayer, and was ready and waiting when opportunity came.

[2] Acts 9:26. They had about as much faith that Saul of Tarsus would be saved in response to their prayers as the church had in 12:12–17 that Peter would be rescued from death in response to their own prayers.

Finally, Ananias was used because he was a man of the Spirit with faith for healing the sick. Luke particularly wants to stress that here, because it's all too easy for us to view gifts of healing as something Jesus gave to the apostles but will not give to us. There's a strangely popular view that God only gave healing miracles to the early apostles to authenticate their ministry until the canon of New Testament Scripture was completed. It's a well-intentioned argument which hopes to protect the finality of Scripture from a perceived threat if miracle-workers are still alive today, but Luke tells us that it is nevertheless misguided. It wasn't just the Twelve who wrote Scripture (for example Luke himself!), and if the purpose of the healing gift was to authenticate the writings of a small group of Scripture writers, then the gift was given to the wrong people. The Corinthian and Galatian churches had stumbled into false doctrine, but they performed more recorded miracles than Mark, Luke, James and Jude put together![3]

No, Luke tells us that it wasn't just the Twelve who performed miracles, but deacons like Stephen and Philip, and ordinary Christians like Ananias.[4] Paul would write later that the healing gift is given *"for the common good"* and *"for the strengthening of the church"*, and not just to authenticate him and his fellow Scripture writers.[5] That's not to say that we will all minister with the same measure of gifts of healing – Luke admits in 19:11–12 that Paul's gifting was unusually strong, and the rank-and-file believers in Joppa needed to send for Peter in 9:38 to come and help them when Dorcas died – but Luke wants to demonstrate that ordinary Christians like you, me and Ananias can see visions of Jesus, call sinners to repentance, heal them, baptize them and commission them for ministry. None of

---

[3] Contrast 1 Corinthians 15:12–14; Galatians 1:6–7 with 1 Corinthians 1:7; 12:9; Galatians 3:5.

[4] Acts 6:8; 8:6–8.

[5] 1 Corinthians 12:7; 14:26.

us is too ordinary for God, because it is *his* extraordinary power that really matters.

Dwight Moody was an uneducated shoe salesman who longed to see the world turn to Christ. One morning he met with his friend Henry Varley to pray, and Varley challenged him that *"The world has yet to see what God can do with and for and through and in a man who is fully and wholly consecrated to him."* The young Moody was captivated by the scope of that promise and refused to let it pass him by. *"Varley meant any man!"* he encouraged himself. *"Varley didn't say he had to be educated or brilliant or anything else. Just a man! Well, by the Holy Spirit in me, I'll be that man."*[6] The ordinary shoe-salesman went on to lead hundreds of thousands of souls to Christ.

The world has yet to see what God can do with and for and through and in *you* too, if you will only believe what Luke is telling you through the life of Ananias. God has more for you to do than you can ever hope for or imagine, because you are not too ordinary for the power of the extraordinary God.

---

[6] There are many great biographies of D.L. Moody. This quotation draws from more than one of them.

Knitting (9:22)

Yet Saul grew more and more powerful and baffled the Jews living in Damascus by proving that Jesus is the Christ.

(Acts 9:22)

Of all the illustrations in the entire world, I have no idea why Luke chooses this one. I can only assume that he wants people like my mother-in-law to know that they have a role to play in the Great Commission too. As Luke draws Part Two of Acts to a close, he reaches for his next illustration of what it means for us to share the Gospel effectively and he tells us that it's time for us to start *knitting*.

If knitting doesn't excite you, bear with me, because the Greek word *sumbibazō* doesn't just mean knitting in an old-lady-by-the-fireside kind of way. It's the word that the Greeks used to describe how bodies are knitted together sinew by sinew,[1] and how arguments are knitted together point by point.[2] There's nothing effete about Luke's teaching in this verse about knitting. Luke simply wants to teach us that effective witnesses for Christ are people who have learned to knit together the different elements of what their listeners believe with the different elements of the Gospel. Challenge and exhortation have their place, but Luke tells us that they are no substitute for

---

[1] Ephesians 4:16; Colossians 2:19. Most English translations take the word in Acts 9:22 to mean that Paul *proved* to the Jews living in Damascus that Jesus in the Messiah.
[2] 1 Corinthians 2:16.

persuading and *reasoning* with people to help them see that the message of Jesus makes sense.[3]

Paul did his knitting in Damascus, in Jerusalem and across the Roman Empire. He found out what people already believed and knitted their thoughts together so they could see their gaps and inconsistencies. Most people don't want to listen to the Christian message because they think that they have already got life sorted. Paul asked questions and started knitting so that they could see that they were wrong. A few years ago, after reading the results of a Willow Creek survey that most non-Christians have never systematically pieced together what they believe, I went to my local shopping centre and started knitting. I started chatting with a lady who was sitting on a bench and asked her questions about what she believed. The results were amazing. She said she didn't believe in God, but prayed every week, thought that Jesus was more than just a man, and that she would probably go to heaven when she died. As we chatted and I did some knitting, I could see her spotting flaws in what she said, and backtracking towards the Gospel. She went shopping as an atheist but came home believing in God, simply because I let her talk and talk and then held up what I had knitted from the woolly ideas that she had given me.

After knitting together what his listeners believed, Paul then knitted together the Gospel itself. When a person knits a sweater, they knit several separate pieces and bring them together to form the final garment. Paul knitted together the different elements of Jesus' life and ministry, and then placed it next to what he had knitted from their beliefs to show that that there was a perfect fit between Jesus Christ and the answers they were searching for.

Let me demonstrate. The Jews of Damascus believed in Yahweh, they read his Old Testament Scriptures, and were

---

[3] For example, Acts 17:2, 3, 4,17; 18:4, 19; 19:8, 26. It's what Paul did in Damascus, and it's what Luke teaches us to do too.

waiting for his Messiah. Paul knitted this together and showed them holes in their current thinking. How could Yahweh be pleased with the Jewish people, yet have handed them over to Roman occupation? How could Yahweh be pleased with their Temple sacrifices, yet keep them standing at a distance and feeling no less guilty than before? Why did their Scriptures end in 431 BC – had God recently lost his voice? These were uncomfortable questions, but they captured his listeners' attention. It was time for Paul to produce the second half of his knitting. Of course they felt guilty and distant from God; their own prophet had confessed that *"Sacrifice and offering you did not desire... burnt offerings and sin offerings you did not require."*[4] Of course God had not lost his voice; they had merely stopped listening to him. The Messiah had come, fulfilling all the Old Testament promises about his life, death, and resurrection, but the Jewish leaders had refused to listen. No wonder Judea was under Roman rule and Jewish life was tough like during the Old Testament periods of apostasy. Suddenly his listeners see how the two pieces fit together. The holes they have discovered in first-century Judaism are perfectly covered by the life of Jesus Christ. It's time to repent and find salvation through the Messiah they have long been waiting for.

Let's try a different scenario, as Paul preaches to the Athenians in Acts 17. Their beliefs were very different, so Paul walks around the city and takes time to chat to people so that he can knit their worldview together.[5] They are thirsty for God and know that their pagan religion only offers them an incomplete picture. They know that they can please or displease the gods, and they busy themselves at their temples in a desperate attempt to earn their favour. Put this way, they

---

[4] David wrote these words in Psalm 40:6. The New Testament applies them to Jesus in Hebrews 10:5–7.

[5] This should encourage you that no Gospel conversation is wasted, even if the person refuses your message. Even when people reject Jesus, they still train you to knit together your culture's particular worldview.

can see that their sophisticated Greek worldview is in fact as threadbare as the Jewish one, so they listen as Paul starts his second piece of knitting. Their unknown god is Yahweh, and he is unimpressed with their images and temples and sacrifices. He is the Creator-God who gives them their very life breath, and he demands far more from them than their own hands can ever offer. He commands them to repent and to receive forgiveness through a man called Jesus, and he has proved that judgment is coming by raising him from the dead.[6] Once again, Paul holds up his knitting and smiles. His Jesus-shaped message is the perfect fit for the hole-ridden worldview of Athens.

Of course, even the best knitting offers no guarantee that our listeners will be saved. The Jews of Damascus tried to murder Paul, and the men of Athens laughed him out of court. Yet, even as they did so, many around them believed in the Gospel through the knitting that they saw. John Stott famously stated that, *"We cannot pander to man's intellectual arrogance, but we must cater to man's intellectual integrity."* When we knit together what people believe, we convince them that they need to hear about Jesus. When we knit together the Gospel message, we show them why he is the answer to what is missing in their worldview. Knitting is very, very simple – but it's very, very effective.

So don't leave knitting to my mother-in-law. It's the basic weaponry of all God's soldiers. We can never be effective with the Gospel unless we learn to persuade and to reason with unbelievers. There is nothing scarier to Satan's forces than the sight of God's army of believers at their knitting.

---

[6] Paul does not actually say the name *Jesus* in Acts 17:22–31 because he is interrupted as he starts talking about him. Luke clarifies in 17:18 that the second half of his knitting was *"Jesus and the resurrection"*.

The Gospel to the Gentiles (37–47 AD)

No Limits (10:1–11:18)

Then Peter began to speak: "I now realize how true it is that God does not show favouritism but accepts men from every nation who fear him and do what is right."

(Acts 10:34–35)

The year was about 40 AD and, for the Devil, things were not going well. Despite his five-columned attack, the church in Jerusalem was booming. What's more, his tactic of scattering Jerusalem's believers had simply spawned a whole network of churches across Judea and Samaria. Even the martyrdom of Stephen had backfired, as the young man's faithfulness in death goaded Saul of Tarsus on towards his own conversion. Only seven years earlier, the 120 unimpressive believers had huddled together like guests at a party which had long since ended. The Day of Pentecost had launched a new and even greater party, and Satan was still reeling from their Spirit-filled artillery. He needed to act, and act quickly, before their unremitting onslaught broke the confines of the Jewish nation and went global.

Satan's plan was simple. If he could not quench the forest fire of Christianity, he would at least try to limit its spread. So far, it was almost exclusively a Jewish phenomenon, and if he could keep it that way then all might not be lost. If he could ring-fence the flames of the Gospel, he might yet hold on to the souls of the Gentiles who accounted for the vast majority of the world's population.

In Peter, he hoped to find a perfect helper. Jesus had entrusted the leadership of his Church to a Galilean fisherman who was ill at ease with change. When Jesus had announced that he must die and rise again, Satan had inspired Peter to try to talk him out of it. When Jesus had been transfigured on the mountaintop, Peter had tried to build tents and preserve the experience forever. When Jesus had announced that every meat was kosher, Peter had refused to listen and insisted that the Jewish food laws were sacrosanct.[1] In short, Peter was a typical first-century Jew: entrenched in tradition and suspicious of change. He possessed the same ethnic short-sightedness which the Lord had rebuked in Malachi 1:5 when he reminded his People that *"Great is the Lord – even beyond the borders of Israel!"* Left to his own devices, Peter's leadership would fall easy prey to Satan's plan to limit the Gospel within the safe walls of Israel. But the Lord had other plans. He had anticipated Satan's strategy and outflanked him brilliantly. He was about to teach the Jewish Church that the Gospel knows no limits.

God's first step was to send an angel to a Roman centurion named Cornelius. Jewish tradition insisted that anyone who entered the house of a Gentile became ceremonially unclean, so God sent his holy angel to a Gentile house to shatter that myth once and for all.[2] Cornelius was not any old Gentile either. He was a centurion in the occupying army, in the pay of Pontius Pilate's successor and working out of the same barracks as the troops who crucified Jesus.[3] For all his passionate devotion to the God of Israel, he was a very unacceptable candidate for salvation.

God's second step was to grant a vision to Peter, the leader of the apostles, as he prayed before lunch at his lodgings in

---

[1] Matthew 16:21–23; 17:1–4; Mark 7:19; Acts 10:9–16.

[2] Acts 10:28; 11:2–3; 22:21–22; John 18:28; Galatians 2:12. Cornelius was a God-fearer but he cannot have been a Gentile convert to Judaism, since such converts were treated as if they were Jews.

[3] The Roman governor ruled from the port city of Caesarea, so the main Roman garrison was there. Troops would go from Caesarea to reinforce Jerusalem whenever there was a major Jewish feast.

Joppa. Eight centuries earlier, Jonah had boarded a ship in Joppa to run away from God's calling to preach to the Gentiles, but now in that same place God would shatter Satan's limitations for good.[4] Peter saw the same vision three times, in which the Lord lowered a sheet from heaven filled with unclean animals and commanded him to kill them and eat. *"No way, Lord!"* protested Peter, oblivious to the irony of calling God his Lord yet refusing what he said.[5] Suddenly, he woke up to hear banging at the door below. Even though the angel had Cornelius' rapt attention, he had deliberately failed to share the Gospel with him. That was a task for Peter to fulfil, for there was much more at stake here than the souls of Cornelius and his friends. Peter needed to learn that *"I should not call any man impure or unclean"*, so that he could spearhead the spread of the Gospel beyond its current Jewish borders.[6] After a final message from the Holy Spirit to break his prejudice, he went down to meet Cornelius' men.

God's third step was even more spectacular. When Peter arrived at the house in Caesarea, taking with him six believers from the church at Joppa for the sake of accountability,[7] he began to explain the Good News of Jesus. What would he do at the end? Could he lead them to salvation and baptize them like Jews? Could he lay hands on them to receive the Holy Spirit? God was gracious and answered all these questions for him. As Cornelius and his friends believed the message Peter preached to them, the Holy Spirit simply fell on them while the astonished Joppa Christians looked on in wonder. Peter concluded that to place any further obstacle in their path would be to oppose God himself,[8] and he leapt to baptize them immediately. God

---

[4] Jonah 1:3. Note that Peter was staying at a tanner's house in Joppa. Since tanners worked with animal hides, the Jews considered it an "unclean profession", so God was already preparing Peter for what was to come.

[5] Acts 10:14. *Mēdamōs kurie* means literally *"No way, Lord!"*, so Peter was repeating the folly of Matthew 16:22.

[6] Acts 10:28.

[7] Acts 10:23; 11:12.

[8] Acts 10:34–35; 11:17.

had utterly shattered the limits Satan tried to place on the spread of the Gospel. The Church was about to turn its localized skirmishes into full-blown world war. Not because of Peter's far-reaching human strategy, but because God is determined to build his Church in spite of her blundering leaders.

Satan's strategies could never stop the Lord from fulfilling his prophecy regarding his Messiah: *"It is too small a thing for you to be my servant to restore the tribes of Jacob and bring back those of Israel I have kept. I will also make you a light for the Gentiles, that you may bring my salvation to the ends of the earth."*[9] He would accept no limitation to his mission to every nation, and neither will he accept them in your life today.

If you learn the lessons of Parts One and Two of the book of Acts, Satan has only one option left to prevent you from wreaking massive damage on his kingdom. He must make you short-sighted, and trick you into limiting the scope of your ministry for Christ. If he can restrict your gaze to Sundays, he will. If he can turn it into private religion, or even corporate church religion, he will do that too. If he can dupe you into ring-fencing your faith away from work colleagues, relatives, neighbours or any of the many people groups in your nation, he still hopes to carry the day.

We mustn't let him. Every limit, restriction, and barricade of Satan must be broken for the sake of Jesus' Gospel. We follow the One to whom the Father promises: *"What are you, O mighty mountain? Before Zerubbabel you will become level ground."*[10]

---

[9] Isaiah 49:6. Isaiah prophesied these words almost 750 years before Peter went to Cornelius' house.
[10] Zechariah 4:7.

Visibly Different (10:44–48)

The circumcised believers who had come with Peter were astonished that the gift of the Holy Spirit had been poured out even on the Gentiles. For they heard them speaking in tongues and praising God.

(Acts 10:45–46)

I'll never forget the day that I brought one of the directors of Procter & Gamble to church. It was exactly the kind of meeting I had hoped to avoid. After three years of witnessing, I had finally managed to persuade him to join me, and I was hoping to ease him in gently. When the first person started speaking in tongues, I have to confess that my heart sank. When they were followed by several other tongues and interpretations, my heart sank further. I tried to catch a glimpse of my guest's expression, but his face was like a poker player's. Next came a prophecy, then some individuals singing in the Spirit. My hope of giving him a gentle introduction to church evaporated amid a half-hour long showcase of the charismatic gifts. I have to confess I was embarrassed.

After the service, the director gave me his evaluation of the meeting with all the razor-sharp clarity which had earned him a job at the top of his field. *"What happened just then was completely outside of my frame of reference,"* he told me. *"But I expected that. You've kept on telling me that God is real and that we can experience him. If I hadn't found anything supernatural in your church, I simply wouldn't have believed you."*

Christianity is a decidedly supernatural affair. I had forgotten that, and needed to be rebuked by my non-Christian manager. I had assumed that a sanitized, risk-free church service would be the most successful way of winning him to Christ, but he expected to be able to see God in us if our Gospel was genuine. Satan lost his fight to restrict the Gospel to the confines of the Jewish race, but he still hopes to limit it through invisibility today.

Luke refuses to let him do so. Being filled with the Spirit is never invisible, Luke tells us. In chapter 2 the Spirit enables believers to speak in foreign languages and love one another with his supernatural love.[1] In chapter 4 he makes them bold, and in chapter 5 he empowers them to heal. In chapter 8 a leading magician tries to purchase the gift of the Holy Spirit, because what he sees is far better than any of his magic shows. In chapter 10 the Holy Spirit enables Cornelius and friends to speak in tongues and praise God with the same unbridled joy as the 120 at Pentecost.[2] In chapter 19 Paul expects the Ephesians to know if they have received the Holy Spirit or not, and when he lays his hands on them they speak in tongues and prophesy. Taken in isolation, any one of these might be dismissed as exceptional, but taken together Luke's message is very clear indeed. Since *"everything that was written in the past was written to teach us, so that through endurance and the encouragement of the Scriptures we might have hope"*,[3] these passages in Acts remind us that being filled with the Spirit should make us visibly different.

Satan wants to fool us into reducing our expectations of the Holy Spirit, and if we refuse to be tricked, he only has two last-ditch tactics left to play. First, he can tempt us into sidelining Luke's teaching about the Holy Spirit altogether. *This hasn't happened to me, we argue, so it can't truly be all that important.*

[1] See Romans 5:5; Philippians 1:8; Galatians 5:22–23.

[2] Acts 10:44–47; 11:15–17. Peter was able to see visibly that *"The Holy Spirit came on them as he had come on us at the beginning"*, and that *"They have received the Holy Spirit just as we have."*

[3] Romans 15:4.

We decide to concentrate on Bible study, prayer, and the nuts and bolts of church life, but in doing so we inadvertently treat being filled with the Spirit as if it were an add-on to the Gospel instead of the Gospel itself. We forget it is the reason Jesus came to earth,[4] the reason why he went back to heaven,[5] and one of the main reasons that he saved us. The Lord *"redeemed us in order that... by faith we might receive the promise of the Spirit"*.[6] Peter held such a high view of being filled with the Holy Spirit that he actually called it *"participating in the divine nature"*,[7] and Luke's highly supernatural book of Acts refuses to allow us to treat lightly what Peter prized so highly.

Second, Satan can trick us into placing too much emphasis on the moment that we are first filled with the Holy Spirit, so that we neglect to go on being filled every day. Luke deliberately downplays the distinction between initial and subsequent infillings of the Holy Spirit because he wants us to focus on the question *"am I full?"* instead of on the question *"was I filled?"*[8] He uses exactly the same verb in 2:4, 4:8, and 4:31 to describe Peter being *initially filled, subsequently filled*, and then *filled yet again* with the Spirit. He uses the same verb in 9:17 and 13:9 to describe Paul being *initially filled* and *subsequently filled* as well. In fact, Luke works very hard in Acts to ensure that none of us reduce being filled with the Spirit to a historical event, but *"go on being filled with the Holy Spirit"* day by day.[9] We must not be

---

[4] Matthew 3:11 was as much part of Jesus' earthly mission as Matthew 1:21.

[5] John 14:23, 28; Acts 2:33.

[6] Galatians 3:14.

[7] 2 Peter 1:3–4. The reference to *"divine power"* links back to Luke 24:49, Acts 1:8, and Ephesians 3:16–17.

[8] Luke uses the term "baptism in the Spirit" in 1:5 and 11:16 to form a contrast with John's baptism in water, and *not* to make a distinction between the initial receipt of the Holy Spirit and later infillings. In the key chapters 2, 8, 10, and 19 he deliberately talks of people being *filled* with the Spirit, *receiving* the Spirit, and the Spirit *coming on* them. He wants us to grasp that our first infilling is simply the prelude to more of the same.

[9] Paul uses a present imperative to say this literally in Ephesians 5:18. He says this to Spirit-filled believers (Ephesians 1:13; 2:22; 4:30) with a prayer that they

duped into forgetting that *"God gives the Spirit without limit"*,[10] and allow the blessings of the past to quench our thirst for the present and the future.

In the 1980s movie, *Crocodile Dundee*, the outback Australian travels to the sophisticated streets of New York. There, amid the cosy trimmings of downtown Manhattan, he is attacked by a mugger with a pocket-knife. *"No, mate,"* Crocodile Dundee corrects him as he draws his own massive bushman's knife and waves it in his assailant's face. ***"This** is a knife."* Satan wants to limit your mindset and reduce your view of being filled with the Spirit to something less than it really is. Luke reminds you that it is not a little pocket-knife. We are called to arm ourselves with *"the sword of the Spirit"*.[11]

So examine yourself, and check that you are not treating being filled with the Spirit as something invisible, peripheral, or historical. Don't settle for less than God offers you. It's time to throw off limitation and live daily by the power of the Spirit.[12]

---

may become *more* Spirit-filled (Ephesians 1:17; 3:16).

[10] John 3:34.

[11] Ephesians 6:17.

[12] We will look practically at *how* to live full of the Spirit in the chapter "Boulevards and Barricades".

Antioch (11:19–30)

Some of them, however, men from Cyprus and Cyrene, went to Antioch and began to speak to Greeks also, telling them the good news about the Lord Jesus.

(Acts 11:20)

God used one local church more than any other to foil the Devil's attempts to insulate the Gentile world from the power of the Gospel. Luke is excited as he comes to describe the church at Antioch. After all, he himself was from Antioch, and was one of the Gentiles who were saved in verse 21 through this pioneering church without limits.[1]

The city of Antioch was everything which Jerusalem was not. It was a Gentile city, founded in 301 BC by the Seleucid kings who emerged from Alexander the Great's divided empire. It was a massive city, whose population of over half a million people was nearly ten times greater than that of Jerusalem. It was an important city, exceeded only by Rome and Alexandria in terms of international influence. It was here that a group of anonymous Christians fled in the wake of Stephen's martyrdom, and founded a church which changed the Roman Empire.

The young church at Antioch refused to place limits on their discipleship. They had lost nothing of their passion in the dispiriting journey from Jerusalem. They were so full of the

---

[1] The *Anti-Marcionite Prologue to the Gospel of Luke*, which was written in about AD 170, says that *"Luke was a native of Antioch, a physician by profession. He was a disciple of the apostles and later accompanied Paul until his martyrdom. He served the Lord without distraction, having neither wife nor children, and at the age of 84 he fell asleep in Boeotia, full of the Holy Spirit."*

Spirit that Barnabas saw visible signs of God's grace in their lives.[2] They were Betty Zanes who devoted themselves to the Scriptures, to prayer, to fasting and to worship.[3] They were so full of God's grace that they accepted even Saul of Tarsus – the man whose persecution had driven many of them to Antioch in the first place! – first as their teacher and then as one of their elders.[4] In short, they were such a faithful reflection of their radical mother church in Jerusalem that Luke tells us they grew just as quickly.[5]

The church at Antioch refused to be limited by their *leadership*. The Jerusalem church had not allowed poor models of discipleship to limit their growth in Acts 2:41–47, and nor did the Antioch church allow poor models of leadership to do the same. They did not appoint a lone pastor whose personal capacity would place a ceiling on their growth. They knew from Exodus 18:18 and Numbers 11:14–15 that such pressure is far too much for any one man to bear. Instead, they developed a leadership team who could carry the church together. It included a wide range of apostolic, prophetic, evangelistic, and teaching gifting, so that together they could prepare the church for all Christ had in store for her.[6]

More than any other church before them, the church at Antioch refused to recognize limits of *ethnicity*. Even before Peter had learned his vital lessons with Cornelius, the Jewish believers at Antioch who had come from Cyprus and Cyrene had

[2] Acts 11:21, 23. When Luke talks about the "hand of the Lord" being on them, he is using an Old Testament expression for the Holy Spirit. See 2 Kings 3:15; 1 Chronicles 28:19; Ezra 7:6, 9, 28; Luke 1:66–67.

[3] Acts 11:26; 13:1–3; 15:35. See also chapter entitled "Betty Zane".

[4] Acts 11:25–26; 13:1. Although Luke does not use the word *elders* in 13:1, the context of 11:30 and 14:23 suggests strongly that these five men comprised the eldership team at Antioch.

[5] Acts 11:21, 24.

[6] We do not know much about the other three elders in Acts 13:1, but Paul and Barnabas alone were a mighty demonstration of what Paul describes in Ephesians 4:11–13.

long since grasped that Jesus was the Saviour of every nation. They had grown up in Gentile lands and were not swayed by the same ethnic prejudices as their Judean brothers and sisters. While Peter was still contemplating his vision on a rooftop in Joppa, the believers at Antioch had already seen hundreds of Gentiles saved, baptized, and added to their number.[7] Once saved, these Gentiles were not treated like second-rate Christians but welcomed to the heart of a multiracial eldership team. Barnabas was a Hellenist Jew from Cyprus. Simeon's Latin name meant *black*, which suggests that he was one of the many black Africans who lived and worked in the Mediterranean. Lucius came from Cyrene and, from his name, was a Roman Gentile. Manaen was a Palestinian aristocrat, who had grown up with Herod Antipas, the immoral tetrarch who had beheaded John the Baptist.[8] Finally, Saul of Tarsus was a Pharisee from Asia Minor, and a former companion of the men who ordered Jesus' crucifixion. Antioch was a very cosmopolitan city, and the church's eldership team was a vibrant demonstration that Christ unites people from all nations and backgrounds through the Gospel.

Above all, the church at Antioch changed the world by refusing to be limited in their *vision*. When an itinerant prophet warned that famine was coming, they immediately sent a gift to the believers in Jerusalem, remembering the needs of others before they set about their own.[9] When the apostles in Jerusalem sent Barnabas to check up on the scandalous rumours which were coming out of Antioch, the church gladly received his oversight and direction. There was nothing small-minded

---

[7] Although Luke uses the word *Hellēnistēs* in Acts 6:1; 9:29 to refer to *Greek-speaking Jews*, in the context of 11:20 it can only refer to *Greek-speaking Gentiles.*

[8] The word *suntrophos* simply means *one brought up with*, so Manaen was either Herod's schoolmate or his foster-brother.

[9] 11:27–30; 12:25. Paul explains some of the motivation behind this gift in Romans 15:27.

or independent about the church at Antioch, which was one of the reasons why God chose this healthy group of Christians to plant similar churches into Asia and Europe. When the Holy Spirit prompted them, the church responded with spectacular generosity and sent away their two best elders, Barnabas and Paul, to a church-planting mission overseas.[10] Through their global heart and vision, they changed the course of the book of Acts and the very course of history itself.

God loves churches which refuse to place limits on his Gospel. They are exactly the churches which he loves to replicate all over the world. Luke commends to you his own local church, and invites you to make it a model for your own.

---

[10] Acts 13:1–3.

Barnabas (11:22–30)

Then Barnabas went to Tarsus to look for Saul, and when he found him, he brought him to Antioch.

(Acts 11:25–26)

"I am only one, but I am one. I cannot do everything, but I can do something. And that which I can do, by the grace of God I will do." Very few people have lived out D.L. Moody's statement as wholeheartedly as the apostle Barnabas. Luke mentions him here because he wants to remind us that God uses visionary individuals as well as visionary churches. The church at Antioch refused to place limits on the scope of the Gospel because one of its elders was Barnabas. He lived the godly life which Luke describes in Part One of Acts, and he had the limitless gaze which Luke commends in Part Three. Barnabas knew God and refused to think small in his service. He was an ordinary person who never forgot he had an extraordinary God.

His real name was Joseph of Cyprus, a Jew from the tribe of Levi, but the apostles were so impressed with his large-hearted vision that they nicknamed him *Barnabas*. Luke translates for Theophilus the Aramaic as *Son of Encouragement*, but he does so using a Greek word which is loaded with meaning. *Paraklēsis* does not just mean *encouragement*. It comes from the Greek word *paraklētos*, or *Counsellor*, which Jesus used as a name for the Holy Spirit.[1] When Luke refers to the *"paraklēsis [encouragement] of the Holy Spirit"* in Acts 9:31, he is telling us that Barnabas was more than just an encourager. He was so full

---

[1] John 14:16; 15:26; 16:7. The word *paraklētos* can be translated *Counsellor*, *Comforter*, *Encourager*, or *Helper*.

of the Holy Spirit that he was able to see with God's eyes and to encourage those around him by telling them what he could see.[2]

Barnabas constantly saw God's big picture for the Church. We first meet him in 4:36–37 when he sells a field and brings the money to the apostles so they can give it to the poor. Here in chapter 11, we find him entrusted with a delicate visit to Antioch. The apostles in Jerusalem are alarmed at the news that Jewish Cypriots in Antioch are leading Gentiles to salvation, and they send Barnabas to investigate, as a Jewish Cypriot himself. Far from clamping down on their evangelistic innovation, Luke tells us that he immediately sees the big picture of what God is doing in the city. He *encourages* them, rejoices with them, and recognizes that their innovation is the shape of things to come. Another way of describing Barnabas' Spirit-filled vision is simply to call him *"full of faith"*.[3] Therefore it comes as no surprise in 13:1–3 that God should choose Barnabas to pioneer a new and risky church-planting venture into Cyprus and Asia Minor.

Barnabas also saw God's big picture for individuals. He was a Son of Encouragement because he just couldn't help himself.[4]

Whenever he looked at an ordinary Christian, he saw what they could become in the hands of their extraordinary God. In 9:27, when none of the apostles believed that Paul had truly been converted, Barnabas saw the best in him and helped to knit him into the church. In 11:25–26, when Paul was living in obscurity in Tarsus, Barnabas saw that he would make a perfect Bible

---

[2] Paul prays in Ephesians 1:17–23 that the Holy Spirit will enable many other people to see God's way too.

[3] Acts 11:24. Paul writes in Romans 4:17 that faith trusts that God *"calls things that are not as though they were"*.

[4] The Jews called James and John *Sons of Thunder* because they couldn't help losing their temper (Mark 3:17; Luke 9:54–56). They called Barnabas a *Son of Encouragement* because he couldn't help encouraging people.

teacher and elder for Antioch and went in person to persuade him to come and pastor the people he had once persecuted. He even recognized on their First Missionary Journey together that Paul should be the leader and main speaker in the team.[5] He was generous-hearted to a fault, and in the end he even fell out with Paul because of it. When Barnabas wanted to give a second chance to his cousin, John Mark, who had failed them in Pamphylia, Paul just couldn't see with the same divine optimism as his partner. In the end, Barnabas decided to form a new team of his own which could accommodate past failures like his cousin. It's a good thing that he did. Even Paul was impressed with Mark's gospel, and he later admitted he was a great man to have on the team.[6]

Every church needs men and women like Barnabas, who have Spirit-filled vision to see the limitless potential which God gives to each church and each church member. Every church needs encouragers, who doggedly refuse to think smaller than their God. Bill Hybels argues that *"Vision is the most potent weapon in a leader's arsenal. It's the weapon that unleashes the power of the church."*[7] Yet Barnabas was more than just a visionary, which Luke hints at strongly in his use of the word *paraklêsis*. The word *naba'* in Barnabas means far more than just *encouragement*. It was the normal Hebrew and Aramaic word for a person *prophesying*, and so Luke hints that Barnabas' encouragement was through more than just kind words. Barnabas encouraged people through the charismatic gift of prophecy.[8]

---

[5] Luke calls them *"Barnabas and Saul"* in Acts 11:26, 30; 12:25; 13:2, 7, but he starts calling them *"Paul and Barnabas"* thereafter. In Acts 14:12 the Lystrans assumed that Paul was Hermes, the messenger-god, and that Barnabas was Zeus, the strong but silent god who remained in the background.

[6] Acts 15:36–40; 2 Timothy 4:11; Colossians 4:10. The word *paroxusmos* in Acts 15:39 means an *angry dispute*. Barnabas was willing to disagree heatedly if he felt that another person's vision was too limited.

[7] Bill Hybels, *Courageous Leadership* (2002).

[8] Luke tells us in Acts 13:1 that Barnabas was numbered among the *"prophets and teachers"*.

Prophecy is a mighty gift which stirs vision in the Church and shatters limitation. God made the church at Antioch strong through the prophets on the inside (13:1) and through prophets like Silas and Judas Barsabbas who visited from the outside (15:32). Luke tells us that one of their most important moments as a church came in 11:27–30 during the visit of Agabus and his team of itinerant prophets. A timely word from Agabus prepared the church for famine as the ancient prophet Joseph had prepared the land of Egypt. Luke is honest with us that modern-day prophecy can be abused and misapplied – Agabus prophesies well in 21:10–14 but gives a poor interpretation – but he refuses to let us consign the prophetic gift to the history-books.[9] He urges us to remember that the Holy Spirit fills us so that we can prophesy (2:17–18; 19:6; 21:8–9), and that the prophetic gift is a vital means of receiving clear vision from God.[10]

Luke loves to tell us about the apostle Barnabas, but he is doing far more than reminiscing about his friend and former pastor. Part Three of Acts is a warning not to let the Devil place limits on our vision for the Church and for the Gospel. Luke uses Barnabas as an example of the kind of person God calls us to be – full of the Spirit, full of big vision, full of encouragement, and eager to be full of prophecy – because he wants you to become a Barnabas too. You are only one, but you are one. You cannot do everything, but you can do something. And that which you can do, by the grace of God make sure that you do.

---

[9] Agabus genuinely prophesied through the Holy Spirit, but foolishly embellished what he received based on what had previously happened to Jesus. This is why prophets submit to church elders and not vice versa, and why we must weigh all prophecy carefully (1 Corinthians 14:29).

[10] I examine the prophetic gifting in much more detail in *Straight to the Heart of 1&2 Corinthians*. The church at Antioch treated the gift very seriously, so we dare not dismiss it lightly today.

Seven Names (11:26)

The disciples were called Christians first at Antioch.

(Acts 11:26)

I am a multi-billionaire. I have in my possession a 5-billion-dollar bill. Unfortunately, because they are Zimbabwean dollars, they are not much use to me. In 1980, when they were worth more than their American equivalent, my 5 billion dollars would have enabled me to live the life of a king. Today, after years of runaway inflation, they are practically worthless.[1]

The word *"Christian"* has also suffered from a similar form of hyper-inflation. In my own country, England, where 72 per cent of people call themselves Christians, only 6 per cent of people go to church on any given Sunday.[2] The name "Christian" is cheap and danger of losing its true meaning like the Zimbabwean dollar. That's why Luke takes time in the book of Acts to describe very carefully what it means. "Christian" is only the seventh name which he gives to the followers of Jesus. He gives six other names beforehand to teach us the true value of that name.

Luke's first name for believers is *the brothers*. It's his favourite name, and he uses it twenty-five times so we will not miss its meaning. Christians are those who have been adopted as children of God, and who have given up their lives to become part of his intimate family. When John Wesley taught that *"The Bible knows nothing of solitary religion",* he was right. The New Testament letters are full of commands to love *one*

---

[1] The Zimbabwean dollar was suspended indefinitely in April 2009.

[2] This data comes from the British government's "2001 Census" and from the "2005 English Church Census".

another, serve *one another*, teach *one another*, and bear with *one another*.[3] Jesus died to save a brother- and sisterhood of believers, not so that they could continue in a Christianized form of individualism, but so that they could become part of his glorious new community.[4] We simply cannot understand the message of the New Testament outside of the context of Christian brotherhood.[5]

Luke's second name is *the believers*. Christians are saved by faith, sanctified by faith, live by faith, and minister by faith. Luke treats "Christian" and "unbelief" as two irreconcilable opposites, and will not have us devalue the name with half-hearted scepticism. Luke's shorthand description for conversion in 11:1 is *"receiving the word of God"*, because the Christian life is a matter of faith *"from first to last"*.[6]

Next, Luke calls the believers *the disciples*. Christians are learners who follow hard after Jesus with a hungry desire to grow into his likeness. Because Jesus taught that *"it is enough for the student to be like his teacher"*, true Christians are always prepared to suffer loss and deprivation for the sake of their Master.[7] They follow in Jesus' footprints and consider it an honour to suffer for his sake.

Luke's fourth name for believers is *those belonging to the Way*.[8] There is nothing static about following Jesus, because it means walking along his path day by day. We may begin our Christian lives by praying a prayer of conversion, but that prayer

---

[3] In the letter to the Romans alone, Paul refers to *"one another"* in 1:12; 12:10, 16; 13:8; 15:7, 14; 16:16.

[4] Since the Jews also referred to one another as *brothers*, this was also a deliberate statement that the Church was the true continuation of Old Testament Israel (Acts 28:20; Galatians 6:16; Romans 11:1–36).

[5] In fact, 1 Peter 2:17 tells us than an integral part of Christianity is to *"love the brotherhood of believers"*.

[6] Romans 1:17. See also the chapters entitled "Glorify God's Word" and "Sanctified by Faith".

[7] Matthew 10:25; 1 Peter 2:21.

[8] Especially in Acts 9:2; 19:9, 23; 24:14, 22.

doesn't make us a Christian. Only those who walk the road of Jesus are truly worthy of that name.[9]

Next, Luke refers to all believers, and not just their leaders, as *the saints* or *the holy ones*. This Greek word, *hagios*, means that Christians have been *set apart* from the world to live lives which reflect their holy God. We are *made holy* by grace through faith, and are called to *live holy* by that same grace through faith. True Christians are visibly different from the rest of the world because the Holy Spirit inside them bears fruit and displays through their lives what their God is really like.

Luke's sixth name for believers is *those who call on the name of the Lord*.[10] He emphasizes that Christians are the spiritual heirs of the patriarchs who called on the name of the Lord in the book of Genesis.[11] We praise the name of the Lord, pray in the name of the Lord, issue commands in the name of the Lord, and take refuge in the name of the Lord. Nobody becomes a Christian by taking that name to themselves, but only by calling on the name of Christ and receiving the salvation which he promises them.

Luke only speaks the seventh name, *Christian*, in 11:26 after he has first carefully qualified its meaning through these six other names. He will not have it devalued like the Zimbabwean dollar, for when Christians treat it lightly they limit the challenge it conveys. When the decadent citizens of Antioch invented the name to insult the *"little Christs"* like Luke who had converted en masse in their city, the believers took the name as a compliment because it summarized what was good about the other six names. Peter even wrote to believers that *"if you suffer as a 'Christian', do not be ashamed, but praise God that you bear*

---

[9] See the chapter on "True and False Conversion".

[10] Acts 9:14, 21; 22:16. Paul also uses this phrase in Romans 10:12–14; 1 Corinthians 1:2; 2 Timothy 2:22.

[11] Genesis 4:26; 12:8; 13:4; 21:33; 26:25.

that name".[12] Luke gives exhaustive definition to what it means to be a Christian because he wants you to praise God that you bear that name too.

Ptolemaeus was a church leader in the city of Rome. One morning in 160 AD, a Roman centurion knocked on his door. *"Are you a Christian?"* the soldier demanded. He was acting on a tip-off he had received from a husband whose wife had recently been converted through Ptolemaeus. When he confessed, *"Yes, I am,"* he was arrested, imprisoned and tortured for his faith in Jesus. Finally, he was taken before a Roman judge to decide his fate.

"Are you a Christian?" the judge asked him, hoping that the torture had weakened his resolve. *"Yes, I am,"* Ptolemaeus repeated, and for those three little words received a death sentence. Suddenly an elderly gentleman named Lucius leapt to his feet in the gallery and shouted, *"What is the basis for this judgment? Why have you punished this man... who has only confessed that he is called by the name of Christian?"* The judge was in no mood for disturbances in his courtroom. *"You also seem to me to be a Christian!"* he sneered. *"I most certainly am,"* confessed Lucius, and was hauled from the gallery to die alongside Ptolemaeus.[13]

Men like Luke and Lucius knew the true meaning of the name Christian, and they will not have us devalue it today. It means *brother*, *believer*, *disciple*, *wayfarer*, *saint* and *one who calls on the name of the Lord*. It meant life or death to the earliest Christians. We must not sell so cheaply today what they once sold so dearly.

---

[12] 1 Peter 4:16. King Agrippa also uses the word "Christian" as a derogatory term in Acts 26:28.

[13] Justin Martyr describes this event as the provocation for his *Second Apology* in about 160 AD.

God's Airlock (12:1–25)

He had James, the brother of John, put to death with the sword. When he saw that this pleased the Jews, he proceeded to seize Peter also.

(Acts 12:2–3)

When I finally see Jesus face to face in glory, I have a long list of questions to ask him. I know the famous story that life is like a tapestry – muddled and confusing on this side of heaven, but gloriously beautiful looking back from above – but I've still got lots of questions, all the same. Why didn't things work out as I expected? What about the things I was sure that God promised me, but never quite came to pass? I've got plenty such questions to ask Jesus, but I may have to wait for him to finish with John first. At the start of 44 AD, King Herod arrested both John's brother James and their friend Peter.[1] God sent an angel to rescue Peter from the jaws of death, but he didn't send one for James. I find it confusing that God delivered Peter but allowed James to be beheaded. For John, it must have been downright faith-shattering.

Don't get me wrong, I'm very excited that God miraculously rescued Peter. It was completely against all the odds. The Jews

---

[1] This was Herod Agrippa I (37–44 AD), the nephew of Herod Antipas who beheaded John the Baptist. He had reunited the tetrarchies of Palestine in 41 AD and was riding on the crest of a political wave. Josephus tells us in his *Antiquities* (19.8.2) that the *appointed day* in 12:21 was the Emperor Claudius' birthday, 1st August 44 AD, and that Herod's symptoms were those of a hydatid cyst caused by tapeworm larvae.

expected him to die,[2] the Church expected him to die,[3] and even Peter himself expected to die.[4] Peter's miraculous jailbreak – a follow-on from his first jailbreak in 5:18–20 – was a wonderful reminder that God can always protect his own.

But this makes what happened to James quite baffling. It's not like James was a minor character in the gospels. He was one of Jesus' inner circle of Three. He was there with Peter and John when Jesus raised Jairus' daughter to life. He was there with them when Jesus revealed himself in glory on the Mount of Transfiguration. He was there with them to support Jesus as he prayed in the Garden of Gethsemane. He even fooled himself for a while that he was the joint greatest disciple along with his brother.[5] Jesus invested more time and energy in training James than any person other than Peter and John, but after only fourteen years of ministry, he became the first of the apostles to die. John must have struggled with that.

When I was twenty-one, I became an overseas missionary. Only two years converted, and filled with bullish self-confidence, I moved to live in Paris as a full-time evangelist. For a whole year I preached the Gospel to anyone who would listen – on the Metro, in the streets, at the universities and in the parks – and at the end of the year I was completely spent. A year of exhaustion had yielded only two converts, and both of those looked pretty shaky. In the end I called time on my missionary endeavour, took the ferry back to England, and licked my wounds in disappointment.

For six months, I felt on the brink of an emotional

---

[2] Acts 12:11.

[3] Although the Church were praying for Peter's release, they wouldn't believe it when it happened. They had more faith to see his guardian angel (see Matthew 18:10) than to see him alive and free. Note that the *James* of 12:17 was not John's brother (whom Peter knew was dead), but the leader of the Jerusalem church.

[4] Men who still hope to live pace their cells at night. Peter slept soundly because he was resigned to death.

[5] Luke 8:51; 9:28; Mark 10:35–45; 14:33.

breakdown. Had the Gospel failed? Had God failed? Had I failed? I took days out to pray and seek God for answers, but nothing came. I trawled from one charismatic meeting to another, desperately hoping for a Holy Spirit encounter which would make sense of my shattered sense of God's calling. Finally, after months of confusion, I had a breakthrough, but it wasn't at all what I was expecting.

I had spent Christmas Day in tears, crying out to God and asking him to explain why he hadn't supported me like I thought the Bible said he would. I had cried myself to sleep on Boxing Day, telling God I couldn't carry on any more with my Pandora's Box of doubt and disappointment. I woke up the following day and drove to see my family. It was snowing and the roads were icy, and suddenly I felt the car slip and go into a skid. It swerved across the road, rolled onto the roof, smashed into a tree, and landed in a ditch. I remember shattered glass, the smell of petrol, the ambulance, the hospital and then what happened when I arrived home. As I stepped across the threshold, I suddenly heard God's voice which had eluded me so long. I felt God point to my near fatal car accident and urge me to view it as closure on my past. By grace, he had given me a future I need not have had, and it was time to stop looking backwards and to start to live life forwards again.

In science fiction movies, spaceships always have an airlock, and it was as if God invited me to step into one of his own. Airlocks have two sets of doors – one to cut off where you come from and another to lead you to your destination – and God told me to let go of the past so I could step into the future. He didn't tell me why my overseas mission was such a failure. He didn't give me any real explanation at all. He simply told me to let go of the past and leave my bitter disappointment behind, so that the questions of my past would not rob me of my future. It was a very, very simple experience, but it was completely life-transforming.

John had never heard of an airlock, and he certainly didn't need a car accident, but only this same process could have saved his heart from sinking when God saved the life of Peter but not James. The death of his brother could have spoiled John for the rest of his life, but we can tell from the rest of Scripture that he let God be God and decided to live looking forwards instead of backwards. As a result, he had fifty years more years as an apostle and wrote five books of the Bible.

You may have questions of your own to ask Jesus about the disappointments and failures of your own walk with him. Perhaps, like John, you have known tragedy in your family life: a loved one who died, a marriage which failed, a child who backslid, a dream which never came to pass. Perhaps, like me, you were involved in a church-plant or missionary endeavour which "failed". If you are like John, me or the whole host of Christians who have struggled with disappointment and despair, I can't give you the answers you are looking for. But I can tell you what to do with your questions.

Step into God's airlock. Hear the doors close tightly shut against your past. Lay your questions at Jesus' feet and then make sure you leave them there. Confess your hurt and disappointment, and then renounce your confusion and complaints. Tell God that you trust him, even without him giving you the answers to your questions, and then hear the doors slide open to your fresh start of walking with God. Feel the pleasant expanse of space and freedom from the constricting walls of confusion.

I thank God for his wonderful airlock. It freed John, it freed me, and if you need it, it will free you too.

The Gospel to Asia Minor (48–49 AD)

Paul's First Missionary Journey, 48 AD (13:1 – 14:28)

Paul and Barnabas appointed elders for them in each church and, with prayer and fasting, committed them to the Lord, in whom they had put their trust.

(Acts 14:23)

When Jesus told them to *"go and make disciples of all nations"*, Paul and Barnabas planted local churches. Whichever way you look at it, that's got to make a difference to the way you invest your life. They didn't simply work for large numbers of conversions. They didn't simply establish a collection of Christian ministries. They didn't even form a network of high-quality Christian meetings. They were satisfied with nothing less than planting vibrant and self-supporting churches like the ones in Jerusalem and Antioch. Paul and Barnabas went to Asia Minor with the power of the Gospel, but their hopes for those they won to Christ were firmly bound up in the local church.

This may seem an obvious point to you, but it isn't. The missiologist George W. Peters bemoans *"an unfortunate and abnormal historical development which has produced autonomous, missionless churches on the one hand and autonomous, churchless missionary societies on the other"*. Sadly, evangelism and the church have not always walked hand in hand. Churches can become so absorbed in sustaining their own internal lives that they leave evangelism to specialist ministries and parachurch organizations. As a result, Christians with the greatest evangelistic fervour can grow disillusioned with their visionless churches and give themselves to pioneering work instead of, or in spite of, the Church itself. Luke's account of Paul and Barnabas' First Missionary Journey makes neither of these two errors. It marks a radical departure from the twelve chapters which have gone before – Paul takes to the fore instead of Peter, and the battleground moves to modern-day Turkey and Europe instead of Israel and Syria – but there is far more continuity than discontinuity between the first and second halves of Acts. Up till now, Luke has focused on the churches in Jerusalem, Samaria, Joppa, and Antioch. Now he focuses on how those churches replicated themselves across the Roman Empire.

Paul and Barnabas planted the Asian churches out of an existing local church. There was nothing independent about their First Missionary Journey. It was prompted by the Holy Spirit as the eldership team of the Antioch church prayed together. It was endorsed by the whole church at Antioch who *"committed them to the grace of God"*. It was carried in the hearts of all the church who stayed behind, so that Paul and Barnabas duly returned and *"stayed there a long time with the disciples"* to share with them all that God had done.[1] Paul and Barnabas were not "missionaries" who went out from an agency in the hope of making converts. They were ambassadors of Christ's church in Antioch who went with delegated authority to reproduce more churches like it.[2] Roland Allen writes the following in his classic book on the missionary journeys of Paul:

> *He did not approach them as an isolated prophet; he came as an apostle of the church of God, and he did not simply seek to gather out individual souls from amongst*

---

[1] Acts 13:1–3; 14:26–28. See also 18:22–23.

[2] I am not denying their own authority as apostles to plant churches (Acts 14:4, 14). I am simply insisting that *apostle* means "sent one", and that 15:24 makes a clear distinction between a "sent one" and a "went one".

the heathen, he gathered them into the society of which
he was a member... The apostle who preached to them
was a member of it, and he preached as a member of it,
and as a member of it he invited them to enter it, to share
its privileges and its burdens, its glory and its shame.[3]

Consequently, Paul and Barnabas gathered their converts into
new local churches with their own teams of elders. It was not
enough for them to save large numbers of souls in Pisidian
Antioch, Iconium, and Lystra. They had been persecuted and
almost martyred in those cities, but they were willing to risk their
lives afresh by returning to gather them into churches under
clearly appointed eldership teams. Roland Allen continues:

Men have wandered over the world, "preaching the
Word", laying no solid foundations, establishing nothing
permanent, leaving no really instructed society behind
them, and have claimed St Paul's authority for their
absurdities... Many missionaries in later days have
received a larger number of converts than St Paul; many
have preached over a wider area than he; but none have
so established churches. We have long forgotten that
such things could be. We have long accustomed ourselves
to accept it as an axiom of missionary work that converts
in a new country must be submitted to a very long
probation and training, extending over generations,
before they can be expected to stand alone.

Paul and Barnabas quickly found leaders who could implement
the lessons of Parts One, Two and Three of the book of Acts.
Their mission yielded far more than new converts to the faith. It
yielded new churches like the one from which they had come.

In fact, Paul and Barnabas had a greater goal even than

---

[3] British missionary Roland Allen in his great work *Missionary Methods: St*
Paul's or Ours? (1912).

planting a new network of churches across the southern half of Asia Minor. They were determined to found churches which shared their limitless vision to start more new churches in the hinterland beyond. When Paul and Barnabas planted a church in the capital city of the province of Pisidia, Luke tells us in 13:49 that the result was that *"the word of the Lord spread through the whole region"*. Once they had planted churches in the four major cities in the area, they returned home to Antioch, convinced that their task of reaching the area was complete.[4] Roland Allen comments again:

> *St Paul's theory of evangelising a province was not to preach in every place in it himself, but to establish centres of Christian life [i.e. churches] in two or three important places from which the knowledge might spread into the country around. This is important, not as showing that he preferred to preach in a capital rather than in a provincial town or in a village, but because he intended his congregations to become at once a centre of light... When he had occupied two or three centres, he had really and effectually occupied the province.*

The beginning of Part Four of the book of Acts opens up an exciting new phase in the history of the Church. No longer were the churches in Jerusalem and Antioch satisfied to share the Gospel with their neighbours and leave the rest of the world alone. From now on, they would take the Gospel on the offensive wherever the Holy Spirit would lead them. First Asia, then Europe, never resting until all the known world had been filled with their teaching.

Yet this turning point does not mark a shift in Luke's focus from "church" to "overseas mission". Paul and Barnabas

---

[4] See also Romans 15:23 where Paul assumes that *"there is no more place for me to work"* in the Eastern Mediterranean because he has planted self-replicating churches in all the major cities there.

Bridges and Walls
(13:16–47; 14:15–18)

We had to speak the word of God to you first. Since you reject it and do not consider yourselves worthy of eternal life, we now turn to the Gentiles.

(Acts 13:46)

On my key ring there are two keys – the key to my house and the key to my car. They are really quite different. If you take my car key and try to get into my house, then you'll be sleeping outside in the cold. On the other hand, if you take my house key and try to start my car, you had better put on your walking shoes. Both keys are on the same key ring, but they are made to unlock two very different doors.

That's pretty obvious, but Luke tells us that the Gospel is like my key ring as well. The Gospel itself never changes, but we need to choose the right way of presenting it if our listeners are to grasp that it is true. Luke demonstrates this with two Gospel messages from Paul's journeys around Asia Minor, with a warning to use the right key in each door. If we preach to Jews as if they were pagans, or to pagans as if they were Jews, we will never succeed in convincing them to follow Jesus Christ.

Some of our listeners will be nominal Christians. They are like the "Jews" of Pisidian Antioch. Our traditional Gospel message of *You're a sinner / Jesus died for you / Repent and follow him* fails to open their door. They think they have already repented, and they immediately assume that our message is for someone other than them. Paul uses a different key from the same Gospel key ring. He builds bridges towards them, calling them *brothers*, and referring to *our fathers*, *our people*, and the message which was sent to *us*.[1] Then he tells them the life story of Jesus as it fits within their own Jewish story. So far he is very well received, because he demonstrates a sympathetic understanding of their history and beliefs. Now for a sudden gear change. Jews and nominal Christians are seldom converted through bridges alone. Why would they be, if all that they hear is what they already believe to be true?

So Paul starts building walls. He tells them that the Law of Moses cannot justify, that Judaism cannot bring forgiveness, and that consequently they are outside the people of God like the Gentiles they despise. They are followers of the rabbis who crucified God's Messiah, and unless they repent they will perish as Habakkuk 1:5 warned they would: *"Look, you scoffers, wonder and perish, for I am going to do something in your days that you would never believe, even if someone told you."* This is the kind of preaching which causes nominal believers to hate you and drive you out of town, but it is also the kind of preaching which causes them to repent and believe the Gospel. Bridge building wins an audience, but only wall building can save them. As if to reinforce this still further, Luke tells us that the following week Paul shook the dust off his feet[2] and turned his attention to the pagans in the city with a final quotation from Isaiah 49:6: *"I have made you a light to the Gentiles."*[3]

In contrast, many of our listeners will be more like the rustic pagans of Lystra. Paul opened their hearts with a different key from the same Gospel key ring. At the synagogue in Pisidian Antioch he quoted from the Old Testament at least six times, but even when he tells the Lystrans in 14:17 that God *"has*

---

[1] Acts 13:17, 26, 31–33, 38.

[2] Jesus commanded his followers to do this in Luke 9:5 as a clear sign that they considered their hearers to be enemies of Christ and that they wanted no share in their judgment. Paul did so again in Acts 18:6.

[3] Note Paul's inference here that the promises of the Servant Songs belong to the Christians and not the Jews.

shown kindness by giving you rain from heaven and crops in their seasons; he provides you with plenty of food and fills your hearts with joy", he makes absolutely no reference to Psalm 104:13–15 or the many other Scripture verses which could reinforce his point. He understands what Luke taught us in the chapter on "Starting Points", and begins with where his hearers are, instead of where he wishes they were. They know nothing of Jesus' life, care little for his teaching, and see no reason why they should surrender their lives to a Galilean carpenter. Therefore Paul has to start by building bridges for the Gospel.

The Lystran pagans were sinful rebels – Paul would make that point himself in Romans 3:10–18 – but he knew that Gospel messages are rarely successful when they begin like a ticking-off from a schoolteacher. Lystra was surrounded by countryside, so he begins by talking about the Creator-God who gives harvests and joyous celebrations to hard-working farmers like themselves. His message is that God is on their side, even though for a period he has *"let all nations go their own way"*. Suddenly the Lystrans are interested. A Jewish Messiah was of no interest to them, but pleasing the harvest god was foremost on their mind. Now they are finally ready to hear about the life of Jesus,[4] and even though Paul is interrupted before he can finish, we can still see what walls he was about to build. He had just healed a lame man by the power of Jesus' name, so his challenge that it is time for the Lystrans to turn from worthless idols to the true and Living God is both natural and convincing. In fact, so many were converted that he needed to return to Lystra later to appoint elders for the church.

Luke tells us that Paul continued to preach differently to Jews and pagans on each of his journeys. In 28:23–28 he preaches the same Jewish message to the Roman Jews, and in 17:22–31 he preaches the same pagan message to the Athenians. In Athens,

---

[4] I'm not speculating here. Acts 16:30–31; 17:7; 18; 20:21; 24:24 tell us what Paul would have said next.

even though he was fuming on the inside at the city's idolatry, he still begins by building bridges. He tells them that *"I see that in every way you are very religious"*, and that God *"is not far from each one of us"*.[5] Paul used the right key from the Gospel key ring to open the hearts of both Jew and pagan, starting with the right bridges and then building the right walls to call them to surrender to Christ.

If you have been taught that the Gospel is a one-size-fits-all message, Luke is telling you that your task is both harder and much easier than you imagined. It is harder because you need first to gauge whether your listeners are nominal Christians or unchurched pagans. Most Westerners need the "pagan" approach if they are to grasp that the Gospel has any relevance to their lives. Most self-assured churchgoers need the "Jewish" approach for them to grasp that they have yet to respond to the Gospel. At the same time it is also much easier, because Luke confirms what we have long suspected – that starting our messages by beating unbelievers over the head with their sin is rarely successful. We build bridges to show people *why* they should follow Jesus, and only then move on to building walls which command them to repent.

Trying to fit the wrong key into a door is a one-way ticket to frustration. Praise God that his Gospel key ring holds the right key for every heart.

---

[5] Acts 17:22, 27. The word *paroxunō* in v. 16 also describes Paul's angry falling-out with Barnabas in 15:39.

Grace is for Other People Too (13:43)

Many of the Jews and devout converts to Judaism followed Paul and Barnabas, who talked with them and urged them to continue in the grace of God.

(Acts 13:43)

It's one thing to have faith that God can use an ordinary person like yourself. It's quite another thing to trust him to use the ordinary people around you. Paul and Barnabas had a major challenge as they neared the end of their First Missionary Journey. After only a few months in the cities of southern Asia Minor, they were about return to Antioch and leave their fledgling new churches to fend for themselves. They must find ordinary men among their converts, and trust the Holy Spirit to finish through those rookies what he had started through themselves.

A lot of Christian leaders stumble at this hurdle. They believe that God can use ordinary people like themselves, but they haven't the same faith to hand over their work to others. They see faults and flaws and a thousand different reasons why it is not yet time to trust those around them to continue what they have started. They consign themselves to mediocrity because they haven't faith to multiply new leaders in their stead. They have forgotten what Paul and Barnabas knew only too well: that they have only borne fruit through God's grace towards them, and that God's grace is also towards other people too.

Paul was acutely aware of his own failings. He told his Lystran disciple, Timothy, that it was precisely because of his history as a persecutor that *"I was shown mercy so that in me,* the worst of sinners, Christ Jesus might display his unlimited patience".[1] He was never under any illusion that his missionary successes were in any way because he was superior to others. Three times he reported back to the Christians in Antioch and Jerusalem that he and Barnabas had only managed to plant such healthy churches because of what "God had done through them".[2] Luke agrees, and reminds us that they were only fruitful "by the grace of God".[3] When we fail to trust others to carry on what we have started, we are actually guilt of crass pride and self-conceit. Paul, in contrast, knew full well that "I planted the seed... but God made it grow. So neither he who plants nor he who waters is anything, but only God, who makes things grow."[4] Because he knew that God's grace was available for other people, and not just for himself, Paul was able to move on to regions new and leave whole teams of new leaders in his wake.

Paul had come to Asia Minor to preach the life story of Jesus and "the message of his grace".[5] When people responded to this Gospel, he simply told them to "continue in the grace of God" and that God would supply them with everything they needed. They had believed by grace and been justified by grace, and so "the word of his grace" would also grow them and strengthen them to lead his work without him.[6] His confidence in his new converts was infectious, and they believed that they could fill his massive shoes simply by continuing in the grace of God.

154

---

[1] 1 Timothy 1:16. Luke tells us that Timothy was from Lystra in Acts 16:1–2.

[2] Acts 14:27; 15:4; 15:12. See also Paul's report in 21:19 on his return from his Third Missionary Journey.

[3] Acts 14:26. Luke also says this about Paul's Second Missionary Journey in 15:40.

[4] 1 Corinthians 3:6–7. Paul wrote this about the church at Corinth which he planted on his Second Missionary Journey, but he evidently had the same attitude on his First Journey too.

[5] Acts 14:3. This was also the message on his Second and Third Missionary Journeys (20:24).

[6] Acts 13:43; 15:11; 18:27; 20:32.

Given the speed with which Paul's converts grew to maturity through his Gospel of God's grace, it is small wonder that the Devil attacked these Galatian churches on this very issue.[7] Paul was forced to write to them the following year to warn them to reject the "Judaizing" infiltrators who had tried to re-enslave them to the Law of Moses. This Law could not justify, Paul had taught them in 13:39, and nor could it gain God's blessing on the work which they had inherited.

Paul was brutally frank with the churches of his First Missionary Journey in the face of this Judaizing threat. *"I am astonished,"* he wrote to them in early 49 AD, *"that you are so quickly deserting the one who called you by the grace of Christ and are turning to a different gospel – which is really no gospel at all."*[8] Their interest in the Law of Moses was not merely a harmless new emphasis which might help the churches to grow alongside the message of grace. Far from it. *"You have fallen away from grace,"* he warned them, and had failed to remain in the only place where they could lead without him.[9] God would fill them daily with the Holy Spirit, but only by grace and never by Law. God would empower them perform great miracles, but again by grace alone.[10] He would strengthen them as mature church leaders, and help them win their cities and plant new churches across Asia Minor, but only by grace and never by Law. *"You were running a good race,"* he warned them. *"How is it that you are turning back to those weak and miserable principles?"*[11]

If you are a Christian, Satan has two strategies to rob you of maturity and fruitful leadership in God's Kingdom. First, he

---

[7] There was a Roman province called *Galatia*, which Paul visited on his Second Missionary Journey (16:6), but the name also referred to a much larger region in Asia Minor. Therefore Paul's letter to the Galatians in 49 AD was written to these four churches in "wider Galatia" – Pisidian Antioch, Iconium, Lystra, and Derbe.

[8] Galatians 1:6–7.

[9] Galatians 5:4.

[10] Galatians 3:1–5.

[11] Galatians 5:7; 4:9.

hopes to persuade you that you could never amount to anything in the purposes of Christ. He tries to make you forget that the grace of God is for you as well, so that you abdicate the Great Commission and drop out of God's army. Second, if you are smart enough to see this full-frontal attack, he tries to seduce you into ministering through something other than God's grace. A little bit of Law and self-effort can make us fall away from grace. We must resist his twin-pronged attack and *"continue in the grace of God"*, for this is the only way that ordinary Christians can ever see extraordinary fruitfulness.

If you are a Christian leader, Satan may already have failed in his first two strategies in your life. Undeterred, he has a third prong to his attack, which may at least place a ceiling on your potential for God's Kingdom. He tries to convince you that what God has done by grace through you, he could never do through the others around you. He convinces you that you are indispensable, so that you get stuck instead of moving on and form a bottleneck to growth.

Paul did not preach a message of grace for salvation but then forget about grace when discipling his new converts. He left Asia Minor very quickly and placed the future of his ministry in the hands of those he trusted. Learn the lesson which made sure Paul's First Missionary Journey was not his last: God's grace is bigger than we thought – it is enough for all the other people around us too.

Glorify God's Word (13:48)

When the Gentiles heard this, they were glad and glorified the word of God.

(Acts 13:48)[1]

I must have been a very annoying child. I liked nothing better than to run the wrong way up and down escalators. The faster they were travelling, the more I enjoyed them, and I must have annoyed a lot of shopkeepers along the way. Given that background, it's no wonder that I love Luke's second reason why Paul's converts in Asia Minor grew so rapidly in their faith. He says they made a roundabout turn in the way they viewed the world around them, and began to run against the flow of the prevailing culture.

Luke uses a wonderful expression to explain how they did so. He tells us literally that they *"glorified the word of God"*. They glorified God himself too, but that isn't the point that Luke is making here. He tells us that they glorified his Word by treating it as the inerrant message of the Creator-God to his creatures. As Paul told the Christians in Thessalonica, who also glorified the Word of the Lord: *"You accepted it not as the word of men, but as it actually is, the word of God, which is at work in you who believe."*[2] In a region which prized its Greek gods and its world-renowned philosophy, the new Christians of Asia Minor had made a very counter-cultural decision. They would glorify

---

[1] Revised Standard Version. The Greek word *doxazō* is a word normally used elsewhere for *glorifying* God.

[2] 1 Thessalonians 2:13; 2 Thessalonians 3:1. Contrast this with 2 Samuel 12:9.

Scripture and the anointed preaching of God's messengers by treating them as God's definitive declaration of truth.

Their honour for the Word of God ensured that their conversion was genuine. Luke's shorthand description for Christian conversion in Acts 11:1 is simply that people "receive the Word of God" for what it really is. If Paul's new followers had merely prayed a prayer of conversion, he could never have left them to fend for themselves in his absence. One of the reasons we expend so much energy in mentoring new believers is precisely because they have not come through on this issue. Paul, on the other hand, was able to lead his converts to rapid maturity because at the heart of their conversion was a surrender to God's Word. They did not argue with its theology or moral teaching, but simply followed it to the letter. They resolved to run the wrong way up and down the escalators of their culture, and to live by faith in what God said in every verse of Scripture. When they were briefly led astray by Judaizing hijackers in 49 AD, they even treated Paul's letter to them with due honour, for by the time he arrived back in Galatia about a year later, he quickly found that *"the churches were strengthened in the faith and grew daily in numbers"*.[3] When people glorify the Word of God at their conversion, they pave for themselves a clear and straight path towards Christian maturity.

Their honour for the Word of God ensured that they grew quickly as disciples. Jesus had commanded his followers in the Great Commission to teach new converts to *"obey everything that I have commanded you"*, and they obeyed him to the letter. Even when Paul and Barnabas were driven out of town, the believers in Pisidian Antioch *"were filled with joy and the Holy Spirit"* and spread the Gospel throughout their region.[4] When Paul was stoned almost to death in Lystra, the believers gathered round him and helped him, even though doing so placed their

---

[3] Acts 16:5.
[4] Acts 13:49, 52.

own lives in danger.[5] In all of the cities on his First Missionary Journey, Paul found his new converts still trusting in their God and in his Word when he returned a few weeks later to appoint elders for each church.[6]

Luke even provides us with a stirring example of what it means to glorify the Word of God in 13:47. Paul and Barnabas are being rejected by the jealous Jews of Pisidian Antioch, when Paul retorts with a quotation from Isaiah 49:6: *"I have made you a light to the Gentiles, that you may bring salvation to the ends of the earth."* The interesting thing about this promise is that God the Father made it to his Messiah at the end of Isaiah's second "Servant Song",[7] and yet Paul treats it as the Lord's command to *himself.* Evidently, he so honoured Jesus' teaching that Christians are the "light of the world", even as he is the "Light of the World",[8] that he reinterpreted the whole of the Old Testament on the basis of what he said. Paul glorified God's Word himself, and taught his converts that they must glorify it too. When they did so, they grew very quickly in their faith.

The new believers' honour for the Word of God also meant that they were well prepared to share the Gospel and minister in power as the natural outworking of their confidence in Scripture. In Psalm 138, David says that he longs to praise God before the "gods" and kings of the earth because his Word is glorified above all else.[9] Since Luke tells us in 13:49 that evangelism is *spreading the word of the Lord*, it should not surprise us that great witnessing for Christ always begins with a prior resolution to glorify his Word.

When Billy Graham started out as a Gospel preacher, he was thrown into a spiritual crisis through a friend who warned

---

[5] Acts 14:19–20.

[6] Acts 14:23.

[7] This is why Paul's quotation in Greek uses the word *su*, meaning *you singular,* and not *you plural.*

[8] John 8:12 and 9:15 compared with Matthew 5:14.

[9] Psalm 138:2.

him that *"Billy, you're fifty years out of date. People no longer accept the Bible as being inspired the way you do."* He writes about his agonized response to that challenge as a turning point in his ministry:

> *As that night wore on, my heart became heavily burdened. Could I trust the Bible?... I had to have an answer. If I could not trust the Bible, I could not go on... "O God! There are many things in this book I do not understand. There are many problems with it for which I have no solution. There are many seeming contradictions. There are some areas in it that do not seem to correlate with modern science.*
>
> *I was trying to be on the level with God, but something remained unspoken. At last the Holy Spirit freed me to say it. "Father, I am going to accept this as Thy Word – by **faith**! I'm going to allow faith to go beyond my intellectual questions and doubts, and I will believe this to be your inspired Word." When I got up from my knees... I sensed the presence and power of God as I had not sensed it in months. Not all my questions were answered, but a major bridge had been crossed. In my heart and mind, I knew a spiritual battle in my soul had been fought and won.*[10]

Paul was able to release his converts quickly into self-supporting churches in Asia Minor because they resolved from the outset to glorify the Word of God. They treated Scripture as the words of the Living God, and ran against the flow of their culture. Whenever people glorify the Word of God like this, God can entrust them with a great future in his Kingdom.

---

[10] Billy Graham in his autobiography, *Just As I Am* (1997).

Honest Truth (14:22)

"We must go through many hardships to enter the kingdom of God," they said.

(Acts 14:22)

Earlier this year, I pretended to be extremely generous to a group of fish. I hired a boat with my two young sons, and we went out to sea to dangle pieces of food in the water. The fish were evidently very hungry, because they were only too eager to take us up on our offer of dinner. Assuming that our motives were altruistic, they hurriedly swallowed our food without suspecting that it concealed a very sharp hook on the inside. Fish are not very clever, and later that evening it was their turn to be dinner for us.

Fishermen need to be deceptive, but that was not what Jesus had in mind when he promised to turn us into fishers of men. On the contrary, Paul told the converts from his missionary journeys that *"we have renounced secret and shameful ways; we do not use deception, nor do we distort the word of God. On the contrary, by setting forth the truth plainly we commend ourselves to every man's conscience in the sight of God."*[1] Therefore Luke tells us that the third major reason that Paul and Barnabas' fresh-faced converts in Asia Minor grew so quickly into mature leadership was that their Gospel message was not like a lump of bait on a hook. They did not promise health, wealth and trouble-free prosperity through the life of Jesus. They simply told their listeners the honest truth, that *"We must go through many hardships to enter the kingdom of God."*

---

[1] 2 Corinthians 4:2.

Many people share the message of Jesus like a fisherman, and not like Paul and Barnabas. They present him as the solution to all life's ills, who makes his followers perpetually happy and prosperous. They repackage the Gospel to major on blessings and conceal the "hook" of suffering. They fail to mention that converting to Christ is a declaration of war as well as an acceptance of peace. It is a decision to refuse the orders of the sinful flesh and to follow the Word of God. It is a decision to be laughed at and persecuted by friends and family. It is a decision to renounce the comforts of peacetime to take a place in Christ's army of missionaries. Becoming a Christian can make life *worse*, as well as better, and Paul's new converts grew so quickly because he told them this honest truth from the outset.

Surprisingly, this unadulterated Gospel message is always more effective at winning people to Christ. When we tell people that *"Jesus will improve your life"*, they treat our happy-ever-after promises like the sales pitch of a used car dealer or a slimy politician. They can see through our baited hooks because they know full well that the Christian life cannot be like a Disney movie as we claim. They know Jesus was betrayed, stripped, flogged and crucified, and that therefore walking along his road is unlikely to be problem free at all. They know that the great Christians of history have been despised and ill-treated, and that the message they are hearing must therefore be too good to be true. People are smarter than fish and hate hidden catches, but they are open to listen to unadulterated truth.

The Gospel message is a proclamation that Jesus is King and that he has proved it through his resurrection. It is a call to follow him, not because he improves our lives (although he does), but simply because he is God and we are not. The Gospel is Christ-centred, not man-centred, and it is powerfully effective when we share it that way.

Take, for example, Paul's vision on the road to Damascus. Jesus reveals himself as the true and risen Lord of the universe

("*Who are you, **Lord**?*"), and warns Paul that he is a sinner facing judgment ("*Why are you persecuting me?*"). There is no smooth sales pitch, and the clearest promise is "*how much he must suffer for my name*".[2] Jesus does not ask Paul to give his life improvement plan a try, but commands him to surrender before his King and do everything he says. Paul's own example and the example of his Asia Minor converts demonstrates that we will not see more converts by packaging the Gospel in brighter colours. We will win them by laying out the Gospel in all its gritty glory.

This unadulterated Gospel message also produces resilient new believers. Jesus warned against the convert "*who hears the word and at once receives it with joy. But since he has no root, he lasts only a short time. When trouble or persecution comes because of the word, he quickly falls away.*"[3] That tends to happen all too often when people have been peddled shallow promises instead of honest truth. When we preach the Gospel as a command to submit to Jesus' rule in spite of every sacrifice, however, we find our converts built into an *army* who want to march instead of an *audience* who want to be entertained. If we tell people that Jesus will improve their lives, we can hardly complain when they expect him to dance to their tune, but when we tell them that Jesus is King, they will amaze us by how willing they are to make sacrifices for his name.

The fact is Jesus *does* improve our lives, and he *did* fill the believers with joy in 13:52. Luke is not denying that such promises are part of the Gospel at all. He is simply warning us that if we only preach prosperity and omit to preach about trials and suffering too, we will never see mature, fast-growing new believers like the ones Paul and Barnabas produced in Asia

---

[2] Acts 9:1–19.
[3] Matthew 13:20–21.

Minor. We will never see converts who rejoice to suffer, to make sacrifices and to be persecuted for the sake of Jesus' name.[4]

The Gospel offers us the blessings of God, but it promises to give them on a road which is potholed with trials. Let's share this honest truth with unbelievers and trust the Lord to cause them to surrender to Lord Jesus, regardless of the cost. This is the message we have been given to proclaim. This is the message which is powerful to save. This is the message which builds up new believers into mature disciples who can lead themselves and others. If you want to see strong new converts like Paul and Barnabas in Asia Minor, Luke tells you very straightforwardly how it is done: Share the honest truth with people and let the Gospel do the rest.

---

[4] Acts 5:41; 16:25. It may have been an even bigger trial for Paul in 17:6–9 when he was forced to watch his new converts suffer too.

Apostles and Elders (15:4)

When they came to Jerusalem, they were welcomed by the church and the apostles and elders, to whom they reported everything God had done through them.

(Acts 15:4)

For a book which teaches us to build Church God's way, Acts contains very little detail about how it should be governed. It's surprising, frustrating, yet at the same time very liberating, that Luke gives principles but not prescriptions. He begins his book with a promise that the Gospel will go to every nation, and he refuses to straitjacket it with an inflexible structure for their churches. The Holy Spirit inspired him to give us a few core principles instead, with a promise to help us as we apply them to our own time and place in history.

165

The first core principle is that churches must be led by teams. Luke is very insistent upon that. When he speaks in detail about the churches in Jerusalem, Antioch and Ephesus, he tells us they were all led by *teams* of elders.[1] When we read about other churches in passing, we find eldership teams in place there as well.[2] We can call these elders by a variety of names – Luke calls them by at least three different names himself[3] – but we dare not neglect what they stand for. Jesus is the Great

---

[1] Acts 11:30; 13:1; 15:4; 20:17; 21:18. See also 1 Timothy 4:14; 5:17.

[2] Acts 14:23; Titus 1:5; James 5:14.

[3] He calls them *presbuteros* (elders), *episkopos* (overseers), and *poimēn* (pastor-shepherds). In Acts 20:28, Luke puts paid to the idea that *episkopos* should be translated *bishop* and treated as a separate category to elders.

Elder, the Senior Pastor, who presides over his Church,[4] and he has determined to govern his churches through teams instead of individuals. There's a practical reason, since very few leaders can operate in all four of the giftings Paul lists in Ephesians 4:11.[5] There's a capacity reason too, since a single church leader creates a bottleneck for church growth much beyond the 200 mark.[6] Most importantly of all, there is a theological reason, helping church leaders to reflect the teamwork of the Trinity and to remind themselves that they are *in* the Church, not over the Church, and *stewards* of the Church, not masters of the Church.[7]

The second core principle is that these eldership teams must be *free to lead under God*. Luke protects them from internal log-jams by indicating that one of the elders should function as the leader of the team. James, the half-brother of Jesus, is mentioned three times as the primary leader of the church in Jerusalem, even though we find him surrounded by his team of elders.[8] Luke also protects them from Athenian-style democracy, by emphasizing that they are to lead through listening to God, and not on the basis of the competing ideas of the people they lead. They are to appoint *deacons* to serve on their behalf in the church so they are never too busy to come before Jesus and hear the words of their true Senior Pastor.[9]

---

[4] 1 Peter 2:25; 5:1–4; Hebrews 13:20.

[5] Without an evangelist, a church loses the heart and ability to share the Gospel; without a prophet, it can become limited in its vision and sense of direction; and without a pastor-teacher, it can grow spiritually weak. Churches need all the Ephesians 4:11 gifts, either within their eldership or from regular outside input.

[6] Exodus 18:14–23; Numbers 11:14–17; Deuteronomy 1:9–18.

[7] Matthew 20:25–28; Acts 20:28; 1 Peter 5:1–4. Acts 15:23 reminds us that elders lead their *brothers*.

[8] Acts 12:17; 15:13; 21:18. Note also that James felt free to write his letter from the church in Jerusalem to the Diaspora Jews in his own name and not simply on behalf of his eldership team.

[9] Acts 6:1–7 does not use the noun *deacon*, but the verb *diakoneō* which means *to serve* or *to deacon*. This ties in with Philippians 1:1; 1 Timothy 3:8–

Luke even protects them from the excessive interference of apostles, through Paul's trusting and highly devolved manner of leadership.[10]

The third core principle is that churches are planted, established, and released by *apostles*. These are Christ-appointed, not self-appointed,[11] and they are recognized by apostles and by churches when they bear the fruit of apostleship in the form of healthy, self-replicating churches like the ones Paul and Barnabas planted in Asia Minor.[12] Luke treats apostleship as a *ground-breaking* role and not as a static position, since he only refers to Paul and Barnabas as apostles after they set out on their missionary journeys.[13] He tells us that their role is to stand firm when others buckle, to establish clear doctrine when others deviate, and to open up new nations for the Gospel when others hesitate.[14] He describes a large number of mutually accountable yet healthily independent apostles, who broke bottlenecks which restricted church expansion and ensured that each new church-plant fully reflected God's plan as embodied Jerusalem and Antioch.[15]

Luke teaches these three principles without prescribing how they must look in every context, but the fact that he uses the word *apostles* thirty times in his twenty-eight chapters should warn us not to relegate apostleship to the history books.

13; Romans 16:1. Deacons free up elders to seek God's direction (Acts 6:2–4; 13:1–3) and to lead the rest of the church forward on the basis of what they hear (Hebrews 13:17).

[10] Acts 14:23; 15:36; 20:25, 32. This may be why Peter urges elders as a *fellow elder*, not *apostle*, in 1 Peter 5:1.

[11] Ephesians 4:11; 1 Corinthians 12:28; 2 Corinthians 10:13–18; Romans 1:5.

[12] The existing apostles gave Paul and Barnabas their *"right hand of fellowship"* in Galatians 2:9. Paul subsequently proved his apostolic gifting through his ministry (1 Corinthians 9:2; 2 Corinthians 12:12).

[13] Acts 14:4, 14.

[14] Acts 8:1; 15:1–31; Ephesians 2:20; 3:4–5; 1 Corinthians 7:1; Romans 15:18–24; 2 Corinthians 10:15–16.

[15] The apostles were independent (Galatians 1:15–24; 2:6), yet mutually submissive (Acts 15:4; 6–31; Galatians 2:2, 9, 11–14).

There are no apostles today like the Twelve, and nor are there any who can write Scripture.[16] Yet Paul tells us in Ephesians 4:11 and 1 Corinthians 12:28 that apostles are still necessary for the Church to be built up for the task Christ has given her, because there is still no shortage of new ground to be broken, new churches to be planted, and doctrinal questions to be answered. The New Testament attributes apostleship to many more people than just the Twelve plus Paul and Barnabas. They include Silas, Epaphroditus, Andronicus, Junias, Jesus' two half-brothers James and Jude, and possibly even Luke and Apollos.[17] Paul warns that there may be false apostles in 2 Corinthians 11:13, but he does not do so by arguing the smallness and exclusivity of their number. Christ appoints great numbers of apostles for his Church, because the work before his Church is still great.

So enjoy the great freedom which Luke gives your church to be structured as best fits your own time and place in history, but do not neglect his three non-negotiable principles. Do not place a ceiling on the health of your church by centring its leadership upon one lone pastor, or by hampering its leadership team with the fetters of committee or democracy. Let your leaders lead, as directed by the great Senior Pastor, Jesus Christ. Let them lead as assisted by modern-day apostles, who break new ground, plant new churches, and continue the great story of the book of Acts.

---

[16] Matthew 19:28; Revelation 21:14; 22:18–19.

[17] 1 Thessalonians 1:1; 2:6; Romans 16:7; Galatians 1:19; 1 Corinthians 9:5. Philippians 2:25 and 2 Corinthians 8:23 also talk literally about *apostles*, this last verse referring to Luke, Apollos, or other unnamed apostles.

When the Past Becomes a Problem (15:1–35)

Why do you try to test God by putting on the necks of the disciples a yoke that neither we nor our fathers have been able to bear?

(Acts 15:10)

When I was much younger, I was given two pet birds. It took me a few weeks to notice the rather obvious fact that they had wings and their cage was small. I felt so sorry for them that I closed all my windows and opened their cage so they could fly around the house. I sat down and waited, and waited, and waited, but they never took me up on my kind offer that morning. Instead, I found them cowering in one corner of the cage, trembling with fright that their cage door was open. They had grown so used to their life of captivity that they found comfort in their cage and had forgotten they were created to fly. The restrictions of their past had killed their vision for the future, and in the end I simply closed the cage door as they wanted.

The Jewish nation had a wonderful past, but they had let it become a birdcage which restricted their future. Paul tells us in Galatians 3 that God gave them the Mosaic Law to guard them as walls of protection until the coming of their Messiah,[1] but now that Jesus had died and been raised to life the Gospel had flung

---

[1] Paul tells us in Galatians 3:23 that God *sunkleiō*, or *locked up*, the Jewish nation securely through the Law to keep them safe and ready for the New Covenant in Jesus. He also tells us in v. 24 that the Law was God's *paidagōgos*, or *bodyguard-slave* who tutored them and kept them safe until Christ came.

their birdcage wide open.[2] Some Jews responded excitedly and learned to fly quickly in New Covenant freedom, but others were unsettled and huddled in the safety of their Jewish Law prison cell. They even demanded that the Gentile believers climb into the cage and huddle there with them too. Paul addressed this issue in his letter to the troubled Galatians at the start of AD 49, and then he set off to take part in what is known as the "Council of Jerusalem".

There is something very impressive about the tone of this gathering of apostles and elders in Acts 15. There is no wrangling or egotism, just a humble desire to discover God's answer together.[3] First, the ultra-Jewish believers lay out their view that the Gentiles must be circumcised and obey the Mosaic Law like themselves. Next it is Peter's turn, as he tells them as *"an apostle to the Jews"* how God taught him through Cornelius that God saves Gentiles by faith, quite apart from the Law.[4] When he sits down, Paul and Barnabas take the floor and recount how God saved the Gentiles in Asia Minor. Finally, James, the lead elder of the church in Jerusalem and the half-brother of Jesus, sums up their conclusions with a radical statement of his own. In about 760 BC, the prophet Amos had promised the nation of Israel that one day the Lord would *"rebuild David's fallen tabernacle... that the remnant of men may seek the Lord, and all the Gentiles who bear my name"*. James says that God will not fulfil this promise from within the Jewish birdcage; he is already fulfilling it in the brave new world of the Gospel, through the

---

[2] God demonstrated this in Matthew 27:50–51 by tearing apart the curtain of the Most Holy Place in the Temple from top to bottom. This showed that God himself had ended the restrictions of their past.

[3] The word *homothumadon*, or *with one mind*, in 15:25 is one of Luke's favourite words to describe the Church in Acts. Note that the Christians developed one mind by facing up to issues, not by avoiding them.

[4] Galatians 2:8–9. This had made Peter the perfect apostle to lead the controversial mission of Acts 10–11.

Church.[5] God's plans had always been bigger than the birdcage, and he had now superseded it with something far greater. It was time for believers to fly out of their cage and not allow the blessings of their past to steal the blessings of their future.

This Jerusalem ruling was of paramount importance to the spread of the Gospel. We can see this in miniature in Acts 21:37 and 22:2. A Roman centurion is uninterested in what Paul has to say because he writes him off as a Jew, but as soon as Paul speaks Greek to him he stops and takes his message seriously. At the same time, the Jewish crowd are uninterested in what he has to say because they consider him a Gentile-loving traitor to his nation, but *"When they heard him speak to them in Aramaic they became very quiet."* That's what normally happens when we bring the Gospel out of the birdcages of our past or of our culture, and ask people to fly freely in the way Jesus intended.

The Council was very respectful to Jewish culture in their ruling. Jewish Christians could be passionate Law-keepers as long as they remembered their new freedom in Christ and that he was the reality to which their shadows had pointed.[6] They could celebrate their national feasts and rituals, so long as they remembered that the Law was *"a yoke which neither we nor our fathers have been able to bear".*[7] The Gentile Christians would need to make a few basic concessions for the sake of Jewish sensitivities, but they would not be forced to squeeze inside the Jewish birdcage. The shadows of the past had been superseded in Christ, and the cage door was open to a future of freedom.

At the same time, the Council unshackled the Gospel from any one culture, so that the Gentiles could receive it as their own message too. James pointed out that *"Moses has been preached in every city from the earliest times and is read in the synagogues*

---

[5] Amos 9:11–12 quoted in Acts 15:16–18. Paul expounds Israel's promises similarly in Galatians 4:26–27.

[6] Acts 21:20–26; 22:12. Timothy was even willing to be circumcised in 16:3 to win a hearing with the Jews.

[7] Acts 18:18; 20:6, 16; 21:26.

on every Sabbath", yet it had singularly failed to convert the Gentile nations to Yahweh. The Gentiles must not be told to step into a Jewish birdcage or the expansion of the Gospel would be stunted forever. When the churches read the letter with the Council's landmark ruling, it's small wonder they *"were glad for its encouraging message"*.[8]

Few readers today are still tempted to huddle in the corner of a Jewish cage, but the battles of the past have been replaced by fresh battles in our own day. The Gospel is viewed in many parts of the world as a Western message, and is viewed by many people in the West as a message which is so rooted in the culture of the past and the sub-culture of the Christian community that its relevance to them is not immediately obvious. We need to learn the lesson taught by Sadhu Sundar Singh, a convert from Sikhism who contextualized the Gospel to reach the villages of rural India: *"You have offered us Christianity in a Western cup... Give it to us in an Eastern bowl and we will drink of it."*[9]

Our challenge is to present the Gospel to people from other nations in the context of their own culture and history so they will sit up and listen. It is also to present Jesus to non-Christians in our own culture so they see why his story is so essential to them. We must not demonize any culture, because what God has made clean we must not treat as dirty.[10] It's time to step out of the corner and fly out from our birdcages. Through Jesus, our God has commanded us to fly.

---

[8] Acts 15:31.

[9] Singh was converted in 1903 and travelled around India as a barefoot missionary. *Sadhu* is the word normally used for a Hindu *holy man*, because he communicated the Gospel in the vernacular of rural India.

[10] See Acts 10:15. Many of the early Christians assumed Acts 1:8 would be fulfilled by the Gentiles doing all the running. At the Council of Jerusalem they agreed to do much of the running themselves

The Gospel to Europe
(50–57 AD)

Paul's Second Missionary Journey, 50–52 AD (16:1 – 18:22)

Paul and his companions travelled throughout the region of Phrygia and Galatia.

(Acts 16:6)

Paul was thoroughly committed to working as part of a team. He refused to minister in any other way. He cut his teeth as one of five elders in Antioch. He partnered on his First Missionary Journey with Barnabas and John Mark. He even took Barnabas and Titus with him on his errand to the church in Jerusalem.[1] He had none of the pride or insecurity which turns church leaders into loners, but recruited, trained and released a whole network of apprentices. Satan feared Paul as part of a team even more than he feared him on his own, so he tried to use the failings of John Mark to destroy his working party. Luke begins his account of Paul's Second Missionary Journey with Satan's scheme backfiring, as Paul and Barnabas recruit two new teams instead.[2]

Paul's commitment to teamwork was on one level purely practical. Building bridges with the very diverse inhabitants of Asia Minor and Europe was not something one man could do on his own. *Silas* was a Jew with outstanding command of the Greek language, so he would be a perfect partner in both the

---

[1] Acts 13:1, 4–5; Galatians 2:1.

[2] In fact, the split with Barnabas enabled Paul to go further with the Gospel. Barnabas revisited Cyprus, so Paul was able to take the overland route through Syria and Cilicia, then press further west into Greece.

synagogues and the marketplaces of sophisticated Macedonia and Greece.³ *Timothy* was half-Jew and half-Greek, and had already impressed Paul in spite of his teenage years. He would help him to reach both Jewish and Gentile young men.⁴ *Luke* was a Gentile doctor from Antioch, and would forge an invaluable link with the educated upper classes.⁵ *Priscilla and Aquila* were a much-needed married couple who joined the team in Corinth, and whose hospitality and heart to disciple young people very quickly reaped dividends.⁶ We can all build bridges to any unbeliever, but a diverse team can reach a wider group of listeners more readily. Paul developed teams because he was wise enough to know his limitations.

Paul's commitment to teamwork was also driven by the size of his vision. He intended to plant churches in as many major cities as possible in little over two years, and this was a task too great for any one man. Paul could only extend the reach of the Gospel as far as others were willing to take it with him, and without his talented team-mates he would have floundered. When he was chased out of Philippi, he was able to leave Luke behind for several years to establish the church on good foundations.⁷ When he was forced to flee Thessalonica, he left Timothy behind and later sent him back for a second visit.⁸ Similarly, when the Jews hounded him out of Berea, he left Silas

³ The Greek of 1 Peter is considerably better than the Greek of 2 Peter, which is probably because Silas helped him write his first letter (1 Peter 5:12). Silas also brought prophetic gifting to Paul's team (Acts 15:32).

⁴ Acts 16:1–3. He must have still been a teenager when Paul took him into his team in 50 AD, because Paul still refers to people looking down on him for his *youth* in c. 65 AD (1 Timothy 4:12). His spiritual maturity owed much to his devout mother and grandmother (2 Timothy 1:5; 3:15).

⁵ Colossians 4:14. We know that Luke was part of Paul's team because he speaks of *we* and *us* after 16:10.

⁶ Acts 18:2–3, 18–19, 24–26; 1 Corinthians 16:19.

⁷ Luke stops saying *we* and *us* when Paul leaves Philippi in 16:40, and starts saying *we* and *us* again in 20:5 when Paul returns to Philippi four years later.

⁸ Paul only stayed in Thessalonica for two to three weeks (17:2), but was able to establish a strong church there because Timothy stayed behind. Paul and

and Timothy behind for a few weeks of intensive teaching.[9] Even as he returned to Antioch at the end of his Second Missionary Journey, he was able to leave Priscilla and Aquila in Ephesus to prepare the ground for his Third Journey.[10]

We must not miss the way Luke laces his account with throwaway comments about Paul's masterful commitment to team. Leadership expert John Maxwell could easily be describing Paul when he teaches that *"Success comes when a leader empowers people to do things with him, significance comes when he empowers people to do things for him, but legacy comes when he empowers them to do things without him."*[11]

Paul's commitment to teamwork was therefore also driven by his plans for the future. His best case scenario was that he would hand his work in the Eastern Mediterranean over to others and pioneer a new work in the West. His worst case scenario was that he would be martyred before he ever got there, and others would need to step into his shoes.[12] Either way, he needed to work today with tomorrow in mind, producing a legion of successors in his wake. Timothy would go on to co-author six books of the Bible, and Luke would write two of his own. Silas, Luke and probably Timothy would later develop into apostles in their own right. Paul did not merely plan to *add* capacity to his own life's work. He planned to *multiply* capacity by releasing many more workers beyond his own lifetime.

Nevertheless, in spite of all these other good reasons, Paul's commitment to teamwork was driven primarily by the communities he was looking to build. He did not spend two and a half years in Asia Minor and Europe for the sake of saving

---

Silas left in 17:10, but Timothy joined them later in 17:14. He also returned to Thessalonica a few weeks later (1 Thessalonians 3:1–2).

[9] Silas and Timothy stayed in Berea all of the time that Paul was in Athens, and only joined him some way into his stay in Corinth (17:14–15; 18:5).

[10] Acts 18:18 – 19:1.

[11] John C. Maxwell, *The 21 Irrefutable Laws of Leadership* (1998).

[12] Romans 15:18–24; Acts 19:21; 20:22–25; 21:13.

isolated individuals. Nor did he build them into churches which were led by a single pastor. He aimed at nothing less than a replication of the healthy church communities of Jerusalem and Antioch. He taught his new converts to love one another as brothers and sisters, and to care deeply for one another. He taught them to submit to plural eldership teams who led them according to the core principles Luke outlines in the rest of the book of Acts. He knew that he could only teach such lessons to the new believers in Asia Minor, Macedonia, and Greece by modelling within his team the way that they should live as churches. His strategy rings out loud and clear in his words to the church at Thessalonica: *"You know how we lived among you for your sake. You became imitators of us and of the Lord... And so you became a model to all the believers in Macedonia and Achaia."*[13]

Paul was given wisdom by the Holy Spirit to increase his effectiveness through harnessing a team of gifted individuals. His team-mates built better bridges in a larger number of cities than he could ever had managed on his own, and in the process they were trained up for future works without him. Most importantly of all, they formed a living demonstration of the church life that they were trying to build. Paul's teams were more than a training school for ministry. They were the church of the first half of Acts in miniature, reproducing themselves in every city where they stayed.

---

[13] 1 Thessalonians 1:5–7. Paul says something very similar in Acts 20:18–19, 34–35 and 1 Corinthians 4:16–17.

God's Satnav (16:6–10)

Paul and his companions travelled throughout the region of Phrygia and Galatia, having been kept by the Holy Spirit from preaching the word in the province of Asia.

(Acts 16:6)

Recently, I got completely lost in the French city of Rennes. I had no knowledge of the city and even less knowledge of its roads, and I didn't have a map in my car. The chances of me reaching my meeting on time were close to zero, except I remembered I had a borrowed Satnav in my glovebox. A few moments later, I was racing through the streets of Rennes, turning left and right at busy intersections like a local. Finding your way in a foreign city is easy when you have a Satnav calling instructions every step of the way.

Paul must have felt like I did in Rennes at the start of his Second Missionary Journey. He had been sent out from Antioch to preach the Gospel to the world, but the sheer choice of destinations must have been baffling. Paul was only able to succeed in his mission because he had learned to listen to God's satnav, and so Luke chooses this place in the story to teach us how to let God guide us on life's journey.

First, Paul simply got moving on the basis of *common sense*. He was from Tarsus in Cilicia and Barnabas was from Cyprus, so it made sense for them to spend their First Missionary Journey in Cyprus and in Asia Minor to the west of Cilicia. Paul doesn't appear to have waited for a bolt from the blue before starting out on his Second Journey either. He simply travelled back to those churches in Asia Minor and then moved north to the next two Roman provinces of Phrygia and Galatia. It is easy to steer a car when it is cruising along the road, but very difficult when it is parked in the garage. Therefore Paul used his common sense and started moving in faith that clearer guidance would come to him as he went.

Second, Paul took his guidance from *open and shut doors*. Common sense was not enough by itself, for he was determined to go where God led him. When he tried to move west to the city of Ephesus, the fifth biggest city in the Empire and by far the most important city in Asia Minor, the Holy Spirit would not let him. When he tried to move north to Bithynia instead, *"the Spirit of Jesus would not allow them to"*. If Luke appears rather cryptic here, it is only because he has already explained to us how this element of God's Satnav works in 14:27, when he talked about God opening a *"door of faith"* on Paul's First Journey. Paul's letters explain it further when he states that he will stay in one city *"because a great door for effective work has opened to me"*, and that his supporters should pray that *"God may open a door for our message"* elsewhere too.[1] Paul even took persecution and Satanic opposition as guidance that God was closing a door on a city.[2] Paul started with common sense and then watched for God's sovereign hand at work in the form of open and shut doors on the journey.

Third, Paul looked for *direct revelation* from the Holy Spirit. Common sense and circumstance were no substitute for this. Sometimes he was guided by a passage of Scripture which the Lord brought to life as he read it.[3] At other times he saw a vision, like the one which drew him to Macedonia, or

179

---

[1] 1 Corinthians 16:8–9; Colossians 4:3. Jesus elaborates on this further in Revelation 3:7–8.

[2] Paul writes in 1 Thessalonians 2:18 that *Satan* stopped him from returning to Thessalonica, but he still took that as a form of guidance from God. The main reason Paul left most cities in Acts was Satanic persecution.

[3] Romans 15:20–22 is a very good example of this.

the one which kept him in Corinth in the face of persecution.[4] Sometimes these revelations would fly in the face of reason, like the angel who told Philip to leave a city in revival and go instead to a deserted road,[5] but Paul was always obedient when they did. He had waited nine long years for the Holy Spirit to fire the starting pistol on his journeys in Acts 13,[6] and he was equally attentive as he went.

Fourth, Paul took his guidance from the *godly advice of fellow Christians*. Acts is a book about Christians finding guidance *together*. Paul began his journeys while praying with his fellow elders in Antioch. He paused to take part in the Council at Jerusalem, where after much discussion the apostles came to a consensus which *"seemed good to the Holy Spirit **and to us**"*.[7] Paul did not even use his divine vision of the man of Macedonia to impose a view on his team-mates, but let the others interpret it with him. There was a reason that Paul appointed a team of elders for each church and why he ministered as part of a wider missionary team. God gives guidance to his People *together*, so that we might know his will as a body, and not as Lone Rangers.

God's guidance is both easier and harder to follow than a satnav. It's easier because there are four different ways of him speaking to us. At the same time, it's harder because we need to weave those four things together into one single strand. In 16:10, Luke uses that word *sumbibazō*, or *to knit*, for only the second time in the book of Acts. God expected Paul and his team to *knit together* these four types of guidance, and to draw a considered conclusion in the light of what they said. He does not

---

[4] Acts 18:9–13. Another example is in Acts 23:11.

[5] Acts 8:26 demanded great faith from Philip, but Luke simply tells us that he obeyed and started out.

[6] Paul learned early on that he was called to go to the nations (Acts 22:17–21; 26:14–18), but he waited until the Holy Spirit told him in Acts 13:1–3 that the right time had now come.

[7] Acts 15:28.

approve of super-spiritual reliance on circumstance or visions at the expense of common sense or accountability, nor does he approve of human reason and committee at the expense of listening closely for his still, small voice in our ear. Instead, he gives us four important ways in which we can hear what he is saying, and lets us knit them together and move forward by faith.

If we truly believe that we are ordinary people, relying on the extraordinary power of the Holy Spirit as the Primary Witness, we cannot afford to miss out on God's Satnav. We want to be where he is working, which means we need to let him take the lead. We combine common sense with open doors and direct revelation with godly counsel so that together we hear clearly the way we should go. This type of clear guidance enables us to say no to great opportunities, like Paul in 18:20, because we know that God has something far better for us. It keeps our path flexible and ready to join in with God wherever we see him.[8] Most of all, it ensures that we fight only where he is fighting and that we are always in the place where he most wants to grant us success.

Don't leave God's Satnav in your glovebox, and don't ignore any of Luke's four principles of guidance. The world is big and your life is short, so you need the constant guidance of your extraordinary God.

---

[8] Peter saw a breakthrough in Acts 3:1–8 when he saw God in action and stopped what he was doing to join him. Paul saw a breakthrough in 16:25–28 when he saw an earthquake as God's invitation to stay, not run away.

Chosen (16:14)

The Lord opened her heart to respond to Paul's message.

(Acts 16:14)

For a book which was written for a non-Christian judge, Acts contains a surprising number of references to the doctrine of *election*. It's strange because we tend not to talk to non-Christians about election in case they use it as an excuse not to respond to the Gospel. Since Luke wrote his book secondly to motivate and equip the Church for evangelism, it's also surprising on another level too. Surely Luke should play down the fact that God has sovereignly chosen some people for salvation, in case Christians take that truth and use it to excuse their laziness and passivity? Since Luke bucks our expectations and insists that God chooses who to save, we need to pause and ask why.

Luke talks about God's election because he is committed to *telling the truth* about the Gospel. The fact is God does choose which people will be saved into his People, and they only choose him because he chose them first. Luke tells us that Lydia was only saved because *"the Lord opened her heart to respond to Paul's message"*, just as he told us back in 13:48 that only those *"who were appointed for eternal life believed"*.[1] He models what he teaches in 20:27 by refusing to downplay God's sovereign election. He states this truth in all its glory, while at the same time dealing with the objection that this makes it unfair for people to be judged for their failure to respond to the Gospel.

---

[1] Luke also uses passive verbs in 17:4 and 34 to emphasize that people *were joined* to the Church by God. The root of the verb in 17:4 is the Greek word *klēros*, or *lot*, which emphasizes God assigning them to salvation.

Luke tells us that God calls *everyone* to repent and that those who refuse to do so reject his perfect purpose for their lives.[2]

Luke also talks about God's election because he is committed to winning *only genuine converts* to the Gospel. It is a terrible mistake for a person to assume that they are doing God a favour by following him. We didn't have to surrender our lives to him, they reason, and so he owes us a reward for our decision. If we are not careful, this can very quickly turn into pride, treating God's gift of salvation as if it were earned. The doctrine of election destroys such self-delusion by reminding us that even our decision to follow Jesus makes us all the more indebted to the God who enabled us to make it. Mark Webb puts it this way: *"God intentionally designed salvation so that no man can boast of it. He didn't merely arrange it so that boasting would be discouraged, or kept to a minimum – he planned it so that boasting would be absolutely excluded! Election does precisely that."*[3] Luke tells us the truth about election because he wants us to produce genuine, humble, God-honouring converts to the Gospel.

Luke also talks about God's election because it is the doctrine which *prevents us from twisting* the Gospel into something it is not. Paul tells us in 2 Corinthians 4 that if we assume we can win people to salvation through our own sweet-talking persuasion, we will be tempted to tamper with the Gospel to make it sound more attractive to non-Christians. What's more, we will be tempted to pressure people into making a response to the Gospel for which they are not yet ready. In contrast, when we remember that people are only saved when the Holy Spirit shines his light into people's hearts, we are reminded to present the Gospel faithfully and to give people space to make a genuine response. Mark Dever challenges us that

---

[2] Acts 2:21, 38; 10:43; 13:24, 39; 17:30; 26:29. See also Luke 7:30.

[3] Quoted by C.J. Mahaney, *Humility: True Greatness* (2005).

If you don't believe that the Gospel is the good news of God's action – the Father electing, the Son dying, the Spirit drawing – that conversion is only our response to God's giving us the grace gifts of repentance and faith, and that evangelism is our simple, faithful, prayerful telling of this good news, then you will actually damage the evangelistic mission of the church by making false converts. If you think that the Gospel is all about what we can do, that the practice of it is optional, and that conversion is simply something that anyone can choose at any time, then I'm concerned that you'll think of evangelism as nothing more than a sales job where the prospect is to be won over to sign on the dotted line by praying a prayer, followed by an assurance that he is the proud owner of salvation.[4]

Pressuring people with slick sales presentations does not produce true and lasting fruit, but giving people space to consider the truth really does.

Finally, Paul talks about God's election because it is the *only thing which will sustain our evangelism* for the long haul. I know that some people use election as an excuse not to evangelize (*"if God has chosen people then he can save them without me!"*), but that simply means that they have failed to understand it. In Acts 18:9–11, Jesus appears to Paul in a vision at Corinth and tells him not to be afraid *"because I have many people in this city"*.[5] In response, Paul does not conclude that he can sit back, concentrate on his tent-making, and wait for the elect to come to salvation without him. On the contrary, Luke tells us that he

---

[4] Mark Dever in his excellent book *The Gospel and Personal Evangelism* (2007).

[5] Jesus actually stresses election even further than most English translations suggest. He uses the Old Testament word for the *People* of Israel to tell Paul that he has a *laos polus*, or a *great People*, in the city.

stayed in the city for eighteen months and worked hard because he was confident that God had an elect for him to find.

Here's the great measure for whether or not you have truly grasped the doctrine of election as taught throughout Scripture: If it makes you passive and blunts your evangelistic fervour, you haven't understood it at all. If it stirs you to busy, faith-filled evangelism, you appear to have understood the same doctrine as Paul, George Whitefield, Jonathan Edwards, William Carey, Charles Spurgeon, and thousands of other great evangelists throughout history.

Therefore Luke speaks to Theophilus plainly about election because he wants to humble him into repentance while God still grants him the chance. He also speaks plainly to us about election because he wants to enlist us into God's army of witnesses through the power and direction of the Holy Spirit. If we treat evangelism as a difficult task which relies on our own skills of persuasion, we will very quickly flag and withdraw from the field. Only if we treat it as an impossible task, which relies on the Holy Spirit alone, will we have the proper perspective to protect us from discouragement and fill us with unyielding determination to seek and save the lost.

D.L. Moody concludes:

That is what we need – [the Holy Spirit's] convicting power, and I am so thankful that God has not put that into our hands. We have not to convict men; if we had I would get discouraged, and give up preaching, and go back to business within the next forty-eight hours. It is my work to preach and hold up the cross and testify to Christ; but it is his work to convict men of sin and lead them to Christ.[6]

---

[6] D.L. Moody, *Secret Power* (1881).

Tour Guides (17:22–34)

"For in him we live and move and have our being."
As some of your own prophets have said, "We are his offspring."

(Acts 17:28)

History has been very kind to ancient Greek culture. Their chief god, Zeus, was a womanizing rapist. Their epic heroes were blood-stained and immoral. Some of their finest citizens, like the philosopher Socrates, lost their lives in political vendettas. When Paul arrived in the city of Athens, he was greatly distressed by its vice and idolatry, and he must have been glad to receive an invitation to speak at the Areopagus.[1] It would give him the perfect opportunity to tell the self-important city exactly what he thought of their sin-steeped culture.

But he didn't. In fact, he treated Greek culture with remarkable respect. As he addresses the Athenian aristocracy in Acts 17, he begins by building bridges: *"I see that in every way you are very religious."* He wants to build more bridges before he tells them the story of Jesus, but he does not choose to do so from the Hebrew Scriptures. Instead, even though Psalm 50:9–12 and Hosea 1:10 would state his message perfectly, he makes those same observations through quotations from the Cretan poet Epimenides (*"In him we live and move and have our being"*) and from Aratus' poem Phaenomena (*"We are his offspring"*).[2]

---

[1] The *Areopagus*, or *Mars Hill*, was probably the supreme court of Athens when Paul arrived there in about 50 AD. Luke may be hinting to Judge Theophilus that if the great Areopagus acquitted Paul, then so should he.

[2] Paul quotes from the poet Epimenides for a second time in Titus 1:12 and refers to him as a *prophet*. He also quotes from the Athenian poet Menander

The quotation from Aratus is particularly striking, because the poem talks about Zeus but Paul applies it to Yahweh instead. Paul is shockingly generous towards Greek culture, and Luke wants to teach us yet another vital principle for effective evangelism.

Paul was careful not to disparage the culture of those with whom he shared the Gospel. He was happy to honour their thinkers because he knew that every culture understands a few basic elements of the Gospel. If their poets grasped things about Zeus which were true about Yahweh, he would take that as his starting point. If they built altars to an "unknown god", this would suit his purpose just as well. He refused to demonize their culture because it offered him ways to build bridges for his listeners.[3] He studied it to find starting points in their own beliefs from which he could explain to them the Gospel.

Rob Bell observes the following:

> *Have you ever heard missionaries say they were going to "take Jesus" to a certain place?... If you see yourself carrying God to places it can be exhausting. God is really heavy... The issue isn't so much taking Jesus to people who don't have him, but going to a place and pointing out to the people there the creative, life-giving God who is already present in their midst... Evangelism is therefore showing people the God whom they were experiencing all along but did not understand. Mission is less about the transportation of God from one place to another and more about the identification of a God who is already there. It is almost as if being a really good missionary means having really good eyesight. Or maybe it means teaching people to use their eyes to see things that have*

---

in 1 Corinthians 15:33.

[3] The clerk at Ephesus was able to say to Paul's opponents in 19:37 that he had not *"blasphemed our goddess"*.

always been there; they just didn't realize it. You see God where others don't. And then you point him out.[4]

Paul makes it easy for his listeners to accept his observations from their culture, without adopting the superior tone of a spiritual know-all. He encourages them in verse 27 that they are not far from finding God, and offers them a face-saver in verse 30 that God has overlooked the shortcomings of their philosophers so far. Because he honours their current beliefs, he makes it very easy for them to listen to his own. Bill Hybels explains:

> *This usually launches me into a tirade, I feel so strongly about it. I've been in situations when strangers are telling me their stories and don't yet know I'm a Christ-follower. A few of their pious remarks or haughty assumptions later, I shut down. They don't care about me. The only thing they care about is getting the roles nailed down: they are the ones with their act together, and I'm the pitiable lost person, substandard in countless ways. There may be no quicker way to send an unbeliever to the hills than to play the piety card. If you want to permanently repulse a person from the things of God, try a little superiority on for size. It works every time.*[5]

Paul builds wonderful bridges with the Athenians through their culture, but he does so in order to confront them with a call to repent. He climbs inside their culture so he can attack it even more effectively from within. He shows them that the Creator-God is affronted, not impressed, by their idolatry and temple worship. He reminds them that God made all nations from one man, and that their arrogant sense of Athenian superiority will

---

[4] Rob Bell, *Velvet Elvis* (2005). I don't agree with all of Rob's writings, but he never fails to provoke me to think.

[5] Bill Hybels, *Just Walk Across the Room* (2006).

not save them from God's judgment. He exposes the error of both the Stoic and Epicurean philosophers with his proof that God is about to judge the world for its rebellion against him. This leads into a brief synopsis of the life story of Jesus and a personal command to repent before him.[6] Many of the Athenians jeered at the idea of Jesus' resurrection, but Paul had built enough bridges by now to lead a handful of listeners to salvation and to win a second audience with many more.

That's what happens when we honour people's culture and shed the superior tone of the self-important know-it-all. It takes time to immerse ourselves in the culture of our world, but it's always worth the effort. Our listeners travel further and faster when we honour their current beliefs and use them to serve as their spiritual tour guide to Jesus.

Let me end with a personal example. A few years ago, when I tried to start a spiritual conversation with my friend, "Katie", she changed the subject by telling me that she had seen an angel when she was a little girl. I groaned on the inside at her New Age mysticism, but I knew I was presented with two choices: I could ignore her story and label it demonic, or I could honour her story and see where it might take us. Having just read Paul's sermon at the Areopagus, I asked a few more questions and listened. Finally, after letting Katie talk and talk, I was able to ask questions from inside of her story:

Me:	Did the angel say anything about Jesus?
Katie:	No. Why?
Me:	Because angels are always messengers of Jesus. Did he tell you to read about Jesus in the Bible?
Katie:	I don't think so. To be honest, I really can't remember.

---

[6] Since the Athenians summarized Paul's message in v. 18 as *"Jesus and Resurrection"*, Paul either gave a much longer biography of Jesus than is summarized in v. 31, or he was about to before he was interrupted.

Respecting her (frankly, rather suspect) story about an angel gave me a chance to start acting as her tour guide, pointing out Jesus where she hadn't see him. Soon, she was investigating Jesus as her own idea, not mine. Several months, the loan of a book, and a few visits to church later, Katie grasped the heart of the Gospel and surrendered her life to Jesus Christ.

Did she really have a vision of an angel as a girl? I don't know, and I really don't care. Luke tells us to stop dismissing people's stories and instead to use them to point people towards Jesus. When we listen for ways to build bridges and point out Jesus where people have missed him, opportunities to call people to repentance are never far away. God is looking for tour guides. Ordinary people like you and me.

God Knows Where You Live
(17:26–27)

He determined the times set for them and the exact places where they should live. God did this so that men would seek him and perhaps reach out for him and find him.

(Acts 17:26–27)

These two verses saved my next-door neighbour's life. They really did. Let me explain how it happened.

Two years ago, my wife and I moved house. It was a horrible experience which dragged on for over a year, but one of the things which kept us smiling and trusting God, even when things got tough, was Paul's teaching here in verse 26. We kept praying and reminding God that he had promised to put us in the right house at the right time. We prayed that verse back to God so many times that we got to know it inside out.

Our prayers didn't change God, but they certainly changed us. By the time we moved into our new home, we were convinced that God hadn't just placed us in this particular house at this particular time, but he had also placed all our neighbours in their houses too. We read back to verse 17 and found that Luke expands this principle still further. Paul's strategy in Athens was simply to go to the shopping centre, start chatting to *"those who happened to be there"*, and assume that they could not have met by accident.[1] Paul was convinced that anyone he met was

---

[1] Luke uses the Greek word *paratunchanō*, which means literally that these people *happened by chance to be present*. He uses tongue-in-cheek language to convince us that we never meet anyone simply by "chance".

brought to him on purpose by God, and we were beginning to be convinced of it too. Those we worked with, those we met through our children's schooling, those we met as we went shopping – all were brought to us by the God of verse 26 because he is also the God of verse 27. He brings people into each of our lives by his sovereign hand, *"so that men would seek him and perhaps reach out for him and find him"*.

So we took a few steps to see what God was doing all around us. We threw a big house-warming party and invited all our neighbours to come. Some of them did, including our next-door neighbour "Barry". He apologized for his wife as we opened the door: she was ill in bed and was sorry to miss the party. I poured him a drink and told him that I pray for people to be healed in Jesus' name and they often get better. If ever they wanted me to pray for "Gaynor", I would be very happy to do so. Then, after thirty seconds of chatting about my rather awkward offer, the conversation turned quickly to football, family, fixing fences, and other neighbourly small-talk.

It was several weeks later that we heard the second half of the story. That night at two in the morning, Gaynor woke up. There was a strange light shining in the garden. She drew back the curtain and saw a magnificent star which lit up her back garden as if it were daylight. She shook her husband awake and whispered, *"Barry! Barry! I think God is trying to speak to us!"* (I still have absolutely no idea how she came to this conclusion!) Barry was tired and in no mood for divine visitations. *"Go back to sleep!"* he protested. *"If you want to talk about religion then talk to the people next door. They're religious."* Somewhere in his sleepy brain was the memory that I had talked about Jesus healing people.

Gaynor went back to sleep, but she woke again a couple of hours later. The bright star was still lighting up her garden as if it were daytime. She shook her husband again. *"Barry! I think God is trying to speak to us!"* Barry was not amused. *"Talk to the people next door,"* he suggested. *"They're religious."* I'm actually very glad she didn't ring us there and then. I'm not very good when woken up in the middle of the night, and she might have found me considerably less religious than Barry thought!

A few weeks later, we threw another party at our house, and again we invited our neighbours. Barry and Gaynor both came this time, and Gaynor finally told us her story. Frankly, I was a bit surprised. To my shame, I couldn't easily see the link between a bright star in the garden and God trying to talk to her. Fortunately, by God's grace, I had read Matthew 2 that morning, and God had prepared me to speak. *"I think you may be right,"* I said. *"God spoke to the wise men in a similar way at the first Christmas. Now what's interesting is that the bright star was not the end of the story but the beginning. God sent them a star to lead them to Jesus."* We talked and talked. We gave her a copy of Mark's gospel and invited her to come with us to church. She came and kept coming, until one morning as she listened to the preacher she felt utterly convicted of her sin and committed her life to Christ. A throwaway comment at a house-warming party had led to sign in the night sky, and this in turn had led her to study Scripture, attend church, and give her life to Jesus. Those two verses had saved her life – they convinced two ordinary messengers like my wife and me that there is no such thing as coincidence, and that we should therefore invite round our neighbours and see what God was doing. Our extraordinary God is at work all around us, if only we will open our eyes to see him.

There's a sequel to this story, because these verses saved Gaynor in more ways than one. We later discovered that her sister is a Jehovah's Witness. On her own confession, if that bright star had appeared over her garden at any point before the night of our party, she would have instantly gone to her sister and attended her Watchtower meetings. Her sister was

Nine Tenths (18:2–3)

There he met a Jew named Aquila, a native of
Pontus, who had recently come from Italy with his
wife Priscilla, because Claudius had ordered all the
Jews to leave Rome. Paul went to see them, and
because he was a tentmaker as they were, he stayed
and worked with them.

(Acts 18:2–3)

I don't know who gave Luke's second book the name "Acts of
the Apostles". Whoever it was, they should have left the job of
naming it to someone else. Luke barely tells us anything about
the actions of nine of the twelve original apostles, and he doesn't
even treat Peter and Paul as the real heroes of the story. They
are the tip of the iceberg, the tenth of the Church which towers
above the water because of the greater nine tenths which lie
hidden beneath the surface. The book of Acts is not the tale of
a handful of apostles. It is the story of thousands of ordinary
church members who were empowered to make a difference by
their extraordinary God. People like you and me.

If you are a woman, it has probably already struck you that
the senior leadership in the Early Church was male. You may
even have concluded that you are somehow less important in
the continuing fulfilment of the Great Commission. You may
not have seen Luke's clues throughout the pages of Acts that
the women of the Early Church were just as vital as the men.
There's the group of godly women who had followed Jesus
around Galilee, and who were part of the hundred and twenty

who founded the first church on the Day of Pentecost.[1] Then there's the hard-working widow Dorcas whose work was so vital to the church at Joppa that Peter raised her from the dead so it could continue.[2] There's the business woman Lydia, who was Paul's first convert in Macedonia and whose house became his first church venue in Philippi,[3] and here – perhaps best of all – Paul's trusted co-worker and team-mate, Priscilla. Perhaps Luke even refers to *Priscilla and Aquila*, rather than the other way around, because he doesn't want his female readers to disqualify themselves from playing the leading role that God has given them. The elders and apostles in the book of Acts are male, but the crucial role of women pops up everywhere.

If you are busy with a full-time job, it may also have struck you that the apostles were "full-time" in their Christian ministry. Again, Luke refuses to let you downplay your importance in God's purposes because you are in secular employment. Priscilla and Aquila were both tent-makers who worked hard for a living but were nevertheless vital partners in Paul's Second Missionary Journey. They befriended him because he was also a tent-maker, and they employed him in their business while he waited for funds to arrive along with Silas and Timothy from Berea. In fact, Paul was so adamant that hard-working Christians were the backbone of his churches that he later told the converts from this journey that *"we worked night and day, labouring and toiling so that we would not be a burden to any of you. We did this, not because we do not have the right to such help, but in order to make ourselves a model for you to follow."*[4] Perhaps one of the main reasons that Paul chose this pair of tent-makers to form part of his team was to demonstrate to the churches that

---

[1] Luke 8:1–3; 23:49; 23:55 – 24:11; Acts 1:14. Peter addresses the *"brothers"* but includes sisters in their number. Interestingly, the women gathered to watch Jesus die while most of his male disciples ran away.

[2] Acts 9:36–42.

[3] Acts 16:13–15, 40.

[4] 2 Thessalonians 3:8–9.

all Christians are "full-time" and that none are too busy at work to be excluded from God's mission.

If you are busy at home, as a parent or a carer, Luke also wants you to see your vital role in the strengthening of the Church. No church buildings are mentioned in the book of Acts, other than borrowed space in the Temple courts or a rented hall in Ephesus. Instead, the Church began in Jerusalem *"in their homes"* and *"from house to house"*, so that Peter knew he was sure to find a group of Christians praying if he went to the house of Mary, the mother of John Mark, and even Saul of Tarsus knew that he could raid the Christian meetings by *"going from house to house"*.[5] The church also met in houses in Philippi, in Corinth, and in Macedonia.[6] Furthermore, Luke tells us that Christians like Simon, Jason, Philip, and Mnason all opened up their houses to facilitate the ministry of others.[7] If you have ever been tempted to write yourself out of the continuing story of Acts because you are in a season where most of your life is spent at home, think again. Homes like Priscilla and Aquila's play a vital role in the spread of God's Kingdom. Nor do workers like Timothy get made without homes, mothers and grandmothers like his.[8]

Finally, if you are tied to one particular place, it may have struck you that men like Paul, Silas, Luke, and Barnabas were all highly mobile. You may even have assumed that because you are not a roving missionary you are somehow second rate in the Great Commission. Again Luke tells you not to write yourself off so soon. Ananias was simply praying at home in Damascus when Jesus appeared to him and used him to reach the nations of the world without ever stepping beyond his city walls. Philip the Evangelist appears to have settled in later life in the port

---

[5] Acts 2:46; 5:42; 8:3; 12:12.

[6] Acts 16:40; 18:7; 20:20. This was also true in every other city. See Romans 16:5 and Philemon 2.

[7] Acts 10:32; 17:5, 7; 21:8, 16.

[8] Acts 16:1; 2 Timothy 1:5; 3:15.

city of Caesarea, and James the brother of Jesus appears never to have left the city of Jerusalem.[9] Even highly mobile Priscilla and Aquila settled quickly in each new city and gave themselves fully to the work of the local church. When Paul took them on to Ephesus to prepare the way for his Third Missionary Journey, they hosted the young church in their home, and when they went ahead of him to Rome they hosted the church in that city as well.[10] Ultimately, your location and your circumstances are entirely secondary. What matters is that you give yourself to the continuing story of Acts in the place where God has put you.

Luke goes out of his way in the book of Acts to make sure that we are not so in awe of the one tenth of the iceberg that we miss the nine tenths which work beneath the surface. Luke's second book contains many of the acts of the apostles, but they were only successful because of the faithful acts of the non-apostles all around them.

Whether you are male or female, whether you have plenty of free-time or are busy at work, and even if you are forced to stay at home or in one fixed town or city, God has a crucial role for you to play in his Great Commission. Don't be put off by the one tenth above water. Nine tenths of the Church's effectiveness is ordinary church members, just like you.

---

[9] Acts 9:10–12; 21:8, 18.
[10] 1 Corinthians 16:19; Romans 16:3–5.

Paul's Third Missionary Journey, 53–57 AD (18:23–20:38)

This went on for two years, so that all the Jews and Greeks who lived in the province of Asia heard the word of the Lord.

(Acts 19:10)

Paul loved cities. Even though less than 10 per cent of the Empire lived in its cities, Paul rushed past the countryside like an intercity express train. He simply wasn't interested in stopping in the suburbs or the villages. He was focused on his mission to the mighty urban centres. Christians today, in contrast, are rather fonder of the suburbs than the cities. Even though over 70 per cent of the Western population is now urban, the Church is strongest in the suburbs and is under-represented in the downtown city centres. If there is a fundamental difference between Paul's mission priorities and our own, we should treat his Third Missionary Journey as a God-given reality check.

Paul's First Missionary Journey took us on a tour of the key cities of Salamis, Paphos, Pisidian Antioch, Iconium, Lystra, and Derbe. His Second Journey sped past minor towns like Neapolis, Amphipolis, and Apollonia in a race to reach the great Macedonian cities of Philippi, Thessalonica, and Berea. It then turned south to Athens and Corinth, respectively the cultural and commercial capitals of Greece. Corinth was the fourth largest city in the Empire, which explains why Paul spent more time there than in all of the other cities combined.[1] He was not concerned to spread himself evenly, but *strategically*. In fact, his bias towards urban centres grew even more marked on his Third Missionary Journey. His journey lasted four years, but he spent three of them in Ephesus,[2] the capital of Asia and the fifth largest city in the Empire.[3] Paul's approach was consistent and deliberate, and we will never mirror his success unless we first accept his methods.

Paul bypassed the countryside and focused on the major cities because they were the places which held the most people. Finding a crowd was never difficult in a city. The churches in Jerusalem and Ephesus attracted tens of thousands of converts, because preaching in cities was the easiest way to reach large numbers of people fast.[4]

Paul also focused on the major cities because he knew that urbanites would be more open to the Gospel than their rural counterparts. For a start, the Jewish population was heavily weighted towards the cities, and their synagogues were the most likely place to find eager new converts.[5] Furthermore, urban Gentiles were far more open to new ideas than those in rural, more traditional communities. The Roman writer Tacitus despaired of the speed with which displaced and disorientated

---

[1] Corinth had a population of 250,000 freemen and women, and 400,000 slaves. It lay at the junction between the Adriatic and Aegean Seas, which made it a very wealthy world trade centre.

[2] Luke tells us in Acts 19:10 that Paul spent two years at the Lecture Hall of Tyrannus, but he tells us in 20:31 that he spent three years in total at Ephesus.

[3] Ephesus had a population only slightly behind that of Corinth. It was such an influential trade centre that Paul tried to go there as early as 50 AD (Acts 16:6).

[4] The size of the Ephesian church is indicated by its haul in Acts 19:20 of 50,000 drachmas, equivalent to over £10,000,000. James tells Paul in 21:20 that *muriades*, or *tens of thousands* of Jews have believed in Jerusalem.

[5] Acts 14:1; 17:2, 10, 17; 18:4, 19; 19:8. Paul preached first to the Jews for theological reasons (Acts 13:46; 18:6; Romans 1:16; 2:9–10), but he also did so for practical ones. It was easier to build bridges for the Gospel with Jews, since they were already waiting for the Messiah.

city dwellers responded to the Gospel. He complained about the growth of the church in his own city, Rome, *"where all things hideous and shameful from every part of the world collect and become popular".*[6]

Paul focused on the major cities because they attracted the nations of the world. *"Every nation under heaven"* came to the pilgrimage city of Jerusalem,[7] and the Christians there did not need to step beyond their city walls to preach Jesus as far east as Parthia, as far west as Rome, and as far south as Ethiopia.[8] The Christians at Antioch, Corinth, and Ephesus could witness to people from all over Asia, Europe, and Africa. These factors are more, not less, the case in our own day. Western cities receive people from every nation, and we can often reach more foreign nationals in our own cities than we can by going to theirs. A few weeks ago, I had coffee with a Saudi student who was about to return home to the Gulf. I was able to tell him the story of Jesus, explain the significance of the cross, raise questions over Islam, and challenge him strongly to give his life to Christ. Had I gone to Saudi Arabia, I might have spent years waiting for a similar opportunity, and I would possibly have risked my life to say the words I did.

Paul focused on the major cities because they are the places where world culture is formed. D.L. Moody toured the large urban centres because *"Cities are the centres of influence. Water runs downhill, and the highest hills in America are the great cities. If we can stir them we shall stir the whole country."* Cities are political centres, which is why Paul was able to befriend and convert key government officials in Corinth, Ephesus, and Rome.[9] Cities are trade centres, which is why Paul met and

---

[6] Tacitus, *Annals of Imperial Rome*, 15.44. See also Acts 17:21.

[7] In the context, Luke is clearly talking only about every nation *in which Jews lived*.

[8] Acts 2:5–11; 8:27.

[9] Acts 18:12; 19:31; Romans 16:23; Philippians 1:13; 4:22. Gallio was the brother of Seneca, the tutor of Emperor Nero. Erastus was the *aedile* of Corinth,

converted business-leaders like Lydia in Philippi. Cities are cultural and media centres, which is why Paul was able to reach Dionysius the Areopagite and many influential Greek women in Athens, Berea, and Thessalonica.[10] Cities are also centres of learning, which is why Paul was able to set up a preaching base in the Lecture Hall of Tyrannus at Ephesus or the house of Titius Justus at Corinth and find that *"all the Jews and Greeks in the province of Asia heard the word of the Lord"*. Even though he didn't leave the capital city of Ephesus, his enemies complained that he won converts *"in practically the whole province of Asia"*.[11]

Once again, this is more, rather than less, true in our own day. Due to the global reach of media giants such as Hollywood, MTV, or even the BBC, it is possible to wield more influence over the hearts and minds of Moroccans, Muscovites and Malaysians from Los Angeles and London than is even wielded by their own national newspapers. We live in a global society, and big cities are the places of big influence.

If you live in the suburbs or the countryside, God still loves your church and the non-Christians it is reaching. Jesus sent one of his seven letters in Revelation 2–3 to the church at Ephesus, but he sent six more letters to the churches they had planted into the hinterland of Asia. Luke does not aim to frustrate you with where you are, but to lift your gaze to the places you are not. As long as there are large cities in your nation with a lack of city churches, Jesus commissions you to plant churches there yourselves.

If you live in a big city, look up and see Paul's God-inspired strategy for reaching the world. Don't complain about your city. Make plans to bless it and transform it with the Gospel. Paul

---

whose name has been found on an inscription there.

[10] Acts 16:14; 17:4, 12, 34.

[11] Acts 19:10, 26. For example, Epaphras from Colossae was converted by Paul on a visit to Ephesus, and then went home to plant churches in eastern Asia without Paul ever going there (Colossians 2:1; 4:12–13, 16).

spent three years in Ephesus and changed the ancient world. You can spend a lifetime in your city and change the modern one as well.

Boulevards and Barricades (19:1–7)

> [Paul] asked them, "Did you receive the Holy Spirit when you believed?" They answered, "No, we have not even heard that there is a Holy Spirit."
>
> (Acts 19:2)

When I used to live in Paris, my apartment overlooked a wide boulevard. Paris is famous for its pretty boulevards, but the city planners did not build them simply for their charm and beauty. From 1789 onwards and for almost a century, revolutionaries would periodically barricade the narrow streets of Paris to hold the city under siege and their governments to ransom. In 1830 they made over 4,000 barricades from barrels, carts, furniture, and rubbish. In 1848 they made 6,000 more. Eventually, the government built the extra-wide boulevards of Paris out of desperation, determined to render such barricades impossible.

God was building boulevards long before the Parisian city planners. He has built a wide and spacious highway for his People to receive the Holy Spirit. Luke has promised in 2:38–39 that if you repent and turn to Christ, *"you **will** receive the gift of the Holy Spirit. The promise is for you and your children and **all** who are far off."* He has promised again in 3:19–21 that if you repent, Jesus **will** fill your heart with his Holy Spirit and refresh you from the inside out.[1] The promise of the Holy Spirit is not given on the equivalent of a narrow back-street, where it may or

---

[1] Even though some English translations use the word *may* in 3:20, the Greek verb is an aorist, which conveys not possibility but certainty. Being filled with the Spirit is a promise, not a perhaps.

may not make it through. It is given on an extra-wide boulevard and is ours for the asking.

Perhaps you know that, because your experience of being filled with the Holy Spirit takes very little conscious effort, rather like Cornelius and friends in chapter 10. Yet perhaps you don't always find it easy to receive the Holy Spirit on a daily basis. The scope of God's promise and the passionate exhortations in Acts to receive more and more of the Spirit can even breed frustration in your heart. Luke knows that Christians need help to live in the good of the promise of the Holy Spirit, and so here in Acts 19 he diagnoses some of our most basic problems with receiving. It turns out that we are as guilty of building barricades as the Paris revolutionaries. God has built a highway for us to receive the Holy Spirit, but like the muddled disciples at Ephesus we need some help to clear the obstacles which can prevent us from receiving him as we are meant to.[2]

One of our barricades can be *ignorance*. This was certainly the case for the twelve Ephesian disciples. God had opened up his boulevard for them to be filled with the Holy Spirit – Paul's question, *"Did you receive the Holy Spirit when you believed?"*, assumes that much – but their ignorance had prevented them from receiving. They tell Paul that they have not even heard that there is a Holy Spirit,[3] and so they have never taken steps to receive what is theirs through Christ. Frankly, there are still many Ephesian-style believers today. They may have been told

---

[2] Some people argue that the dozen Ephesians were not truly converted, because they believe that everybody automatically receives the baptism in the Spirit at conversion, whether or not they know it. They argue that Luke calls them *mathētai*, or *disciples*, because they were non-Christian followers of John the Baptist or Apollos. There are many flaws in this argument: Luke clearly uses the same word, *mathētai*, in v. 9 to refer to Christians; Luke tells us in v. 6 that when they were filled with the Spirit they knew it visibly; and Luke tells us plainly in 8:15–17 that baptism in the Spirit is *not* automatic at conversion.

[3] Most people assume that this is shorthand for *a baptism in* the Holy Spirit. Since the Holy Spirit appears in only the second verse of the Old Testament, they must have been aware of his existence but not his promise.

that the baptism in the Spirit belonged only to the Early Church, or that they have it and it just looks different today. They have been sent a gift but failed to receive it and enjoy it. They need someone like Paul to come and correct their theology, then lay hands on them to help them to receive.[4]

Another barricade can be *feelings of inadequacy*. There's plenty of this around. Perhaps people misunderstand verses like Acts 5:32, which say that God gives the *"Holy Spirit to those who obey him"*.[5] Perhaps they have been taught that "the Holy Spirit only fills clean vessels". It's hard to believe such a view when Scripture tells us that he filled the philanderer Samson and the murderer Paul.[6] It is also difficult to reconcile with the fact that Luke calls the baptism in the Spirit four times a *gift* of God's grace,[7] and with the teaching of both Jesus and Paul that we receive the baptism through *faith* that it is ours through the Gospel.[8] Our feelings of inadequacy come from looking at ourselves when we should instead be looking at Christ. We can receive the Holy Spirit like these newly converted Ephesians simply because God *"purifies our hearts by faith"* in the finished work of Jesus.[9]

Still another barricade is *fear*. The promise of being filled with the Holy Spirit was new to these Ephesians, but they didn't resist Paul's teaching because it was outside their current experience or their comfort zone. Jesus links receiving

---

[4] People often assume they haven't received because they haven't prayed and asked long enough like the 120 in 1:4, 14. Yet Jesus tells us in John 7:37–39 that they waited because *he* was not yet ready, not them. He has now built his great boulevard for us; we simply need help to remove our barricades.

[5] Peter's point here is not that Christians need to work on their obedience to be fit to receive the Spirit. He is telling the Sanhedrin that their disobedience to Christ means that they are outside of God's People, and therefore also of his promise. God will not empower non-Christians to rebel even more effectively!

[6] Judges 15:14; 16:1; Acts 9:17.

[7] The Greek word *dōrea* in 2;38; 8:20; 10:45; 11:17 means a *gift* freely given.

[8] Luke 11:9–10, 13; Galatians 3:5; Ephesians 3:17.

[9] Acts 15:8–9.

the Spirit to trusting that the Father will only give good gifts to his children.[10] The understanding of the twelve Ephesians was only basic, but at least they offered God their basic trust.

A final barricade is *lukewarmness*. Jesus tells us in John 7:37 to come to him *thirsty* for the Spirit. In Luke 11:9–10 he uses present imperatives to tell us to *go on asking, go on seeking*, and *go on knocking*. Note how readily the Ephesians leap to obey Paul's teaching in verse 5. They were willing to wait no longer, and neither should we be. Of course, this lesson is equally true for the way that we go on receiving the Spirit afresh each day of our lives too. Paul told the converts from his journeys that unless they remained thirsty for more and more of the Spirit, they would *put out* his activity in their lives instead of *fanning it into flame*.[11]

If you have not yet been filled with the Holy Spirit, or it has been a long time since you were refilled, Luke wants you to learn from the dozen ordinary disciples in Acts 19 and to be filled with the Spirit today. However big your barricades, God's boulevard is wider. If you know somebody who can help you as Paul helped the Ephesians, lay hold of them until they do, but even if you must ask alone, Luke sits with you and shows you how.

So don't read the book of Acts and leave its promise to others. God doesn't merely promise that you *can* be filled with Spirit. He promises that you *will* be filled if you rid the road of barricades. So remove your barricades and ask God to give you his Spirit as he has promised. If you are a believer, God has built a Holy Spirit boulevard to you!

---

[10] Luke 11:9–13.

[11] 1 Thessalonians 5:19 and 2 Timothy 1:6 are addressed to people converted and filled with the Spirit on Paul's First and Second Missionary Journeys. We can assume that he gave similar instruction on his Third.

How to Heal the Sick
(19:11–20)

Jesus I know, and I know about Paul, but who are you?

(Acts 19:15)

Chapter 19 of Acts is a place for finding answers. Luke is not satisfied with answering our practical questions about how to be filled with the Holy Spirit. He now moves on to an event which shows us how, and how not, to pray for the sick. Doctor Luke has left us in no doubt that our extraordinary God wants to heal and drive out demons through ordinary people like us. Therefore Luke continues coaching us with some practical do's and don'ts.

Don't assume that healing is beyond the likes of you and me. Luke is very clear with us in verse 11 that Paul's miracles were *extraordinary*. He says this not to place them beyond our reach, but to make sure we don't get discouraged and assume that healing is for far greater people than us. Faith for healing is like a muscle which grows stronger and stronger with exercise, so we need to start small and keep on going. I have never seen anywhere near 3,000 people saved through any of my sermons, but that may simply show me that my evangelistic gifting is still immature compared to Peter's. The fact that your healing gifting looks very immature next to Paul's is not a reason to give up. It is an invitation to fan it ever more into flame.[1]

Don't think that God will heal people through you if only you find the perfect formula. The seven sons of Sceva had a

---

[1] Acts 2:41; Romans 12:6; 1 Timothy 4:14; 2 Timothy 1:6.

brilliantly crafted formula for casting out demons – *"In the name of Jesus, whom Paul preaches, I command you to come out"* – but healing comes through speaking on behalf of Jesus and not through spiritual abracadabras. Don't rely too heavily on techniques such as laying on hands, anointing with oil, speaking commands rather than prayers, or ending with the words *"in the name of Jesus"*. All of these things are biblical, but they will not suffice in themselves.

Luke and his fellow gospel writers deliberately contrive to stop you from relying on well-worked formulae. If we only had Matthew's account of Jesus healing Peter's mother-in-law, we would assume that laying on hands was the key factor in her healing; if we only had Mark's, we would assume it was helping her to her feet; and if we only had Luke's, we would assume it was rebuking her fever![2] Again, if we only had Matthew's account of Jesus healing blind Bartimaeus, we would assume that the key factor was laying on hands; if we only had Mark's, we would assume it was proclaiming over him that *"Your faith has healed you"*; and if we only had Luke's, we would assume it was commanding him to *"Receive your sight!"*[3] Luke is speaking to us loud and clear: Don't place your hope in formulae.

Do, however, place your hope in your relationship with Jesus. Luke tells us in verse 15 that demons flee because they fear Jesus and anyone they know can speak for him. No wonder Jesus called the Twelve *"that they might **be with him** and that he might send them out to preach and to have authority to drive out demons"*.[4] If Jesus was only able to heal because he communed intimately with the Father through *"prayer and fasting"*,[5] and if

---

[2] Matthew 8:14–15; Mark 1:29–31; Luke 4:38–39.

[3] Matthew 20:29–34; Mark 10:46–52; Luke 18:35–43.

[4] Mark 3:14–15.

[5] Mark 9:29. Luke tells us in Luke 5:17 and in Acts 2:22 and 10:38 that Jesus did not just heal because he is God, but because he was a man filled with the Holy Spirit. He is not simply our Lord, but our model as well.

Paul was known in hell because he walked closely with Jesus on earth, we will not find any short-cuts to healing ourselves.

Do also learn to feel the heart of Jesus towards the sick and demonized people around you. Paul spent his three years in Ephesus weeping over the needs of its citizens,[6] and it is no coincidence that his tear-drenched handkerchiefs were therefore used to heal and deliver those he had prayed for. One modern-day pastor attributes the many healings he sees to his experience of the love of God for people:

> *It was as though the Lord broke off a little piece of his heart and placed it inside me... I was learning that the power of God was to be found in the **love** of God... The healings came almost as a by-product. I learned that only love can make a miracle.*[7]

Godly compassion was one of the key factors in Jesus' healing ministry, and it must be in ours too.[8]

Jesus doesn't just feel love towards those who are sick and demonized. He also feels angry and affronted by the devastating work of Satan in their lives.[9] One of the main reasons that we do not see as many healings as Paul is that we acquiesce to the presence of sickness and effectively broker a truce with Satan. Those who hope to see healings which change cities are those who feel provoked like Jesus and his servant, Paul. Another twentieth-century pastor describes how he began to see God heal people through him:

---

[6] Acts 20:19, 31.

[7] Mahesh Chavda in his autobiography, *Only Love Can Make a Miracle* (1990).

[8] Matthew 9:35–36; 14:14; 20:34; Mark 1:41.

[9] Acts 10:38 tells us that sickness is spiritual as well as biological, and in Luke 13:16 Jesus even treats severe backache as the work of Satan. Mark 3:5 tells us he was furious when he saw religious leaders who more interested in their programmes than the sick in their midst.

A great cry to God, such as had never before come from my soul, went up to God. She must not die! I would not have it! Had not Christ died for her?... No words of mine can convey to another soul the cry that was in my heart and the flame of hatred for death and sickness that the Spirit of God had stirred within me. The very wrath of God seemed to possess my soul![10]

Do have faith that God will bring many people to salvation when they see him healing people in response to your commands in Jesus' name. If you stand up to sickness and demons like Paul did in Ephesus, if you love the sick and hurting like he did too, and if you walk closely with Jesus and full of his Spirit, you will see breakthrough beyond your wildest dreams. Luke tells us in verse 20 that *"In this way the word of the Lord spread widely and grew in power."* It's the way that God has chosen, because it is so clearly something done by him and not by us – the extraordinary God revealing himself through ordinary people like you and me. Paul saw so many people saved in Ephesus that his bonfire of magic-scrolls was worth over £10 million in today's money, and those engaged in false religions were forced either to convert to Christ or to chase him out of town. Luke tells you that you only need a small amount of faith to get started in praying for the sick, because little steps of faith can move big mountains.[11]

If you have read this far into the book of Acts and not yet concluded that God wants to use you to heal the sick, you may need to go back and read it again. Healing miracles are on almost every page, and in Acts 19 Luke shows you how you can take part in the action. Luke writes these things for you and not just for others. You are an ordinary person, and he is your extraordinary God.

---

[10] John G. Lake, *Adventures in God* (c. 1930).
[11] Luke 17:5–6; Acts 3:16.

Magnified Vision (20:24)

I consider my life worth nothing to me, if only I may finish the race and complete the task the Lord Jesus has given me – the task of testifying to the gospel of God's grace.

(Acts 20:24)

If you have never started a fire using a magnifying glass, I recommend you have a go. It's really very simple. If you focus the sun's rays into a single dot of heat, on a sunny day that dot is over 250 degrees centigrade. After that, it's up to you what you want to do with it. You can set fire to bits of paper or kindling, you can melt the head of a plastic soldier to simulate battle injuries, or you can really have some fun if your brother has fallen asleep in the sunshine. Go ahead and try it, but don't blame me for what your brother does to you when he catches you. Just tell him you were applying an important spiritual lesson you read in the book of Acts.

We are at the end of Paul's three missionary journeys, and are about to enter the final section of the book. Luke wants to make sure that we haven't fallen into the trap of viewing Paul as an exceptional, inimitable hero on a pedestal, so at this point he tells us the simple secret of Paul's effectiveness. Paul was an ordinary person, empowered by his extraordinary God, but he did something important with the power which God gave him. He didn't dilute it in an ocean of multiple priorities. He focused it all into one single dot of heat to pour the whole of his life into the *race* he had been given. Luke turns to this now so that you can do the same, and pour the extraordinary power of God into his single red-hot purpose for your life.

Paul did not formulate a vision for his life, and neither must we. From the very outset, Jesus told him that *"You will be told all that you have been assigned to do."*[1] Paul spent nine long years in the obscurity of Damascus and Tarsus, but those years were not wasted as he discovered his race and learned to pinpoint his energies like a magnifying glass. At first he protested, pleading with Jesus that as an ex-Pharisee he was ideally placed to preach the Gospel to Jews, but in the end he submitted to the race he was given.[2] God clarified this focus as he read Isaiah 52:15, and he will clarify it to us in the same way as we study his word and pray over what it means for our lives.[3] Luke has already told us that in Acts 13:25 John the Baptist had a *race* and in 13:36 that David had one too. Now he urges us to believe that God has marked one out for us, and it is worth taking the time to discover it.

Paul clear sense of God's racetrack for his life gave him courage to say no to many bright opportunities. He exchanged fruitful ministry in Antioch for the dangerous lifestyle of a travelling preacher. He said no to an open door in Ephesus but yes to imprisonment in Jerusalem.[4] He understood Jesus' teaching that the human heart can only carry a finite number of priorities, and he would rather die than be diverted from this one great mission for his life. In fact, Luke tells us that he unequivocally *"handed his life over for the name of the Lord Jesus"*.[5]

Sure enough, as Paul pinpointed his life's energy on one

---

[1] Acts 22:10. The Lord used similar language to appoint another messenger to the nations in Jeremiah 1:5–10.

[2] Acts 22:17–21, which took place after 26:15–18.

[3] Paul explains that this verse underpins his understanding of his life's mission in Romans 15:20–22.

[4] Acts 13:1–3; 18:20; 20:22–25; 21:13.

[5] Luke 21:34 and a literal reading of Acts 15:26. See, for example, Philippians 3:12–14 and 1 Corinthians 9:23–27.

single goal, he experienced the magnified power of clear vision. Luke tells us that the Holy Spirit gave him limitless stamina to overcome all the trials which he met on his journeys. He was almost stoned to death in Lystra, but went back into the city and began a sixty-mile journey by foot the next morning to carry on his work in Derbe![6] He worked night shifts in Corinth to be free to spend his day shifts preaching the Gospel, and had no sooner arrived back at Antioch in 18:22 than he set off again for his Third Journey in 18:23![7] In Ephesus he spent his siesta times preaching to the city,[8] and even after preaching all night long to the church at Troas, he still had the energy to walk twenty miles to reach Assos.[9]

Frankly, we might find Paul's boundless energy depressing were it not for two factors which God tells us were in play. First, Paul tells us that he worked with *God's* energy, as he was continually replenished through the power of the Spirit. The same energy which was at work in Paul is also available to you and me today.[10] Second, Luke assures us that we can focus our lives in a similar way on the race God has given us, and discover the same magnified fruitfulness too. Luke is bringing Paul home from his Third Missionary Journey, and he will spend the remainder of the book of Acts in chains. Luke's purpose in this chapter is to teach you to focus your life in the same way as Paul so you can know his same power on the racetrack which God has apportioned to you. He wants you to say no to the good, so you can focus your life on achieving God's best. D.L. Moody concluded that *"The trouble with a great many men is that they*

---

[6] Acts 14:20.

[7] Acts 18:1–3; 20:34–35; 1 Corinthians 9:6, 12; 2 Corinthians 6:3–5.

[8] A few less reliable Greek manuscripts tell us that Paul taught in the Lecture Hall of Tyrannus *"from the fifth hour to the tenth"*. If we assume that this later insertion was based on fact, this was 11 a.m. to 4 p.m., when most Ephesians were asleep and it was presumably too hot for Tyrannus to fill his lecture hall himself.

[9] Acts 20:1–13.

[10] Colossians 1:29; Philippians 4:13.

spread themselves over too much ground. They fail in everything. If they would only put their life into one channel, and keep it in, they would accomplish something."[11] He was merely echoing Luke and his heartfelt exhortation for us to learn the great secret of Paul's magnified vision.

Ten years after Paul spoke to the Ephesian elders at Miletus, Paul would write his final letter to Timothy, who was at that time working in Ephesus. He was in prison in Rome and was under no illusions that his life would be spared. As he waited on death row for his executioners to come, he closed off his letter by looking back on his life. *"I have fought the good fight,"* he told Timothy. *"I have finished the race, I have kept the faith."*[12] Luke ends his account of Paul's Third Journey, hoping that Theophilus will not make it his last, and he takes this opportunity to urge you to focus your life for magnified fruitfulness. If the Kingdom of Heaven in just one of your priorities, then of course you will conclude that Paul's fruit was exceptional. But if you focus your life with the same magnifying glass he used, there is simply no limit to the Gospel fires you can start.

---

[11] Saying of D.L. Moody quoted by George Sweeting in the February 1985 edition of *Moody Monthly* Magazine.
[12] 2 Timothy 4:7.

Job Description (20:17–38)

When they arrived, he said to them: "You know how I lived the whole time I was with you, from the first day I came into the province of Asia."

(Acts 20:18)

We have reached the end of Part Five of the book of Acts. Luke has told us about the churches of Jerusalem and Judea, and outlined how they spread across Asia and Europe. He is about to move into Part Six of his book: Paul's journey as a prisoner to Judge Theophilus in Rome. Therefore he begins to exhort us to take our own place in his story, and he turns his attention to the pivotal issue upon which the Church's future depends. He gives a detailed account of Paul's message to the elders at Ephesus and uses it as a job description for each one of us as we serve in our churches today. Whether you lead a church or a home-group or even just your family, this teaching is for you. Through it Luke passes you the relay baton from the manacled hands of the prisoner Paul.

The first item on the job description is a heart which is full of *God's love*. That's important to note alongside Paul's magnified vision and focus. Luke will not let us depict his team leader as a task-driven activist. He was full of relational warmth and love, sharing his life with the Ephesians from the first day he arrived in Asia.[1] He spoke to the Ephesians *with tears* every night and day for three years because he genuinely loved them as brothers and sisters, and they reciprocate his love by weeping

---

[1] Paul expands on v. 18 when he writes in 1 Thessalonians 2:8: *"We loved you so much that we were delighted to share with you not only the gospel of God but our lives as well, because you had become so dear to us."*

over him here.[2] We must not grow so focused on mission and management that we forget that church leadership is founded first and foremost on God's love. The Lord works through hearts of love and compassion, and Paul warns us that otherwise we are toiling in vain.[3]

Next on Luke's job description of a leader is a reminder of our need to work hard on *God's mission*. Church leadership is not a nice indoor job which doesn't require any heavy lifting; it is a commitment to shepherd the people whom God bought at the cost of Jesus' blood. It is an appointment made by the Holy Spirit, and one for which we will be called to account. Although Paul calls eldership *"a noble task"*, James qualifies this with a reminder that *"Not many of you should presume to be teachers, my brothers, because you know that we who teach will be judged more strictly."*[4] That's the substance behind Paul's concern in verse 26 to declare himself *"innocent of the blood of all men"*. He takes any form of church leadership extremely seriously, and Luke warns us that so must we. Paul worked hard as a tent-maker to provide for himself and his team members, because he was determined to be a model for the whole church at Ephesus that Christians *give*, not just take, from God's People.[5]

The third non-negotiable item on Luke's list is that Christian leaders must minister the whole of *God's Word* to those around them. Every church leader, and not just those who feel called to be evangelists, is called to shepherd both the lost and the saved in their communities. Paul preached tirelessly *"to both Jews and Greeks that they must turn to God in repentance and have faith in our Lord Jesus"*, and so must we. Paul was no armchair general,

---

[2] Acts 20:31, 37–38. See also 21:1, where Luke says *"After we had torn ourselves away from them..."*

[3] 1 Corinthians 13:1–3.

[4] 1 Timothy 3:1; James 3:1.

[5] Paul's quotation of Jesus' teaching in Acts 20:35 does not appear in any of the gospels. It reveals Paul's strong concern that each local church should demonstrate the Gospel by serving the poor (Galatians 2:10).

commanding his congregations to share the Gospel with others while he stayed in his office and worked hard on his sermons. He was so eager to share with the non-Christians in Ephesus that even when the mob tried to kill him, his friends had to beg him not to go out to preach to them.[6] Paul also taught the church in their large meetings and home-groups, warning them with tears to watch out for false teachers and lay hold of all that God had in store for them. He preached the whole of God's Word, both the palatable and the unpalatable, because he knew that church leaders who short-change their people will be short-changed themselves in the age to come.[7]

Finally, Luke tells us that the fourth essential item on his job description is that we never lose our focus on *God's grace*. Paul refers to his message in verse 24 as *"the Gospel of God's grace"*, and he commits the team of elders in verse 32 to that same *"word of grace"*. He himself ministered *"with great humility and with tears"* because he was keenly aware of his utter dependence on God's grace for every area of his ministry.[8] He was willing to leave the team of Ephesian elders to lead in his absence because he was utterly confident that the Lord would also enable them to fend off the "wolves" by his never-ending grace.[9] This grace, he told them in verse 32, would *build them up*, would *sanctify them*, and would ensure that they gained their *inheritance* from God. It was the reason he could cope with the pressures of church leadership, as he let Jesus sustain his Church and remembered

THE GOSPEL TO EUROPE (50–57 AD)

218

---

[6] Acts 19:31. For me, this verse epitomizes Paul's red-hot zeal to tell non-Christians about Jesus, at any cost.

[7] Acts 20:20–21, 26–31. Paul's words in verses 26–27 are a New Testament echo of Ezekiel 33:1–9.

[8] This is also Paul's constant teaching in Romans 1:5; 15:16–16; 1 Corinthians 3:10; 15:10; 2 Corinthians 3:4–6; 4:1; Galatians 2:9; Ephesians 3:2, 7.

[9] Paul's reference to false teachers as *wolves* in v. 29 contains a hint that false teachers will often hunt in packs. Never assume that a new emphasis is biblical simply because it is adopted by many teachers.

it belongs to him.[10] Church leadership is a crushing burden if we forget the grace of God, but by God's grace we can lead those he has entrusted to us.

Now, as Luke draws Paul's three journeys to a close, he hands you this job description and invites you to step up and play your own role to the measure you have been given in Christ. It doesn't matter if that means leading a church, a small group, or merely your family; what matters is that you are faithful where God places you and fulfil the job description which Luke gives you. Will you love those around you? Will you work hard for them, teach them, confront them, and protect them? Will you do so by God's grace and have faith that his grace is for them as well as you? Paul will soon be in chains, and the book of Acts will soon end, but you can still play your part in its sequel.

Bill Hybels defines the local church as *"A community of people who are radically devoted to Christ, irrevocably committed to each other, and relentlessly dedicated to reaching those outside God's family with the gospel of Christ. The church is an unstoppable force for good in the community and a testimony to God's unfailing grace."*[11] Can you honestly think of any greater privilege than to be asked to play a role in leading even part of this blood-bought community? Luke hands you this job description as Paul goes into captivity, and invites you to take your own place in Church history.

---

[10] In 2 Corinthians 11:28; 12:9, Paul confesses to the Corinthians that he feels the crushing pressure of church leadership, but then tells them that God's grace is sufficient to carry it for him.

[11] Read Lynne and Bill Hybels, *Rediscovering Church* (1995).

The Gospel to Rome (57–62 AD)

Paul's Journey to Rome (21:1 – 28:31)

After Festus had conferred with his council, he declared: "You have appealed to Caesar. To Caesar you will go!"

(Acts 25:12)

Unless you know who Theophilus is, you'll find the last eight chapters of Acts very confusing. What begins with a rip-roaring tumult of conversions, miracles and adventure ends with several chapters of legal speeches. They can seem to us like a bit of an anticlimax, like a brilliant novel which goes awry in its final pages. If you do know who Theophilus is, however, you'll find these last eight chapters a brilliant conclusion.

Luke wrote both his gospel and its sequel for a man named Theophilus.[1] He calls him *"most excellent Theophilus"*, and gives us an important clue as to his identity. The lawyer Tertullus addresses a Roman judge and governor as *"most excellent Felix"* in Acts 24:3, and Paul addresses his successor as *"most excellent Festus"* in 26:25.[2] Luke therefore speaks to Theophilus after the manner of a Roman courtroom, because he and Paul did not arrive in Rome as tourists or Christian guest-speakers. Paul arrived in chains as a prisoner whose final appeal was to be heard by Caesar's judges. Put this together with the abrupt way in which Luke ends his account with Paul still awaiting trial, and the final eight chapters make perfect sense. Theophilus

---

[1] Luke 1:3; Acts 1:1.

[2] Antonius Felix was the Roman procurator of Judea from 52 AD to 59 AD, and Porcius Festus from 59 AD to 62 AD.

was probably the judge who would pass the verdict on Paul's appeal, which makes Acts much more than a first-century history book. It is Luke's summary of Paul's case so far, to help Judge Theophilus to acquit his prisoner and send a message to the Empire that the Christian faith was tolerated by Caesar.

If you still need some convincing, let's go back over Acts so far. Having stated three times in his gospel that Governor Pilate found Jesus innocent,[3] Luke sets out to prove to Theophilus that the Christians are also the clean-handed victims of a nasty smear-campaign. The Jews have plagued them at every turn out of jealousy and prejudice,[4] but the Christians have responded with great virtue. Their bold reply to the Sanhedrin echoed the famous reply of Socrates to the wicked judges of Athens,[5] such that even the Rabbi Gamaliel feared they might be opposing God himself.[6] When Paul stood before his first Roman judge in 13:6–12, Procurator Sergius Paulus was such *an intelligent man* that he actually became a Christian. The magistrates at Philippi deeply regretted arresting Paul, and the Roman governor Gallio of Achaia threw his accusers out of court.[7] The Roman clerk at Ephesus threatened and dismissed Paul's unlawful accusers, and the two Roman commanders Lysias and Julius both intervened to save his life. Luke even adds some humour to his challenge by pointing out the ignorance of some of Paul's detractors: Lysias originally assumed he was an Egyptian terrorist who led a secret guerrilla army![8] In fact, Paul is so undeniably innocent

[3] Luke 23:4, 14–16, 22. Verse 25 also stresses that an *insurrectionist* and *murderer* was released in his place.

[4] Acts 6:8–10, 9:23, 29; 12:3; 13:45, 50; 14:2, 5, 19; 17:5, 13; 18:6, 12–17; 20:3, 19; 21:27; 23:12, 27; 24:27; 25:7–11; 26:21.

[5] See p.55, footnote 4.

[6] Acts 5:33–39. The Romans were very superstitious and lived in constant fear of offending the gods.

[7] Acts 16:19–40; 18:12–17. Gallio was the brother of the famous Seneca who was tutor and courtier to Emperor Nero. Luke offers a veiled threat to Theophilus that it would be foolish to overturn Gallio's verdict.

[8] Acts 19:35–41; 21:30–39; 27:1–44.

that Theophilus deserves an explanation for why he has not been acquitted long before he ever reached the highest court in the Empire.

That's why the last eight chapters of Acts are so important. Paul's first trial shows the vindictive hatred of the Jewish Sanhedrin, who beat him unlawfully, turn on one another, and then plot to murder him in transit. The second trial reveals the corruption of Governor Felix, who recognizes he is innocent but wants a bribe. His successor, Governor Festus, knows immediately that he is innocent, but he also knows that handing him over to the Jews will ingratiate himself nicely with his new subjects. Finally at his fourth trial King Agrippa, the ruler of Galilee, dares to pronounce him innocent, but because of a legal technicality he needs this decision ratified by Caesar's own judges in Rome.[9] On his journey to Rome, Luke reminds Theophilus that Paul is more than just an innocent man. God saves him from a shipwreck and a venomous snakebite, and then blesses the Roman ruler of Malta because he helped him in his time of need. All of this leaves Theophilus with very little room to manoeuvre, because his prisoner is not just an innocent Roman citizen, but a prophet with divine protection.[10]

Judge Theophilus was clearly impressed with Luke's briefing paper, because Paul's letters reveal what he did after reading it. After two years of house arrest in the imperial capital, Paul finally stood before his judge in person. He was acquitted in around February 62 AD, and released to plant churches in the Western Mediterranean as planned. After more than a year in Spain and the west, he headed back east to Crete, then on to Ephesus, Colossae, and Philippi.[11]

But something very significant happened in 64 AD, which

[9] 23:1–15; 24:25–27; 25:10; 26:31, 32; 28:18.

[10] Luke stresses four times that Paul is a Roman citizen in 16:37–38; 21:39; 22:25–29; 23:27. The *Lex Julia* and *Lex Valeria* stipulated severe punishment for any ruler or judge who mistreated a Roman citizen.

[11] Romans 15:24, 28; Titus 1:5; 1 Timothy 1:3; Philippians 2:23–24

made Luke's victory in his Christian test case very short-lived. On the night of 18th July, a fire broke out near Rome's chariot-racing stadium, and it quickly spread across the city. Rome burned for a week, and the blame was directed towards the amoral Emperor Nero, whose ambitious plans for urban redevelopment had suddenly received suspicious new impetus.

The historian Tacitus tells us what happened next:

> To quash this rumour, Nero fastened the guilt and inflicted the most exquisite tortures on a class hated for their abominations, called Christians by the populace. Christ, from whom the name had its origin, had suffered the death penalty during the reign of Tiberius at the hands of one of our procurators, Pontius Pilate, and a most mischievous superstition, thus checked for the moment, again broke out not only in Judea, where the evil began, but even in Rome... A large number were convicted, not so much for the crime of setting fire to the city as for the fact that people hated them. Mockery of every sort was added to their deaths. Covered with the skins of beasts, they were torn by dogs and perished, or were nailed to crosses, or were doomed to the flames and burnt, to serve as nightly illumination when daylight had expired.[12]

Paul was arrested in Troas, brought back to Rome, and beheaded in around 67 AD.[13]

This doesn't mean, however, that Luke wrote the book of Acts in vain. It failed to save the Church from persecution, but God had a much bigger goal in view. Paul fell, but millions like him have risen. Because believers have read Luke's book and modelled their churches on Jerusalem, Antioch, and Ephesus, the Church was saved from the inside out. The Gospel was

---

[12] Tacitus, *Annals of Imperial Rome*, 15.44.

[13] 2 Timothy 4:13. Paul may even have left his cloak and scrolls behind when he was suddenly arrested.

preserved and would spread beyond Rome and Spain to the nations of North and South America, Australia, and Japan – places which Paul and his friends did not yet know existed. The book of Acts has served as far more than a legal briefing for Judge Theophilus. It is the marching manifesto of God's missionary army. Roman emperors and modern dictators can never stop its soldiers, because the Church which Luke describes in Acts still marches on through you and through me.

Shut (21:30)

Seizing Paul, they dragged him from the temple, and immediately the gates were shut.

(Acts 21:30)

Like all great historians, Luke sees evocative symbolism in the simplest of actions. He uses it here as he begins his conclusion in order to shock and stir his readers into action. Part Six of Acts brings Luke's two-volume history to a close and issues a repeated challenge for his readers to make a decision and play their own role in its continuing story. For Theophilus, this would mean acquitting and releasing his innocent prisoner, Paul. For the rest of us, it means surrendering wholeheartedly to Jesus and picking up the baton from where Peter, Paul, and the generations of Christians in between have carried it. Therefore the first chapter of Part Six resounds with a symbolic action by the Jews, which Luke uses to warn us that God takes our choices very seriously. The mob slam the Temple gates shut on Paul and his Gospel, and in doing so provide a case study in what happens to those who reject their place in God's story.

God was immeasurably patient with the Jewish nation. From the early days at Sinai when they worshipped a golden calf, to the end of the Old Testament era when they killed the prophet Zechariah, the Jewish nation had constantly rejected God's calling on their lives. God gave them his Law, his Covenant, his Scriptures and his promises, but in spite of his grace they stubbornly refused to listen. God sent John the Baptist, and their king executed him. God sent Jesus his Messiah, and they rejected him out of hand too. They ignored Jesus' warnings that this would call down God's wrath on their nation,[1] but goaded their unwilling Roman governor into crucifying him like a common criminal.

Incredibly, God continued to extend grace patiently towards the Jewish nation. Jesus appeared after his resurrection to his few remaining followers with a command for them to *"stay in Jerusalem"*.[2] God had not given up on the city and was about to pour out his Holy Spirit on over 3,000 Jews as they gathered for one of their Jewish festivals. On the Day of Pentecost, only seven weeks after God's Son had been lynched by the Jewish nation, the Spirit fell on a room just a few hundred yards from the mount of crucifixion and planted a vibrant mega-church at the heart of the Jewish capital. For three whole years God added Jewish converts daily to the burgeoning church in Jerusalem, showering grace on whoever would listen. Then, tragically, the Jewish leaders rejected their calling once again. They murdered his young servant, Stephen, and drove most of the Christians from their city.

Even at this late stage, God continued to be patient and refused to turn his back on his hard-hearted capital city. The decimated church in Jerusalem arose from the ashes, as radically beautiful as before. When Paul visited the city for Pentecost in 57 AD, James excitedly told him that God had saved and added tens of thousands of Jews to their number.[3] The successful missions to the Gentiles were not evidence that God had given up on the Jewish nation, but that he loved them so much that he was determined to make them jealous – a tactic which was most definitely working.[4] Now in 21:30, however, the Jewish leaders rejected God's calling on their nation yet again. With

---

[1] Matthew 21:33–46; Luke 19:11–27.

[2] Luke 24:49; Acts 1:4.

[3] The Greek word *muriades* in Acts 21:20 means literally that *tens of thousands* of Jews had believed in Jesus.

[4] Paul explains God's strategy to convert the Jewish nation in Romans 11:11–14. He has not yet completed it.

chilling symbolism, Luke tells us that the Jews dragged Paul out of their Temple *"and immediately the gates were shut"*. Twenty-seven years after they crucified their Messiah and twenty-four years after they stoned his servant Stephen, the Jewish nation refused God's grace once more. They rejected God's purposes for their lives and for their nation, and God reluctantly ratified their stubborn act of suicide.[5]

For most Jews in Jerusalem it felt like a day like any other, but Luke's symbolic detail is a warning that big decisions are often made through little actions. When the Jewish mob slammed the door shut on the Christian message they set their course for national disaster. Thwarted by the Roman troops and judges in his lust to kill Paul, the high priest seized his chance when Governor Festus died unexpectedly in office in 62 AD and executed James in defiance of Roman law. In retaliation, Rome deposed the high priest and was so heavy-handed that it provoked the Great Jewish Revolt of 66 AD. General Titus quashed the rebellion in 70 AD by leading his Roman legions into Jerusalem, and he razed both the city and its Temple to the ground. According to the eyewitness Josephus, over a million Jews were killed and almost a hundred thousand enslaved,[6] and the Gentile historian Philostratus tells us that even Titus refused to wear a victory-wreath in celebration since he saw *"no merit in vanquishing people forsaken by their own God"*.[7] As a final insult, in 132 AD, Emperor Hadrian built a new pagan city in the rubble of Jerusalem, and erected a temple to his god Jupiter on the site of the old Jewish Temple. However insignificant the thud of the Temple doors may have sounded to the Jewish mob in Acts 21:30, its echo resounded through many centuries of history.

---

[5] Luke uses this very phrase in Luke 7:30, without contradicting the message of the earlier chapter, "Chosen".

[6] The ancient Jewish historian Josephus in his *War of the Jews*, 6.9.3. He adds in 7.1.1 that Jerusalem was so thoroughly destroyed that *"nothing was left there to make visitors believe it had ever been inhabited"*.

[7] Philostratus II, *The Life of Apollonius of Tyana*, 6.29.

Theophilus, of course, did not yet know all that lay ahead for the Jewish nation, but such poignant, door-slamming symbolism cannot have escaped his experienced judicial scrutiny. Theophilus was a Gentile, one of those whose inclusion in the Gospel message had provoked the Jewish mob to riot against Paul. They preferred to turn their back on God rather than watch him turn his face towards the Gentiles, and Luke hoped that their slammed doors might yet open a door for Theophilus' salvation. If God permitted even the nation of Israel to refuse his Gospel and set their course for destruction, he warned tacitly, a pagan judge in Rome must take his two books very seriously indeed. We know that Theophilus acquitted Paul and ruled in favour of the Christians, so he may even have gone one step further and accepted Luke's passionate Gospel appeal.

Unlike Theophilus, however, we do know what happened to the Jewish nation, and we have even more reason than him to heed Luke's tragic national case study. God displays enormous patience towards sinful rebels and half-hearted followers, but Luke warns us that there comes a day when he ratifies our choices and lets us reap the consequences. In Part Six of Acts, Luke challenges you to respond to his message while you still have the chance. None of us can ever presume upon tomorrow; God takes it very seriously when we slam doors shut on him today.

Heavenly Protection
(22:23–29)

Those who were about to question him withdrew immediately. The commander himself was alarmed when he realized that he had put Paul, a Roman citizen, in chains.

(Acts 22:29)

In 20 BC, the city of Cyzigus in Asia Minor made a terrible mistake. They flogged and killed some Roman citizens in error, and their whole city was enslaved by the furious Emperor Augustus.[1] A few decades later, when they did it again, they received fresh reprisals from the Emperor Tiberius.[2] In 44 AD, when the island of Rhodes dared to crucify some Roman citizens, an irate Emperor Claudius annexed their island in retaliation.[3] Again and again in Rome's history, she left the world in no doubt over how they must treat all her citizens. Mistreat a Roman citizen and you would certainly live to regret it.

Claudius Lysias had therefore committed a cardinal error. He and his soldiers had quelled a riot and saved Paul from the lynch mob, but they had assumed he was an Egyptian terrorist or a Jewish nobody who could be stripped and flogged to obtain a confession.[4] Lysias had not registered above the din of the

---

[1] Cassius Dio, *Roman History*, (54.7.6; 54.23.7). Augustus only gave them back their freedom in 15 BC.

[2] Cassius Dio, *Roman History*, (57.24.6); Tacitus, *Annals*, (4.36.2); Suetonius, *The Life of Tiberius*, (37.2–3).

[3] Cassius Dio, *Roman History*, (60.24.4).

[4] In v. 24 he orders his troops literally to *"investigate him with flogging"*. This use of torture in lieu of questioning to extract a confession would embarrass

crowd when Paul warned him in 21:39 that he was *"a citizen of no ordinary city"*, and as a result he had clamped a Roman citizen in chains like a barbarian troublemaker. He could easily lose his life for a mistake of this magnitude, so he suddenly became Paul's most zealous protector. That's why he wrote a weaselly letter to Governor Felix to claim that he had rescued Paul from the crowd *"for I had learned that he is a Roman citizen"*.[5] Lysias knew that to abuse a Roman citizen was to abuse the very emperor himself, and he was scared, very scared.

Paul had played this to his advantage seven years earlier in Philippi. He had been chased out of the cities of Asia Minor on his First Missionary Journey, and he was determined to set a test case for the churches of Macedonia. When he and Silas were dragged before the city magistrates in 16:19, they decided not to disclose their Roman citizenship too early. Only once they had been stripped, beaten, severely flogged and imprisoned did they finally reveal to the magistrates what a dangerous mistake they had made. Philippi had sinned against the emperor and was in very grave danger of going the same way as Cyzigus. No wonder Luke tells us that the magistrates were alarmed and appeased them before begging them to leave the city. Paul and Silas had shed their blood to buy some breathing-space for the new church in Philippi, which meant that Luke could spend four fruitful years establishing a mighty new church in that city, safe in the knowledge that the magistrates would not dare tamper with them again in a hurry.[6]

The emperor's commitment to his citizens was so full and so fearsome that even modern nation states have drawn inspiration from it for their own foreign policies. The British

---

Judge Theophilus, Roman citizen or not.

[5] Acts 23:27.

[6] Luke refers to *we* and *us* on the Second Missionary Journey up until Paul leaves Philippi in Acts 16:40, and starts referring to *we* and *us* again in 20:5 as soon as Paul returns to Philippi four years later.

Prime Minister, Lord Palmerston, led the way in 1850 when he told Parliament that

> As the Roman, in days of old, held himself free from indignity, when he could say Civis Romanus Sum [Latin for "I am a Roman citizen"]; so also a British subject, in whatever land he may be, shall feel confident that the watchful eye and the strong arm of England will protect him against injustice and wrong.

Today this has become a maxim for many powerful nations. To abuse a citizen is still considered, in effect, as abuse towards the whole of their nation.

Luke is sounding a stern warning to Judge Theophilus here that he had better think twice before condemning his prisoner, but he also has a second point to make from Paul's safeguarded status as a citizen of Rome. In Acts 9:4, when Paul – then Saul of Tarsus – had his vision of Jesus on the road to Damascus, the Lord asked him a question which echoed the commitment which put terror into the heart of both Lysias and the magistrates of Philippi. He asked him, *"Saul, Saul! Why do you persecute me?"* Not *my Church*, not *my Christians*, but *me*. It's such a surprising way of speaking that Luke repeats it twice more in 22:7 and 26:14. He wants the Suffering Church to be in no doubt at all that when they suffer trial and persecution on behalf of his Kingdom, Jesus considers it an attack upon him personally, and he will not be outstripped by Caesar in his commitment to avenge his People.

Paul wrote to the Ephesians from his house arrest in Rome while he waited to appear before Judge Theophilus, and he told them: *"Consequently, you are no longer foreigners and aliens, but **fellow citizens** with God's people... with Christ Jesus himself as the chief cornerstone."*[7] We were not born as citizens, but as

---

[7] Ephesians 2:19–20.

foreigners, yet we did not purchase our citizenship at a very high price like Claudius Lysias.[8] On the contrary, Paul tells us in Acts 20:28 that we are those that *"he bought with his own blood"*. We are not mere subjects who appeal to our Saviour as Paul appealed to Caesar, with a hope that he will answer our cry of distress. Our great Ruler has purchased our citizenship by shedding his blood on a cross like the ones used at Rhodes. He has been treated far worse than a citizen of Rome, so that he can protect us far better as citizens of heaven.

If you are experiencing persecution for your faith, this should come as great comfort to you. Even if you are suffering from the normal troubles of life, this should encourage you to look to the Lord Jesus as well. You have been saved by the God about whom Isaiah said, *"In all their distress he too was distressed."*[9] You are a subject of the King who says to the world that *"Whatever you did for one of the least of these brothers of mine, you did for me."*[10]

So have confidence that the Lord Jesus will never leave you, never forsake you, and never abandon you to your troubles. He affords greater protection that a Roman emperor, a British prime minister, or an American president.[11] When you are threatened, he will deliver you. If you are martyred, he will strengthen and avenge you. For not one teardrop, not one anguished cry, and not one single drop of blood will ever escape Jesus' notice. He offers heavenly protection to the citizens of heaven, so appeal to him now – he is listening.

---

[8] Acts 22:28.

[9] Isaiah 63:9.

[10] Matthew 25:40.

[11] Paul wrote to the Philippian Christians for whom he had kept his Roman citizenship silent, and told them in 3:20 that *"Our citizenship is in heaven. And we eagerly await a Saviour from there, the Lord Jesus Christ."*

Credit Rating (23:11)

The following night the Lord stood near Paul and said, "Take courage! As you have testified about me in Jerusalem, so you must also testify about me in Rome."

(Acts 23:11)

The Lord has done it again. He never seems to stop. Here, in the midst of riots and lynch mobs and trials and murder plots, Jesus appears to Paul in his room at the Roman barracks to tell him that he is in control. It's absolutely incredible. To any outside observer, it surely seems that the Devil has the upper hand, Paul is on the ropes, and the Gospel is about to take a major blow. Jesus, on the other hand, tells us the view from the control-room of heaven. Things are going exactly according to plan, and the Sovereign Lord is about to display his death-defying wisdom.

This is one of Luke's major themes in the book of Acts, and it needs to be. Church history has been full of knock-backs, hurts, and disappointments, and Christians without a big view of God will never hold their nerve. Many people have dropped out of the race, giving up on Church, giving up on themselves, and even giving up on God himself. Others still look like they are running, but in their hearts they dropped out long ago. Therefore Luke crams his thirty-two year snapshot of Early Church history with vital perspective for the years that will follow. He sets our expectations that Satan will often look like he is winning, but then he shows us the hidden workings of the Sovereign Lord of History.

Luke starts with the life story of Jesus. Has anything ever

looked quite so catastrophic as the violent crucifixion of God's own Son? Luke tells us that this happened *"by God's set purpose and foreknowledge"*, because *"they did what your power and will had decided beforehand should happen"*.[1] If Jesus' death was his path to victory, surely nothing is beyond our God. When we meet with setbacks and surprises, disaster and defeat, we are merely walking on the same road as God's Son.

Luke repeats this lesson frequently in Parts One to Three of Acts. When Peter and John are arrested, God uses it to gather all of Israel's leaders together for a showdown with the Gospel. When Ananias and Sapphira threaten to destroy the Church from the inside out, he uses them to wake up sleepy Jerusalem to the holiness of their God. When Satan tries to distract the apostles with discontented voices inside the Church, God uses it to release men like Philip and Stephen, whose preaching cannot be silenced. When the Jerusalem believers scatter and their city church is decimated, God births more churches nationwide and their reach grows ever stronger. Whenever Satan looks like he is winning, God lays his cards out on the table and outwits him every time.

In Parts Four to Six of Acts, it is the same. As Paul and his friends take the Gospel westward, they treat persecution, stoning and imprisonment as vital stepping stones to victory.[2] When Judaizers try to hijack the Gospel, the apostles meet to clarify and it sends the Gospel to the Gentiles even faster than before. When Paul falls out with Barnabas, their capacity is effectively doubled.[3] Even the accidental death of a teenager

---

[1] Acts 2:23; 4:28. See also 3:18; 4:11.

[2] Acts 14:22.

[3] Paul says in Romans 15:23 that there are no more big cities left without churches in the whole of the Eastern Mediterranean. Since he never went to Alexandria, the second biggest city in the Roman Empire, we must assume that Barnabas and other preachers went south from Cyprus and reached Egypt without him.

during a church meeting at Troas grants an opportunity for God to demonstrate his power as Paul raises him back to life.

If you have ever applied for a mortgage or a personal loan, you have been given a *credit rating*. This is a statement made by financial institutions about how trustworthy they consider you to be. If you have defaulted on debt in the past, they tend to give you a poor credit rating for the future. If you have never missed a repayment, they tend to set your rating high.

Luke wants you to consider whether God should be awarded high or a low credit rating. He fills the book of Acts with dark days and crushing setbacks, but reminds us that God never once defaults on his promises. He lets us see the Christians at their lowest – like Paul here in the Roman barracks in Jerusalem – and builds up a credit history which is second to none. Paul is about to spend two years languishing in prison at Caesarea,[4] before being shipwrecked on his way to Rome and being placed under house arrest in the metropolis he had hoped to criss-cross with the Gospel. Luke shows us the Church at the very worst of times and tells us that God's credit rating is undented.

The Bible tells us that God gives *us* a credit rating too. Strangely, it does not depend on our ability to deliver against our promises, but on our trust in him to deliver against his own. Scripture tells us that Abraham trusted in God's ability to *"call things that are not as though they were"*, and that as a result he *"believed God, and it was **credited** to him as righteousness"*.[5] Just stop and consider that for a moment. God gives you a credit rating based on how you treat his own credit rating towards you!

Paul trusted God, and his credit rating passed the test. The two frustrating years in Caesarea gave Luke the chance to write his gospel, and Paul the chance to preach to all the leading

---

[4] Acts 24:27.

[5] Genesis 15:6; Romans 4:3,17, 23–24; Galatians 3:6; James 2:23.

people of the city.[6] His shipwreck meant a chance to preach to a shipful of pagans and the hitherto ignored island of Malta.[7] His two years in prison in Rome gave him unprecedented access to soldiers, judges, and even the household of Emperor Nero himself.[8]

His house arrest simply forced him to turn his living-room into a new preaching centre in Rome like the Lecture Hall of Tyrannus, and meant that he reached all Italy without ever leaving home. Paul gave God the credit he was due, and God credited it back to him.

That was then and this is now, and the victories of the past must be repeated in the present. As we look around us today at our churches and our nations, we need Luke's credit check more than ever. Is God still able to call things that are not as though they were? Is his credit rating just as high for the circumstances stacked against us? Ultimately, it is not God's credit rating which is in question, but our own. He has not changed and nor has his ability to deliver on his promises. He is simply looking for people of faith who will take him at his word and persevere.

Abraham and Paul believed in God and their credit rating soared. Let's follow their lead and give God the credit he deserves. His People never received all his blessings in any other way.

---

[6] Luke refers to *we* in 27:1, and the chronology of his life dictates that he did the research of Luke 1:1–4 while he waited with Paul in Caesarea. Paul could never have gathered the guest list of Acts 25:23 any other way.

[7] Luke refers to the Maltese people in Acts 28:2 literally as *barbarians*. They would normally not have visited them.

[8] Acts 21:37; 27:1; Philippians 1:13; 4:22. There might not even have been a book of Acts had Paul and Luke not come into contact with Judge Theophilus.

Religio Licita (24:14–17)

I admit that I worship the God of our fathers as a follower of the Way, which they call a sect. I believe everything that agrees with the Law and that is written in the Prophets.

(Acts 24:14)

For a multicultural, pluralist society, the Roman Empire was surprisingly intolerant. In theory, there were as many Roman gods as temples, and its people could worship them in any way they chose. In practice, however, Rome was as intolerant as Henry Ford when he decided that *"A customer can have a car painted any colour that he wants so long as it is black."*

The only "colour" which was tolerated in the Roman Empire was its own sophisticated pantheon of Jupiter, Venus, Mars, and friends. Greeks could worship their own deities so long as they admitted that they were merely the Roman gods under different names. Egyptians could continue to worship Isis so long as they identified her with the Roman goddess Ceres and paid lip-service to the rest of their crowded pantheon. The Empire believed in widespread religious toleration, just so long as it all took place under the umbrella of Roman mythology. So long as people played by those rules, everyone could be happy.

The Jews, of course, refused to cut a deal with the Roman gods. Very quickly after the Romans annexed Palestine in 63 BC, they realized that the race which had worshipped Yahweh under the Babylonians, Persians and Seleucids was not about to change its mind for Rome. Therefore Julius Caesar granted them a major concession, that Judaism would be a *religio* licita*, a *permitted religion*, and be tolerated alongside the Roman gods.[1] Henceforward, the practitioners of any other religion which defied the Roman pantheon would continue to be severely punished, but the Jewish worshippers of Yahweh would be indulged in a category of their own.[2] This distinction was therefore paramount for Luke and his Christian friends. If the Gospel was a form of Messianic Judaism, the Church could claim legal protection from the emperor, but if it was a cult or a sect outside of Judaism, the Church was a community of outlaws. Much of Luke's defence-brief for Theophilus revolves around this central question: *Should Christianity be considered a religio licita?*

For the Jews who rejected Christianity, there was a very simple answer. By worshipping a prophet from Nazareth, these people had become sub-Jewish, a heretical cult which was blasphemously opposed to the religion of Moses. In the words of their prosecuting lawyer, Tertullus, they were simply *"the Nazarene sect".*[3]

Paul and his Jewish converts saw things very differently indeed. He claimed he was on trial for *"the hope of Israel"*, because he believed in *"what God promised our fathers"*, and because he was waiting for *"the promise our twelve tribes are hoping to see fulfilled"*. He followed the same Scriptures as the Jews, with the *"same hope in God"*, and therefore expected the same legal protection.[4] If Christianity was a sect, he argued, it was only so in the same sense as the Pharisees, who used the

THE GOSPEL TO ROME (57–62 AD)

240

---

[1] Josephus records this in his *Antiquities of the Jews* (14.10.17–26). Caesar did not personally use the term *religio licita*, but this is how it came to be known.

[2] The Romans did not always honour this concession consistently. The Jews were exiled from Rome in 19 AD and 49 AD (Acts 18:2), and the Philippians slandered Paul in Acts 16:18–19 by calling him a Jew who was *"advocating customs unlawful for us Romans to accept or practise"*.

[3] Acts 24:5.

[4] Acts 13:32–33; 24:14–18; 26:6–7; 28:20–22.

word to emphasize that they were *more*, not less, committed to religion of Moses.[5]

Governor Gallio of Corinth was convinced by these arguments and treated Christianity as a flanker brand of Judaism. Theophilus appears to have been convinced by them too, but Paul and his friends were ultimately fighting a losing legal battle. The real issue was not whether the Christian Gospel fell under the remit of Julius Caesar's historical concession. The issue was that Christians had an unlimited vision, which eluded the Sanhedrin. The leaders of Judaism wanted to be left alone and were largely willing to leave the pagan world to perish as a price for their toleration. The leaders of Christianity were determined to fulfil their Great Commission to make disciples of every nation. It was therefore an issue of zeal and ambition rather than of history and theology which caused the Emperor Domitian to declare Christianity a *religio illicita*, an *illegal religion*, in the 80s AD.[6] He was not decreeing that the Church had deviated from Moses, but that their message was too radically ambitious to be shut up in a corner.

The Jews had not compromised the identity of Yahweh, but they had done a shameful deal with Rome which renounced their national mission. They agreed to personalize, or at least nationalize, the message of the Living God for the sake of a quiet life. The Christians refused to cut such shady deals and insisted that the worship of Yahweh was not just a private affair. Even when Roman poets such as Lucretius and Juvenal poked fun at the Roman pantheon, they did not dare to question its worship, but the Christians commanded their listeners to turn away from lifeless idols to follow the one true God.[7] If the retort was that

---

[5] Acts 26:5.

[6] The Romans also referred to Christianity as a *superstition*, to differentiate it from lawful religion. Suetonius called it a *"new and dangerous superstition"*, Tacitus a *"detestable superstition"*, and Pliny the Younger an *"unreasonable and limitless superstition"*.

[7] Acts 14:15; 17:29; 19:26; 1 Corinthians 8:4; Galatians 4:8; 1 John 5:21.

the gods would judge the Empire for their so-called "atheism", they replied that the whole Empire needed to repent or it would be judged by the God to whom they bore witness.[8] They demanded out-and-out conversion which deeply offended to the quasi-pluralism of their day. When the Romans saw that the Christians would not stop preaching their Gospel, they resorted to killing them instead.

The Jews had forged a compromise with the emperor's rule, telling their governor that *we have no king but Caesar*.[9] The Christians, on the other hand, were both his most loyal and his most defiant subjects at one and the same time. They offered him complete submission under God and went about doing good in every place they gathered, yet they refused point blank to submit to him when he went against their God.[10] Since the Roman emperors considered themselves to be gods in their own right and demanded unquestioning loyalty from their subjects, they could not tolerate the Christian message. It preached that Jesus was Lord, not them, and that the Son of God had not sat on a Roman throne but in a Galilean carpenter's workshop instead. In an empire where Caesar lusted for the position which only Jesus can hold, the Christians refused to play along, even when it cost them their lives.

But here's the fascinating thing, which is as relevant today as ever. When the Christians eschewed interfaith dialogue and embraced evangelism; when they decided that the Gospel was not theirs to change and preached it in all its counter-cultural glory; when they refused to accommodate and demanded unilateral surrender instead; when they refused to be swayed by mockery, despising, hatred, persecution and even martyrdom, the Gospel spread like wildfire. Far from silencing this *religio illicita*, the Roman pantheon crumbled before its fearless message of a risen Christ.

[8] Acts 17:29–31.
[9] John 19:15.
[10] Luke 20:25; Romans 13:1–7; 1 Peter 2:17, contrasted with Acts 4:19; 5:29.

The Christians discovered what is still true today when they obeyed their God without fear for the consequences. They found that in every place people said to them the words of Acts 28:22: *"We want to hear what your views are, for we know that people everywhere are talking against this sect."*

Mañana (24:25; 26:28)

That's enough for now! You may leave. When I find it convenient, I will send for you.

(Acts 24:25)

If Acts 24 and 26 had a theme tune, it would be "Mañana" by Dean Martin. *Mañana*, the Spanish word for *tomorrow*, was how both Felix and Agrippa responded to the Gospel. They were alarmed, interested and almost convinced, but they put off a decision until later. In the words of Dean Martin, they sang *"Mañana, Mañana – Mañana is soon enough for me."* Since Theophilus and his friends must have known Felix and Agrippa, by reputation at the very least and probably in person, Luke uses these members of the imperial aristocracy to shock his readers into action of their own. He does not merely want to brief Theophilus and his other Roman readers about Christianity. He wants to challenge them to respond to the Gospel themselves, and not to put it off until *mañana*.

Everybody knew Antonius Felix. He was the younger brother of Pallas, one of the richest men in Rome and the former favourite of Emperor Claudius. They knew that he was a rogue who had recently been recalled to Rome in disgrace for his cruelty towards his subjects. When Luke writes that *"Paul discoursed on righteousness, self-control and the judgment to come"*, he knew it would make his Roman readers sit up and listen.[1] They knew that Felix had won his governorship of Judea in 52 AD because he was married to a relative of Emperor Claudius, but that he had quickly abandoned her when Claudius died two years later.

---

[1] Acts 24:25.

They knew he had seduced Drusilla, the beautiful married sister of King Agrippa, away from her husband with the spells of a hired magician.[2] They disapproved of his political marriage to this beautiful girl who was young enough to be his daughter. The historian Tacitus accuses him of *"indulging in every kind of barbarity and lust, exercising the authority of a king with the mind of a slave".*[3]

Felix was a political outcast who had been given a chance to respond to the Gospel. This was a turning point in his life, as he put God's apostle on trial but found his own soul in the dock instead. He was scared and convicted, but then suddenly started singing *"Mañana"*. He wouldn't reject the Gospel outright – just put it off until tomorrow. *"That's enough for now!"* he quickly interjected. *"You may leave. When I find it convenient, I will send for you."* He would frequently send for Paul to continue their discussions, but he kept putting off his response till *mañana*. Two years later he was deposed and disgraced, never to recover his reputation or position. Drusilla and their son were both killed in the eruption of Vesuvius in 79 AD. Felix himself simply disappears from the history books. Warning one for Theophilus, for his friends and for us: don't *discuss* the Gospel and put it off until *mañana*. Respond to it today, while you still have a chance.

Porcius Festus was a more virtuous replacement as governor, but he too would prove a chilling example to Luke's readers. He knew Paul was innocent, but was more interested in winning favour with his new Jewish subjects than with their God. His ignorance is shocking, as he refers to the most famous Jew of his day as *"a dead man named Jesus"*, and so is his refusal to engage with his story when given the chance. He dismisses Paul as an over-educated madman, all to the sound of *"Mañana, Mañana"* in the background.[4] Two years later, a few weeks after

---

[2] Josephus, *Antiquities of the Jews*, (20.7.2).

[3] Tacitus, *The Histories*, (5.9).

[4] Acts 25:19; 26:24.

Paul arrived in Rome and a short while before Theophilus read the book of Acts, Festus died suddenly in his prime while still in office in Judea. Warning two for Luke's readers: dismiss the Gospel at your peril.

The third judge, King Agrippa II, was as much a rogue as his brother-in-law Felix. He had been a seventeen-year-old courtier of Emperor Claudius in Rome when he heard of his father's death as reported in Acts 12:21–23. After fifteen years of scheming, he had finally become ruler of Galilee. It was a shrewd move on the part of Festus to involve Agrippa in Paul's trial; one false step at the trial of this Roman citizen and the ambitious Agrippa would make a bid for his job too. Luke does not mention that Bernice was Agrippa's incestuous lover as well as his sister, although the public knew these rumours only too well.[5] When Paul challenged King Agrippa that Jesus' resurrection had taken place in public and not *"in a corner"*, he was calling him to repent publicly and put his faith in the Gospel.[6] Once again, Luke baits his Roman readers' interest and captures their undivided attention.

Sadly, Agrippa was more concerned for his reputation than for his soul. He was embarrassed to be put on the spot in front of a hall-full of Caesarea's nobility. He laughed off Paul's challenge and used a term of abuse to dismiss his Gospel message: *"Do you think that in such a short time you can persuade me to become a* **Christian***?"*[7] Yet another Roman ruler sings *"Mañana, Mañana"*, and yet another Roman ruler learns his mistake the hard way. His ambitions were thwarted, and he was exiled back to Rome after the Jewish revolt of 66 AD. His lover Bernice became the mistress of the Roman General Titus, who destroyed both Jerusalem and its Temple. Agrippa would later die childless as

---

[5] Josephus, *Antiquities of the Jews*, 20.7.3. He eventually married her off to quash the rumours.

[6] Acts 26:27.

[7] Acts 25:23; 26:28. This is the only time the abusive name *"Christian"* is used in Acts other than in 11:26.

the last of Herod's dynasty and another sad example of fatal delay. He was warning three for Theophilus, for his friends, and for us. The time has come for Luke to turn and bring a call for decision.

In 26:29, Paul challenges the crowded courtroom that *"I pray God that not only you but all who are listening to me today may become what I am, except for these chains."* Luke is pressing home his challenge to Theophilus and his Roman friends, urging them to respond where these three rulers had failed. Felix had *debated* the Gospel instead of embracing it, and he was now a political has-been in a shady corner of Rome. Festus had *dismissed* the Gospel as the foolish talk of a street preacher, and he had been struck down dead in his prime as a warning of God's judgment. Agrippa had *disdained* the Gospel for the sake of reputation, and would now be a lonely and frustrated man, despised by the very courtiers whose praise he had held so dear.

Yet it was not too late for Theophilus and friends to respond to the Gospel and find blessing instead of cursing from the hand of Paul's God. It is not too late for you either, if you have read this far into Acts and not yet surrendered your life to the Lord Jesus. Luke's message is for you as much as for Theophilus, and it is a warning of judgment for all who hear the Gospel and yet leave it till *mañana*. Don't delay or dismiss or disdain this glorious message. Paul warns you as he warned the great rulers of Rome: *"We urge you not to receive God's grace in vain... I tell you, **now** is the time of God's favour, now is the day of salvation."*[8]

---

[8] 2 Corinthians 6:1–2.

Raised to Life (25:19)

> *Instead, they had some points of dispute with him about their own religion and about a dead man named Jesus whom Paul claimed was alive.*
>
> (Acts 25:19)

When I received my first formal training in how to share the Gospel, I was warned not to "leave Jesus in the tomb" by forgetting to mention the resurrection. I've been issued the same reminder on many training courses since then, which makes me very troubled when I read the book of Acts. Paul and the other early Christians simply didn't need a reminder to mention the resurrection, because they treated it not as a tag-on to the Gospel, but as the very heart of the Gospel itself. Since Luke summarizes it very simply as *"the good news about Jesus and the resurrection"*,[1] this should set alarm bells ringing over what distorted message we may be sharing with the world instead.

It's not that we shouldn't be focusing on the cross of Jesus. Paul told the converts from his Second Missionary Journey, *"I resolved to know nothing while I was with you except Jesus Christ and him crucified."*[2] It's just that Luke goes out of his way to model for us Gospel messages which focus at least as much on the resurrection as they do on the cross. He only uses the word *cross* three times in the whole of the book of Acts, but he uses

---

[1] Acts 17:18. In fact, since the Greek word *anastasis*, or *resurrection*, is a feminine noun, Luke is probably telling us here that the Athenians misunderstood Paul and assumed that he was advocating two new *"foreign gods"*: one named *Jesus* and the other a consort-goddess named *Anastasis*.

[2] 1 Corinthians 2:2. See also 1 Corinthians 1:17–18.

the word *resurrection* eleven times.[3] He only speaks of Jesus being *crucified* nine times in Acts, yet speaks of him being *raised to life* sixteen times.[4] None of the early Christians needed to be reminded not to "leave Jesus in the tomb" when they preached the Gospel across the Roman Empire because they understood clearly that *"Jesus Christ, raised from the dead… is my gospel"*.[5] As he draws the book of Acts to a close, Luke wants us to rediscover the fullness of the Gospel for ourselves.

First, Luke wants us to understand that the resurrection is the *substance of the Gospel*. He refers to the Gospel in 5:20 as the *"message of this new life"*, and he constantly reminds us that the thing to which we are called to be witnesses is above all the resurrection.[6] This was *"the hope of Israel"* in the Old Testament and is still the Christian hope in the New.[7] Because Jesus died and was raised to life, sinners can be raised to life with him by believing that *"the one who raised the Lord Jesus from the dead will also raise us with Jesus"*.[8] When we preach a Gospel message which is all about the cross and little about the resurrection, we reduce the mission of Jesus to nothing more than forgiveness for our sins and deliverance from judgment. That's only a part of the Gospel which Luke describes in Acts. Forgiveness is not the goal of salvation but simply the means by which we are admitted to the new life which Jesus gives us through his

---

[3] Luke doesn't use the word *stauros*, or *cross*, at all in Acts. He uses the word *xulon*, or *tree*, in 5:30; 10:39; 13:29, and the word *anastasis*, or *resurrection*, in 1:22; 2:31; 4:2, 33; 17:18, 32; 23:6, 8; 24:15, 21; 26:23.

[4] Luke only speaks of him being *crucified* in 2:23, 36, and 4:10, but also speaks of him being *killed* or *executed* in 3:13, 15; 5:30; 7:52; 10:39; 13:28. He talks much more about him being raised to life in 1:3; 2:24, 32; 3:15; 4:10; 5:30; 10:40, 41; 13:30, 33, 34, 37; 17:3, 31; 25:9; 26:8.

[5] 2 Timothy 2:8. Paul carries on by telling Timothy in vv. 17–18 that those who spiritualize the resurrection and rob it of its vital place in the Gospel message *"destroy the faith of some"*.

[6] Acts 1:22; 3:15; 4:2, 33; 24:21.

[7] Acts 24:15; 26:6–8; 28:20.

[8] 2 Corinthians 4:14. See also Romans 6:4; 1 Corinthians 6:14; 15:22; Ephesians 2:4–6.

resurrection. It enables our dead spirits to be raised to the new life which Jesus won instead of the old life which Adam lost, both now and forever in resurrection bodies in the age to come. The Gospel is not just a message of forgiveness, but a message of resurrection, restoration and eternal glory with the Father.

Second, Luke tells us that the resurrection is the *reason why the Gospel is the only means of salvation*. Paul insists three times in Part Six that *"I stand on trial because of my hope in the resurrection of the dead"*,[9] convinced that it was the resurrection and not just the cross which had shattered the empty hopes of Roman paganism and first-century Judaism. Paul explains this in more detail in his letter to the Romans when he tells them that Jesus *"was delivered over to death for our sins and was raised to life for our justification"*.[10] We are not justified through the cross alone, or Paul would not have written that *"if Christ has not been raised, your faith is futile; you are still in your sins"*.[11] We are justified through his resurrection too because only this divine vindication confirms to us that his blood sacrifice has fully paid the price for human sin. The cross is not the only means of salvation simply because the Son said *"It is finished!"*[12] but because the Father shouted his loud *"Amen!"* when he raised him from the dead. On Easter Sunday, God fully endorsed Jesus' sacrifice as the only way for people to be saved, and in doing so sounded the death knell on every other man-made religion.

Third, Luke tells us that the resurrection is the *definitive proof that the Gospel is true*. It was very convincing when Jesus commanded his followers to witness to his resurrection in the city of Jerusalem where it had recently taken place. When Peter preached the resurrection on the Day of Pentecost only

---

[9] Paul did not simply say this as a ruse to divide the Pharisees and Sadducees, because having said it to the Sanhedrin in Acts 23:6–9, he also said it to Governor Felix in 24:15, 21 and King Agrippa in Acts 26:6–8.

[10] Romans 4:25. This is also the logic behind Romans 8:33–34.

[11] 1 Corinthians 15:17.

[12] John 19:30.

seven weeks and several hundred yards from the empty tomb itself, his enemies could say nothing to prevent thousands of his listeners from flocking to believe.[13] Nevertheless, Jesus also commanded them to witness to his resurrection *"to the ends of the earth"*, hundreds of miles and even hundreds of years in the distance. The truth is the message of the resurrection is such incontrovertible evidence that Paul told the far-off Athenians in 17:31 that God *"has given proof of this to all men by raising him from the dead"*, and the far-off Romans that, even for them, Jesus was *"declared with power to be the Son of God by his resurrection from the dead"*. [14] The facts of Jesus' resurrection are so well documented, and the emergence of the worldwide Church from 120 dispirited disciples is so compelling, that Luke urges us to preach the message of the resurrection to any audience and to ask them: *"Why should any of you consider it incredible that God raises the dead... because it was not done in a corner"*?![15]

As Luke moves the book of Acts towards its cliff-hanger ending, he speaks more, not less, about the importance of preaching the resurrection at the heart of the Gospel. He doesn't simply remind us to tag it on to the end of our messages about the cross. He urges us to share it as an essential element of the Gospel message itself. We are saved through the cross *and* the empty tomb, because the resurrection is the substance of the Gospel, the reason why the Gospel alone can save, and the definitive proof that the Gospel is true.

We are to preach like Paul to all who will listen that: *"If you confess with your mouth, 'Jesus is Lord,' and believe in your heart that **God raised him from the dead**, you will be saved."*[16]

---

[13] Peter's message on the Day of Pentecost did *not* quote from Psalm 22 or Isaiah 53 to focus on the reasons for the crucifixion, but from Psalms 16 and 110 to focus on the resurrection. Interestingly, the Jewish leaders didn't even try to argue the resurrection had not happened, but simply ordered them to keep silent about it.

[14] Romans 1:4.

[15] Acts 26:8, 26.

[16] Romans 10:9.

Sanctified by Faith (26:18)

Turn them from darkness to light, and from the power of Satan to God, so that they may receive forgiveness of sins and a place among those who are sanctified by faith in me.

(Acts 26:18)

My working life used to involve one crisis after another. Every time the phone rang there would be a new problem to solve. One day a major customer would threaten to renege on a several-hundred-thousand-pound deal. The next day industrial action at the French ports would bring my deliveries to a standstill. On one occasion a disgruntled ex-employee even sabotaged our factory. Every single day there was another pressing crisis which demanded my attention, so you can imagine my relief when my mobile phone rang with an urgent disaster a few days after I left the company. *"I'm sorry I can't help you,"* I was able to say to my troublesome caller. *"I don't work for you any more."*

Those words felt good to say, and Luke wants to teach each one of us to say them to our former boss, Satan. He skilfully words his abridged summaries of Paul's legal defences in the final chapters of Acts in order to equip us to carry on the Church's story. He writes Acts 26:18 to equip us to live holy lives by the power of the Holy Spirit, and to teach every believer how to overcome sin on a daily basis. We do not become more like Jesus by gritting our teeth and giving ourselves pep-talks on how we must try to be more godly; that's the attitude which caused Paul to ask the Galatian Christians: *"Are you so foolish? After beginning with the Spirit are you now trying to attain your goal by human effort?"*[1] We do so by co-operating with the Holy Spirit through the Gospel. Paul tells King Agrippa here that any ordinary Christian can be transformed to live like Jesus because he has promised them a place among those who are *"sanctified in me."*

The Greek word *dikaioō* means *to justify* or declare somebody legally righteous in God's sight. We are justified instantly at conversion because the Father counted sinless Jesus guilty in our place, and counts us righteous through his sacrifice. The nineteenth-century theologian William Plumer reminds us that:

> *Justification is an act. It is not a work, or a series of acts. It is not progressive. The weakest believer and the strongest saint are alike equally justified. Justification admits no degrees. A man is either wholly justified or wholly condemned in the sight of God.*[2]

The Greek word *hagiazō*, however, which Paul uses here, means *to sanctify* or be made more and more righteous through increasing conformity to the example of Christ. Unlike justification, this is a process which continues throughout our lives and which demands our constant attention. One of the biggest errors which we can make as we follow Jesus Christ is to mistake the call to holiness for a call to self-improvement. Luke quotes Paul's teaching here because he wants to save us from a life which can never truly sanctify. We are sanctified *by faith* in exactly the same way as we were justified, because it is God himself who sanctifies us and who makes Jesus the source of our *sanctification* as well as our justification.[3] Rules and resolutions

---

[1] Galatians 3:3.

[2] William Swan Plumer, *The Grace of Christ* (1853).

[3] 1 Thessalonians 5:23; 1 Corinthians 1:30. Both of these verses talk about *hagiasmos*, or sanctification, as God's gift of grace towards us through Christ. See also Exodus 31:13.

can never sanctify us in the long term, because only the Gospel which freed us from the penalty of sin is able to free us also from its power.[4]

Paul taught his converts that the Gospel was not merely their hope of being *declared* righteous because Jesus died for them, but also their hope of being *made* righteous because they died with him too. This probably sounded as strange to them as it does to you and me, but Paul insisted that anyone who had been saved into Christ's new people had effectively *died with Christ* on the cross, been *buried with Christ* in his tomb, and been *raised with Christ* to a new life of salvation.[5] Satan would still come knocking to tempt them to live as they did before their conversion, but they could tell him that they had long since come off his sinful payroll: *"I died to you and have been raised in Christ. I don't work for you any more!"*

Although Luke has to point us to Paul's letters for a more detailed explanation of how this principle works in daily practice, he is as eager for us to be sanctified through the Gospel as he is for unbelievers to be justified through it. Christians are those who have been saved *"from darkness to light, and from the power of Satan to God"*, he tells us in verse 18, so unless the message of Acts changes a person's lifestyle they cannot truly have understood it. Genuine believers will read Scripture to find out what pleases and displeases God, and will believe the Bible's message that we have died to sin and been raised to a new righteous way of living by the power of the Spirit. They will come to the Holy Spirit and ask him in faith to apply what is objectively true to their day-to-day lives through the Gospel.[6]

---

[4] Colossians 2:23; John 8:34–36.

[5] Colossians 2:12, 20; 3:1, 3. Paul tells us in Romans 6:6 and Galatians 2:20 that we have been *sustauroō*, or *crucified with* Jesus, which is the same word used in Matthew 27:44 and John 19:32 to describe the two robbers being crucified with Jesus at Calvary. Although our old nature feels very much alive, we have no more right to doubt the Bible when it tells us we were crucified with Christ than we do when it tells us the robbers were.

[6] 2 Thessalonians 2:13.

This is the liberating message of Christian sanctification by grace through faith, which Paul wrote about and preached about throughout the Roman Empire:

> *Count yourselves dead to sin but alive to God in Christ Jesus... Do not let sin reign in your mortal body... but rather offer yourselves to God, as those who have been brought from death to life; and offer the parts of your body to him as instruments of righteousness. For sin shall not be your master, because you are not under law, but under grace.*[7]

Christians have been called to live like Jesus in contrast to the world, but they have not been called to do so through a straitjacket of rules and regulations. The Gospel is the Good News that we have died with Jesus and been raised to a new life in the power of his Spirit to enjoy by grace what we could never achieve by our own human effort. It is the message that Jesus sets us free from sin through our faith in the Gospel and through our partnership with the Holy Spirit. It is the promise to every Christian that we are *"sanctified by faith"*.

---

[7] Romans 6:11–14.

Actions Speak Louder Than Words (26:20)

THE GOSPEL TO ROME (57–62 AD)

256

> *[I] declared first to those in Damascus, then in Jerusalem and throughout all the region of Judea, and also to the Gentiles, that they should repent and turn to God, performing deeds in keeping with their repentance.*
>
> (Acts 26:20)[1]

You've probably heard the story of the young man who wrote a text-message to his girlfriend. *"Sweetheart, I love you,"* he told her. *"I love you so much that I'd climb the highest mountain just to look into your eyes. I love you so much that I'd swim the deepest river, sail the widest ocean, and cross the hottest desert just to be by your side. P.S. I'll come over tomorrow night if it isn't raining."*

Actions do speak louder than words. It's very easy to make a verbal profession of commitment to Christ, but what matters is whether we do as we say. Luke refers to God twice in 1:24 and 15:28 as the *kardiognōstēs*, or the *One-Who-Knows-the-Heart*, and he returns to this theme as Paul speaks to King Agrippa, to remind us that God isn't fooled by empty promises. The book of Acts is in its final pages, so Luke asks us what we will *do*, not just say, at the end of the story.

For some it will be genuine conversion, which Luke tells us means more than just saying a "sinner's prayer". It means *repenting and turning to God* from the other false gods who compete for our devotion. The book of Acts is strewn with sobering examples of people who tried to follow Jesus *and*

---

[1] English Standard Version.

something else. In chapter 1 Judas Iscariot died a bloody, shameful death after he betrayed Jesus his Master for a bagful of coins. He had once been such an impressive, miracle-working apostle that when Jesus announced at the Last Supper than one of the Twelve would betray him, none of his colleagues imagined it could be him. Even when he slipped out for a late-night rendezvous with the wicked chief priests, the Eleven assumed that he must have left to minister to the poor.[2] Judas looked the part of the perfect disciple, but paid the price for continuing to serve his god Money on the inside.

In chapter 5 Ananias and Sapphira pretended to be wholly devoted disciples of Christ, but the One Who Knows the Heart was angered by their barefaced hypocrisy and deception. They lost their lives as a sober reminder that it is better not to make promises to God at all if we are secretly planning to continue to serve the tyrant-god of Self. A few chapters later in Samaria, Simon Magus tried to follow Jesus and Power, and even tried to purchase the power of the Holy Spirit. Peter cursed him with hellfire for his shallow conversion, which lacked the raw passion of the magicians at Ephesus in 19:18–19.[3] Luke wants his readers to examine their own hearts and renounce the false gods which steal their devotion away from God alone.

For others, the issue is not so much serving other gods too much as serving the true God too little. Paul reminds us in verse 20 that those who truly convert to Christ must then *"perform deeds in keeping with their repentance"*.[4] In 1879, a criminal named Charlie Peace was being marched to the gallows in the city of Leeds, when a chaplain ran up to him and started reading

[2] Luke 22:21–23; John 13:27–29.

[3] Acts 8:9–24. Luke tells us in v. 13 that Simon genuinely believed the Gospel, but that he failed to repent and turn to God from idols, which Paul insists to King Agrippa is the hallmark of genuine conversion.

[4] The Greek word *axios* means *worthy*, but it is a mistake to translate this as *"acts worthy of repentance"*. Paul uses the word in a normal secular sense in 2 Thessalonians 1:3, which shows us that Paul uses it here to mean *in keeping with*.

from the Anglican Prayer Book. Charlie Peace angrily pushed him away and poured scorn on the Church's lacklustre lifestyle. *"Sir,"* he sneered. *"If I believed what you and the Church say you believe about heaven and hell – even if England were covered with broken glass from coast to coast, I would walk over it, if need be on my hands and knees, and think it a worthwhile living just to save one soul from an eternal hell like that."*[5] The chaplain could give no answer to Charlie Peace's challenge, for he was simply repeating the challenge of Paul here in Acts 28:20. People who truly believe the Gospel cannot help but live like Paul.

With the exception of John Mark, the would-be missionary who deserted Paul when the going got tough on his First Missionary Journey,[6] the book of Acts is full of people who rose to Charlie Peace's challenge. Peter and John were so transformed by the Gospel that they stood up to the Sanhedrin and rejoiced that they could suffer for the sake of Jesus' name. Paul and his team-mates suffered untold imprisonments, beatings, floggings, and dangers for the sake of those Jesus had died to save.[7] The Gospel caused Ananias to risk his life, Dorcas to spend her life on the poor, and Timothy to be circumcised to reach the Jews. It caused Jason to side with the apostles even in the face of a mob attacking his home, it caused Dionysius to endure the ridicule of his fellow Areopagites, and it made Priscilla and Aquila relocate across the Aegean to pioneer a new church-plant into Ephesus.[8] The book of Acts is crammed full of ordinary radicals who performed deeds in keeping with their repentance towards Jesus, and now Luke turns to us and urges us to do the same.

The nineteenth-century bishop J.C. Ryle gave the following

---

[5] Charlie Peace was such a notorious criminal that even Sherlock Holmes mentions him in Sir Arthur Conan Doyle's "The Adventure of the Illustrious Client" (*The Case Book of Sherlock Holmes*, 1924).

[6] Acts 13:5, 13; 15:37–38. John Mark was restored and served faithfully in Colossians 4:10 and 2 Timothy 4:11.

[7] Paul describes these trials for the sake of the Gospel in more detail in 2 Corinthians 11:23–28.

[8] Acts 9:10–19, 36, 39; 16:3; 17:5–9, 32–33; 18:18.

definition of what it means to be zealously devoted to Christ in the manner which Luke is describing:

> *A zealous man in religion is pre-eminently a man of one thing. It is not enough to say that he is earnest, hearty, uncompromising, thorough-going, whole-hearted, fervent in spirit. He only sees one thing, he cares for one thing; he is swallowed up in one thing; and that one thing is to please God. Whether he lives or whether he dies – whether he has health or whether he has sickness – whether he is thought wise, or whether he is thought foolish – whether he gets blame or whether he gets praise – whether he gets honour, or whether he gets shame – for all this the zealous man cares nothing at all. He burns for one thing; and that one thing is to please God, and to advance God's glory. If he is consumed in the very burning, he cares not for it – he is content. He feels that, like a lamp, he is made to burn; and if consumed in burning he has but done the work for which God appointed him. Such a one will always find a sphere for his zeal. If he cannot preach and work and give money, he will cry and sigh and pray... This is what I mean when I speak of "zeal" in religion.*[9]

This is what Luke also means when he reminds us here that actions speak louder than words. The *One-Who-Knows-the-Heart* is not fooled either by counterfeit conversion or by bargain-basement discipleship. He calls each one of us to play our own role in Church history by performing deeds in keeping with our repentance.

---

[9] J.C. Ryle, *Practical Religion: Plain Papers on the Daily Duties, Experience, Dangers and Privileges of Professing Christians* (1878).

God Wants You to Be Ignored (27:10–11)

> "Men, I can see that our voyage is going to be disastrous."... But the centurion, instead of listening to what Paul said, followed the advice of the pilot and of the owner of the ship.
>
> (Acts 27:10–11)

Have you ever stopped to wonder why Luke spends forty-four verses on the detail of Paul's sea voyage from Caesarea to Malta? That's more verses than the Day of Pentecost, more verses than the Council at Jerusalem, and more verses than the whole of Paul's three years in Ephesus. There must be an explanation, and it can't simply be that he is building our suspense for Paul's arrival in Rome – after all, he only devotes four verses to the whole of his journey from Malta to Rome itself! Perhaps it is because he wants to demonstrate to Theophilus that Paul is under divine protection, but he also has a deeper, more urgent goal in view.[1] Luke knows that the book of Acts is about to end, and that his ordinary Christian readers are about to carry on where he leaves off. Therefore he uses this long chapter to teach us an essential insight for winning our friends or our nations to Christ: God wants you to be ignored.

The truth is we all like being listened to. We like to be taken seriously, and we quickly lose heart when we are not. Very few of us have the resilience of Winston Churchill, who for many years

---

[1] If the length of this account doesn't strike you as strange, then note it is the most detailed account of ancient seamanship in any classical work, including Homer's *Odyssey* which is mainly based on a ship!

kept on preaching the dangers of Nazi Germany to a deaf nation which was drunk on disarmament, appeasement and "peace in our time". Shut out in the political wilderness, he was dismissed as nothing more than a maverick with a grudge, but it was only because he kept on speaking when ignored that the nation turned to listen to him later. Historian William Manchester tells us that *"He had come to power because he had seen through Hitler from the very beginning"*,[2] and Churchill himself wrote in his memoirs that *"My warnings over the last six years had been so numerous, so detailed, and were now so terribly vindicated, that no one could gainsay me."*[3] Luke wants us to learn the same lesson here from the voyage of Paul. Unless we are willing to speak and be ignored today, we will never have a chance to be listened to later.

Paul was a man who heard God, and Luke paints him for Theophilus in the colours of a venerable prophet. When the ship's captain and owner proposed to set sail from Crete at the beginning of the stormy season in October,[4] Paul prophesied to them that *"I can see that our voyage is going to be disastrous."* Centurion Julius and the majority of the crew-members decided to ignore him, but this did not mean that he had spoken in vain. Being ignored today is the price of being listened to tomorrow.

The storms begin. The ship is so battered and buffeted that even the hardened sailors begin to fear for their lives. Luke drops hints to his readers that he has spiritual lessons in view, by using the word *sōzō*, or *to save*, seven times in this passage.[5] This is not just a story about an ancient maritime disaster – it is an up-to-date lesson on how we win crowds to salvation. It was

---

[2] William Manchester, *The Last Lion: Winston Spencer Churchill; Alone: 1932–1940* (1988).

[3] Winston Churchill in Volume 1 of his World War Two Memoirs, *The Gathering Storm* (1948).

[4] *"The Fast"* in Acts 27:9 was *Yom Kippur*, the Day of Atonement. This took place on 5th October in 59 AD.

[5] He uses the word *sōzō*, *to save*, and its companion word *diasōzō* in 27:20, 31, 34, 43, 44, and in 28:1, 4.

only because Paul was ignored back in Crete that the centurion and crew sit up and listen to him when he says, *"Men, you should have taken my advice... Last night an angel of the God whose I am and whom I serve stood beside me... So keep up your courage, men, for I have faith in God that it will happen just as he has told me."* Nobody is laughing now, and no one is ignoring him either. When we speak God's warning before the storm comes, we pave the way for people to listen to us later when disaster comes. When we shrink from rejection and keep silent because we are afraid of being ignored, we lose our chance to speak with authority later.

This is how I became a Christian. My brother and I were both nominal Christians, until one day he started to follow Jesus for real. I laughed at him, poured abuse on him, and generally despised him, but he simply refused to stay silent. For three whole years I threw questions and objections and derision in his direction, but then my life got stormy and I started to listen. Storms always come in the lives of those around us; it's simply a question of whom they turn to when they come. My brother hadn't flinched and hadn't been flummoxed during three years of criticism and abuse, so as soon as the storms came I did what these Roman sailors did to Paul. I turned to the only person who had been talking sense all along. A series of phone-calls, letters, and Christian meetings later, I had come to know Jesus for real as well.

Don't miss the startling nature of the turnaround at the end of chapter 27. Roman prisoners were so despised that a soldier would kill them with barely a second thought,[6] and yet Paul the prisoner is suddenly treated like the ship's captain. They follow his advice even when he tells them to get rid of all their lifeboats, and he is the one who calls them to dinner and says grace over their food. Centurion Julius and the crew-

---

[6] Acts 27:42. The soldiers were trying to avoid reaping the same fate as their colleagues in 12:18–19.

members start to dance to his tune, because he started to play it long before the storms came.

If you want to see people saved through your life, you need to get used to being ignored in the short term. People rarely respond the first time they hear the Gospel, so you need to keep speaking until they do. Mark Dever reminds us that

We do not fail in our evangelism if we faithfully tell the Gospel to someone who is not converted; we fail only if we don't faithfully tell the Gospel at all. Evangelism itself is not converting people; it's telling them that they need to be converted and telling them how they can be.[7]

They may ignore you and laugh at you and even abuse you, but you need to remember that the storms are coming. Unless you preach God's Word in the good times, they will never turn and listen to you in the bad times.

The book of Acts is almost over, but the task of world evangelization still looks like it has a long, long way to run. Luke wants you to resolve in your heart that you will never purchase comfort with silence, but will always build a platform for tomorrow by enduring rejection and laughter today. Bringing those around you to salvation is easier than you think if you will speak up whatever the consequences. Don't be put off when they refuse to listen. God wants you to be ignored.

---

[7] Mark Dever, *The Gospel and Personal Evangelism* (2007).

Rome (28:11–31)

For two whole years Paul stayed there in his own rented house and welcomed all who came to see him. Boldly and without hindrance he preached the kingdom of God and taught about the Lord Jesus Christ.

(Acts 28:30–31)

The apostle Paul was completely unstoppable. No trouble, hardship, setback or trial ever seemed capable of denting his resolve. He arrived in Rome as a prisoner, deprived of his liberty and defending his life. He had almost been killed by his over-eager guards, and might have died of a snake-bite after the soldiers sent him to gather firewood like a common servant. For a Roman citizen like Paul, who must have dreamed his whole life of visiting the mother city, his arrival in chains must have been a terrible disappointment.

Yet Paul was not dismayed. He truly believed the Gospel that he preached, and it was this Gospel which gave him strength to make the best of his terrible circumstances.

Paul was placed under house arrest, which meant he could gaze out at the city through his windows but not wander its streets to talk to its million free residents plus slaves. He was penned inside the four walls of his home, but he refused to be daunted. He quickly set about turning the house into a preaching-centre like the house of Titius Justus in Corinth or the Lecture Hall of Tyrannus in Ephesus.[1] He received the Roman Christians to whom he had written five years earlier from Corinth, and who

---

[1] Acts 18:7, 11; 19:9–10.

loved him so much that they journeyed forty miles from Rome to provide him with an escort into the city.[2] He also received the Jews, who had returned to Rome in large numbers since their exile was rescinded. He even received a runaway slave named Onesimus, who was converted and went back to his Christian master in Colossae.[3] Far from locking Paul away in a prison house in the suburbs, the Roman state had simply forced him to fall back on the same strategy with which he had formerly reached Achaia and Asia, and with which he would now reach the whole of the western Empire.

He was guarded by Roman soldiers, but even their hovering presence could not dampen his spirits. A guard meant an audience, and an audience met an opportunity to tell somebody new the story of Jesus. He turned his captors into his own captive audience and persuaded each new guard to repent and surrender to Jesus. In his letter to the church at Philippi, he told them that *"what has happened to me has really served to advance the gospel. As a result, it has become clear throughout the whole palace guard and to everyone else that I am in chains for Christ."* What was more, he told the Philippians, his imprisonment had made his team members (as well as his jealous rivals) all the more eager to preach the Gospel in his place. The enemies of Christ who had clapped Paul in irons had not restricted the Gospel, but propelled it to reach the Praetorian Guard and even Caesar's household.[4]

Paul was the prisoner of Caesar, but this had not dented his faith that he was serving the King. Twice, in verses 23 and 31, Luke stresses that Paul kept preaching about the Kingdom of his God. It didn't matter to him that Rome was filled with the palaces of Caesar or the temples of the Roman gods. It was his

---

[2] The *Forum of Appius* and the *Three Taverns* in v. 15 were forty-three and thirty-three miles respectively south of Rome.

[3] Philemon 10. Paul wrote to Philemon and asked him to forgive and release Onesimus.

[4] Philippians 1:12–18; 4:22.

King Jesus who had healed all the sick on the island of Malta – not doctor Luke with his Roman medicine or the islanders with their Roman gods. No matter how much the Emperor Nero told the masses he was a god, it was Paul and his team who had arrived in the city as the true sons of God.[5] In fact, Paul's four letters from his house arrest – Ephesians, Colossians, Philemon, and Philippians – are packed full of statements about the supremacy of Christ.[6] Caesar left Paul waiting two whole years in his prison in Rome, but Paul never stopped believing that Jesus was still his true Lord and King.

He was in the city of the great orators Cicero and Mark Anthony, but Paul was not ashamed to preach the simple message of Jesus. He gathered the Jews and built bridges as before, speaking to his *brothers* about *our people* and *our fathers*, and explaining from their Law and Prophets that Jesus was *the hope of Israel*. He did not beg them for their audience but built walls as clearly as before, warning them not to become like their forefathers whom the Lord had told Isaiah were too spiritually deaf and blind to see the truth. Luke ends the book of Acts by telling us that Paul's boldness was completely unhindered, and that for all of Nero's posturing the Gospel still marched on.

In view of all this background, Luke has a question to ask us as he draws the book of Acts to a close: *What is hindering you from sharing the Gospel with people today?* He has already called us to do so several times in his concluding section, but now he particularly focuses on our excuses. Are you stuck at home through age or illness or the demands of your young family? Paul was stuck at home too, but shared the Gospel with anyone who came to see him. Are you stuck in an office or a factory or

---

[5] Luke tells us in v. 11 that the figurehead on their ship was of the *Dioskouroi*, which literally means *the children of Zeus*. There seems no reason for him to give this detail unless either Castor and Pollux were Theophilus' patron-gods, or else Luke wants to point out that Paul and his team were the sons of the true God.

[6] Philippians 2:5–11; Ephesians 1:17–23; Colossians 1:15–20.

some other workplace? Paul was stuck in the Roman soldiers' workplace too and took every chance to share with them on the job. Are you disappointed with God or with the Church or with yourself? Paul had more reason to be disappointed than you, but he refused to make excuses for himself.

Paul had decided not to let his circumstances dictate his role in God's plan, but to keep on sharing in whichever place he found himself. Paul wrote to the Philippians from his prison cell that: *"I press on to take hold of that for which Christ Jesus took hold of me... One thing I do: Forgetting what is behind and straining towards what is ahead, I press on towards the goal to win the prize for which God has called me heavenwards in Christ Jesus."*[7]

If the Lord Jesus Christ has taken hold of you as one of his ordinary followers, there is no legitimate excuse for neglecting that for which he did so. Let's silence our excuses and strain towards what is ahead. If Paul was not dismayed by his house arrest in Rome, we must follow his example and keep on sharing.

---

[7] Philippians 3:12–14.

Conclusion: Ordinary People, Extraordinary God

As Peter entered the house, Cornelius met him and fell at his feet in reverence. But Peter made him get up. "Stand up," he said, "I am only a man myself."

(Acts 10:25–26)

Rick Hoyt of Massachusetts, USA, has competed in over 1,000 races, including around 250 triathlons and seventy-five marathons. That's pretty impressive by anyone's standard, but for Rick Hoyt it is astonishing. Rick has cerebral palsy and has been quadriplegic from birth. When the starting pistol fires to begin a triathlon, Rick's father does the swimming and pulls his son two and a half miles in a tailor-made dinghy. Next, he cycles over a hundred miles while Rick sits in a seat on the front of his bike. Finally, he transfers Rick to a wheelchair and runs twenty-six miles to complete the triathlon. On his own, Rick is unable to walk even a single step, but with the help of his father he competes alongside Ironmen. In his own words to his father in a television interview: *"Dad, when we're running it feels like my disability disappears."*[1]

The book of Acts is written like a Greek or Roman history book, but don't let that fool you. Its content is far more like the story of Rick Hoyt than one of the heroic adventure stories which the Greeks and Romans loved reading. They loved fiction like Homer's *Odyssey* (about the Greek hero Odysseus) and Virgil's *Aeneid* (about the Roman hero Aeneas). They loved history

---

[1] You can read more about Rick Hoyt's amazing story at http://www.teamhoyt.com.

268

books like Xenophon's *Cyropaedia* (about the heroic King Cyrus of Persia). They loved anything about strongmen and despised stories about ordinary people who needed a helping hand. They loved stories about people who deserved their hero worship, which is exactly the kind of story which Luke refuses to give them. The book of Acts is not a hero story. It's a story about ordinary people and their extraordinary God.

Many people finish the book of Acts with the mistaken impression that the early Christians were superhuman and deserve our reverent praise. Luke was one of them and he disagrees. In the first half of the book, it is Peter who is dominant, and who turns to the reader in 10:26 to insist that *"I am only a man"*, who should be copied as an example instead of worshipped as a saint. In the second half of the book, it is Paul who takes his place, and who also turns to the reader in 14:15 and asks with frustration: *"Men, why are you doing this? We too are only men, human like you."* Luke quotes these words from Peter and Paul because he doesn't want your admiration, but your *action*. He wants you to see what was achieved by a ragtag bunch of nobodies and to step up to the plate yourself to continue his ordinary story.

Other people make the opposite mistake and finish the book of Acts in a state of excited optimism. They resolve to imitate the passion and strategy of the Early Church, hoping to see similar fruit themselves, but Luke warns us not to join them on their path of disappointment. In the first half of Acts, he refers to *God* about a hundred times, to *the Lord* about seventy times, to *Jesus* over forty times, to *Christ* over fifteen times, and to *the Holy Spirit* over forty times. That's well over 250 times between them, and twice as often as *Peter*, *John*, and *Paul* put together. Luke sets this balance carefully because he wants to stir us to action, not to activism. The book of Acts is not a spiritual pep-talk which urges Christians to fulfil their hidden potential. It is a book which pulls no punches to inform us that without God we have absolutely no potential at all. Our optimistic activism is no more able to make us fruitful than Rick Hoyt's optimism is able to win him races. It's not that ordinary Christians have terrific potential, but that they have an extraordinary God to carry them.

Perhaps the biggest mistake that people make when they finish the book of Acts is to assume that it is a story of the past and not of the present. That's why Luke ends his book, frankly, in a very strange manner. It's so abrupt and incomplete that one enterprising conman even tried to convince the world in 1871 that he had discovered the manuscript to the "missing final chapter" of Acts.[2] Luke doesn't end the book of Acts in the polished style of a Greek historian, or with any of the commentary we might expect if it were written to chart the spread of the Gospel from Jerusalem to Rome. He ends his book in mid-air because he wants to show us that it hasn't finished. Theophilus must continue it by releasing Paul from prison, and every other reader after him must finish by how they live the rest of their lives. It has been said that *"When Cicero spoke, people marvelled; when Caesar spoke, people marched."* Luke ends the book of Acts in such an abrupt and sudden manner because he didn't write it to make his readers marvel. He wrote it unequivocally to make them march.

We live in a world where the call to be Jesus' witnesses to the ends of the earth is still as urgent as ever. Over 4,000 of the world's 10,000 major people groups are without any local church of their own. That's 2.75 billion people for whom Jesus died, who have no hope-filled community in their midst to convince them that his Gospel is true. As for the 4 billion people in the other 6,000 people groups, many of them are in countries like my own, where over five times as many people watched the final of *Britain's Got Talent* on television than went to church

---

[2] This *Sonnini Manuscript* was discovered in London in 1871 and claimed – wait for it – that Paul was released from prison and went to preach the Gospel in ancient London! Scholars were unconvinced.

that same weekend.[3] The challenge of the Great Commission is as over-sized for us as it ever was for the 120. It's as impossible for us as it is for Rick Hoyt to run a triathlon, but we have a Father who is far, far stronger.

That's why Luke doesn't want you to put down his book with a sense of defeatism that our task is unattainable, nor with a sense of optimism that our task is achievable. He wants you to put down his book with a sense of heavenly realism that, however impossible our task may be, it is not impossible when we are carried by our Almighty God. He is the one who chose us from the beginning, who has entrusted us with his Gospel, who fills us with his Spirit, who has endowed us with his authority, who guides us with his Satnav, and who carries us to victory through his Son. It is only carried by his power that we can write the conclusion to the book of Acts with every day of the rest of our lives. In his arms every single one of us can go, live like Jesus, pray, share, heal, plant churches, and proclaim the vital message that God's Kingdom has come.

Hudson Taylor once wrote that *"All God's giants have been weak men who did great things for God because they reckoned on God being with them."* Luke tells us that we are weak men and women, but that our God is with us and will never let us go. As we end the book of Acts, this is very good news. After all, we are ordinary people and he is our extraordinary God.

---

[3] *The Sunday Telegraph* reported on 31st May 2009 that 19.2 million people had watched the *Britain's Got Talent* final that weekend. Only 3.7 million people had gone to church.

OTHER BOOKS IN THE
STRAIGHT TO THE HEART SERIES:

ISBN 978 1 85424 988 3

ISBN 978 1 85424 990 6

For more information please go to **www.philmoorebooks.com**
or **www.lionhudson.com**.